HISTORIC
CLAPHAM

HISTORIC CLAPHAM

MICHAEL GREEN

To Christine and James

First published in 2008

Reprinted with corrections, 2009

The History Press
The Mill, Brimscombe Port
Stroud, Gloucestershire, GL5 2QG
www.thehistorypress.co.uk

© Michael Green, 2008

British Library Cataloguing in Publication Data.
A catalogue record for this book is available from the British Library.

ISBN 978 07524 4122 1

Typesetting and origination by
The History Press
Printed in Malta

CONTENTS

FOREWORD

Despite a century and a half of almost uninterrupted development, London is still a metropolis of villages. Some of those villages are easily discernable today, like Wimbledon or Hampstead, others, like Stepney, have been almost completely expunged by redevelopment. Clapham falls into the former category – a part of London that was and is still a distinct settlement. Walking through the old town, along North Side and across the Common, Clapham's early eighteenth-century buildings give the village a strong air of history. They are, however, only a veneer; the oldest standing parts of a history that stretches back to prehistoric times.

Clapham's remote history is not well known, even to historians. I lived in Manor Gardens on Larkhall Rise for seven years and never understood whose manor the gardens belonged to. I was not alone in my ignorance; many residents have only the vaguest idea of how their streets and parks, gardens and property boundaries came to be. No one has, until now, succeeded in explaining how modern Clapham was shaped over a period of a millennium.

This book brings the eye of a historian and the hand of an architect to the problems of Clapham's past. Through a minute analysis of both documentary and archaeological evidence Michael Green has given substance to the evolving topography of Clapham from prehistoric times to the eighteenth century. A series of maps demonstrate how ancient trackways, Saxon Estate boundaries, Roman Roads and medieval field systems make up the structure of modern Clapham. Several key documents and buildings are the building blocks he uses to peel back, layer by layer, Clapham's history and explain the place we know today.

His research into the archives has turned up illustrations that have long been hidden from the public and these are explained with a clarity and precision that is enviable.

In short this book is a fascinating quarry for both the serious researcher and the resident who wants to know why their road runs the way it does. Having read it, for me, at least, Clapham will never be the same again.

Simon Thurley

ACKNOWLEDGEMENTS

This study would not have been possible without the valued help of various friends, colleagues and institutions. Dr Simon Thurley MA FSA, Chief Executive of English Heritage, has supported and helped with the research from the outset and, not least, has kindly provided a foreword to *Historic Clapham*. Nicholas Long gave me access to the late E.E.F. Smith's historical archive of Clapham in 1998 and thus provided leads to the location of various drawings and papers. I am indebted to Mrs. Alyson Wilson and Peter Jefferson-Smith of the Clapham Society who have helped with the research in various ways. Fred Uhde has given unstinting support. I am deeply grateful to my typists without whom the book could not have been prepared, my wife Christine Insley Green, Iona Meek and especially Pam Baldwin who bore the brunt of the work. David McLean and Claire Fry advised on publication issues. I am indebted to the Reverend Deborah Matthews for permission to photograph the monuments in St Paul's Church, Clapham.

Robin Densem and Derek Seeley kindly gave permission for the results of their 1980-81 excavation in Rectory Grove to be used in this study. Wilf White reported on Roman finds from Clapham Common. Bob Cowey helped with the preparation of the Saxon report. Mr and Mrs Rawlins, owners of No. 13 The Chase, gave permission for work to identify the remains of Clapham Place during building excavations on their property. I am grateful to Mrs Tina C. Hampson for transcribing medieval documents and Lydia Wingfield Digby for help with the Anglo-Saxon documents. John Harris OBE FSA, Dr Timothy Mowl D. Phil. FSA, Guy de la Bédoyère, Dr Christopher Thacker MA and George McHardy MA FSA all helped in different ways with the research into Clapham Place.

Finally I am indebted to librarians, curators and other staff of the following institutions and societies for help in the preparation of this study:

Black and white illustrations 1, 12, 13, 16, 21, 32, 38, 47 and 78, and use of Geological Survey material are reproduced by permission of the British Geological Survey © NERC. All rights reserved. IPR/94:03C.
The British Library
Steven Tomlinson of the Bodleian Library, Oxford
Dr Mike Howe of the British Geological Survey

Philip N. Gale of the Church of England Record Centre

English Heritage: Lydia Szaslaraska of the London region; Liz Brown and Graham Deacon of the National Monuments Record; Robert Whytehead of the Greater London Archaeology Service; Barry Taylor of the London Sites and Monuments Record

Dr D.J. Tolhurst and Mrs Janet M. Morris of Emmanuel College, Cambridge Guildhall Library, London

National Trust staff at Ham House, London

John Henderson of the Lambeth Archives Dept., Minet Library, Lambeth

Mrs Clare Brown of Lambeth Palace Library

Andy Chopping of the Archaeological Service, Museum of London

Rhys Griffith of the London Metropolitan Archives,

The National Archives, Kew; Karen E. Gaffney of the Archive Centre, Norfolk Record Office; Dr R. Luckett and Mrs Aude Fitzsimons of the Pepys Library, Magdalene College, Cambridge; Charles Wheelton Hind of the Drawings Collection of RIBA

Colour plates 4, 16 and 20b, black and white illustrations 22, 23, 28 and 98, and use of Ordinance Survey material are reproduced by permission of the Ordinance Survey on behalf of HMSO © Crown Copyright 2007/8. All rights reserved. Ordinance Survey Licence number 100047602.

Adrian James, FSA, Assistant Librarian of the Society of Antiquaries of London Surrey Archaeological Collections

Surrey History Centre

Surrey Records Society

Meridith Davis and David Aynsworth of the Wandsworth Local History Service The Wandsworth Museum

Picture Library of the Victoria and Albert Museum

Lastly I am grateful to Peter Kemmis Betty, Wendy Logue, Abigail Green and Tom Vivian of The History Press for seeing the book through to publication.

I would like to thank my secretary Mary Coales, Miranda Embleton-Smith and Tracey Moore for organising the reprint of *Historic Clapham*.

INTRODUCTION

It was the London judge, Lord Bowen, who in 1903 coined the phrase 'the man on the Clapham omnibus', as in 'we must ask ourselves what the man on the Clapham omnibus would think', when faced with yet another example of aberrant human behaviour. The man in the judge's mind was the touchstone of ordinariness: moderately intelligent and reasonably well intentioned. In fact, everything that a decent, upstanding Englishman should be!

By extension, Clapham as a place might be thought an embodiment of normality. For most of the last thousand years, Clapham was a small, very ordinary Surrey village on the periphery of London. Its basic concern was agriculture, as was that of nearly all rural settlements in England at the time, with absolutely no other special characteristics whatsoever. It is always dangerous to speak of a 'typical' medieval community, but Clapham really was one such in the Home Counties, and this, strangely, is perhaps what makes it of special interest. Furthermore, in the eighteenth century it produced the *Clapham Sect*, and historians and moralists have wondered ever since how such a dull, respectable community could have managed to inspire one of the greatest civilising movements of all time – the abolition of the global slave trade.

All local antiquarians back to the late eighteenth century have managed to produce a paragraph or two about Clapham. The article by Lilian Redstone in the *Victoria County History for Surrey* in 1967 brought together all that could reasonably be said about the formal history of Clapham (Redstone 1967, 37-41), but the fact of the matter is that it is not possible to write a comprehensive, joined-up, early history of the place and this is for a very good reason. The lords of the manor, the Atkins family and their affiliated branches, comprehensively destroyed all the manorial records, probably when they retired to their country estate in the eighteenth century. The loss of the estate maps, mentioned in parish records of the time, is especially grievous.

This study, the result of a decade of work, is the fruits of a trawl through national and local archives for the slightest scrap of material of earlier periods in Clapham, particularly that of a topographical nature. From the seventeenth century onwards, the sources of historic information begin to become relatively plentiful, particularly as wealthy suburban families began to settle around the Common. As a consequence, local historians have tended to concentrate on family histories and none more so than the late Eric Smith (1907-1990) who for the best part of 50 years brought together an impressive body of material, now republished by the Clapham Society. It has not been the writer's intention here to regurgitate this material, nor re-examine in detail the existing historic buildings in Clapham. This has been done with considerable competence by current Clapham historians (Wilson, 2007). Neither am I concerned with scampering through the history of the last two centuries, which has been more than adequately published by Gillian Clegg (1998).

The emphasis of this study, therefore, is essentially on the early topographical and social history of Clapham; topographical because of the need to re-examine the place of the village, its fields and landscape in the light of its underlying geological and geophysical structure. It is a social study of Clapham's earlier inhabitants because the lives, needs and constraints of the ordinary, inarticulate people of the past need to be heard.

> And what the dead had no speech for, when living,
> They can tell you, being dead: the communication
> Of the dead is tongued with fire beyond the language of the living.
>
> T.S. Eliot, *Little Gidding*

One cannot come away from such an encounter with the past without enormous admiration for the ordinary villagers of Clapham. Their resilience, indeed bravery, faced with starvation and disease, compounded by the extortionate demands of the State, Church and Manor, is quite extraordinary. How would the present generation face up to something like the Black Death if such a pandemic struck today?

What emerges from this study, therefore, is essentially an *early* history of Clapham: what made it what it was and is today. In essence it takes the form of a series of thematic essays centred on either archaeological excavations or some major historical document which has managed to survive to our time. In doing this an attempt has been made to try and provide a linking thread of continuity from the Palaeolithic period of 300,000 years BP to the Age of Enlightenment in the eighteenth century.

It is also a detective story. What happened to those distant people is hidden, sometimes carefully hidden, in the dry texts of the historical record, or the muddy features of an archaeological trench. It is all there, but nothing can be accepted at face value; it all has to be teased out to reveal such things as the subterfuges of Merton Priory, the tyranny of the lords of the manor or the misery of the Gauden family at Clapham Place when they fell on hard times. I consider the result a compelling tale of survival in an ancient community, which, writ large, is the story of the British nation itself.

1

'LAND VERY BAD'

Time before and time after …
Driven on the wind that
sweeps the gloomy hills of London

T.S. Eliot, *Four Quartets*

In the Minet Library of Lambeth under a folio title *The Rectory of Clapham* are a collection of notes mostly concerned with tithe and glebe rentals (p.26). Under the heading *Bleak Hall Farm in 1803* is an entry for Mr Mason, butcher, who farmed 34 acres. Scribbled beside it is a poignant note which reads in full 'Land very bad and in very bad condition'. This introduces us at once to the *leitmotiv* of farming in Clapham, probably from earliest times. Why this should be so and how the community coped with the situation down the centuries is the subject of this and the following chapters. Mason's remark is an authentic voice from old Clapham about the real conditions of the time and will be heard again in this study in various contexts from different people. It must have been with a collective sigh of relief for the surviving Lord of the Manor, the Rev. W.H. Atkins-Bowyer and the last members of the farming community, that the remaining fields began to be systematically bought up and developed for housing in the mid-nineteenth century. Indeed, the only manorial papers which the present Lord of the Manor, Lord Denham, holds are those which gave the family title to their old demesne lands.

For in the story of Clapham, as elsewhere in England, everything hinged on *land*: acquisition, ownership, management, disposal and, of course, value. Where a community has to feed itself from the produce of its own agricultural land, these matters are critical. First then, there must be consideration of the geophysical and geological factors which made Clapham a focus of human settlement 5000 or more years ago (*colour plate 1*).

THE ANCIENT LANDSCAPE (*1* & *2*)

The underlying geological formation of the Clapham area is the London Clay, the primary deposit of the Palaeogene System in the London Basin. It was laid down in a deep marine gulf as alluvium some 60 million years ago. Where exposed, as in the south-

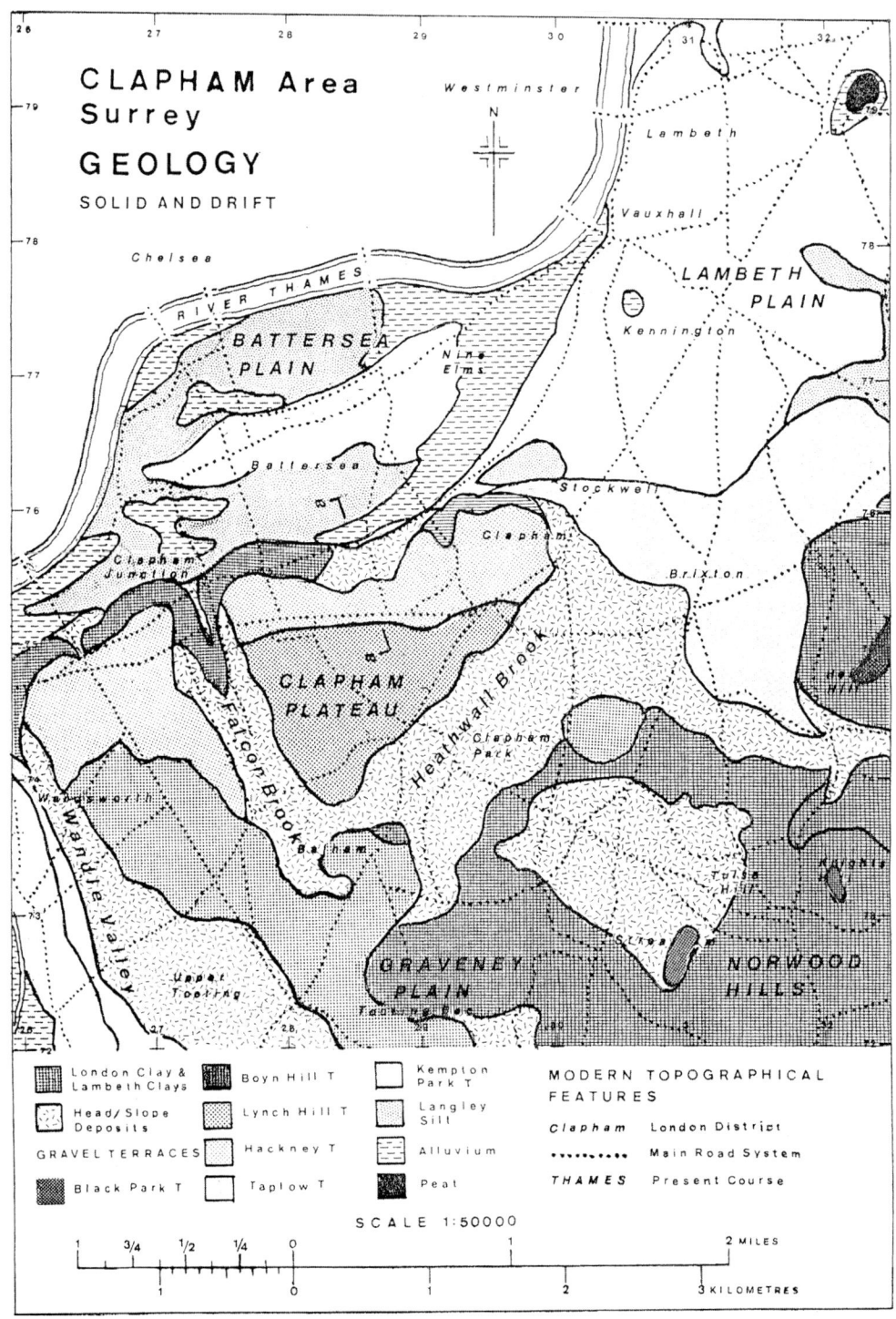

1 Geological map (solid and drift) of Clapham area. *H.J.M. Green based on the British Geological Survey published 1998. By permission of the B.G.S.*

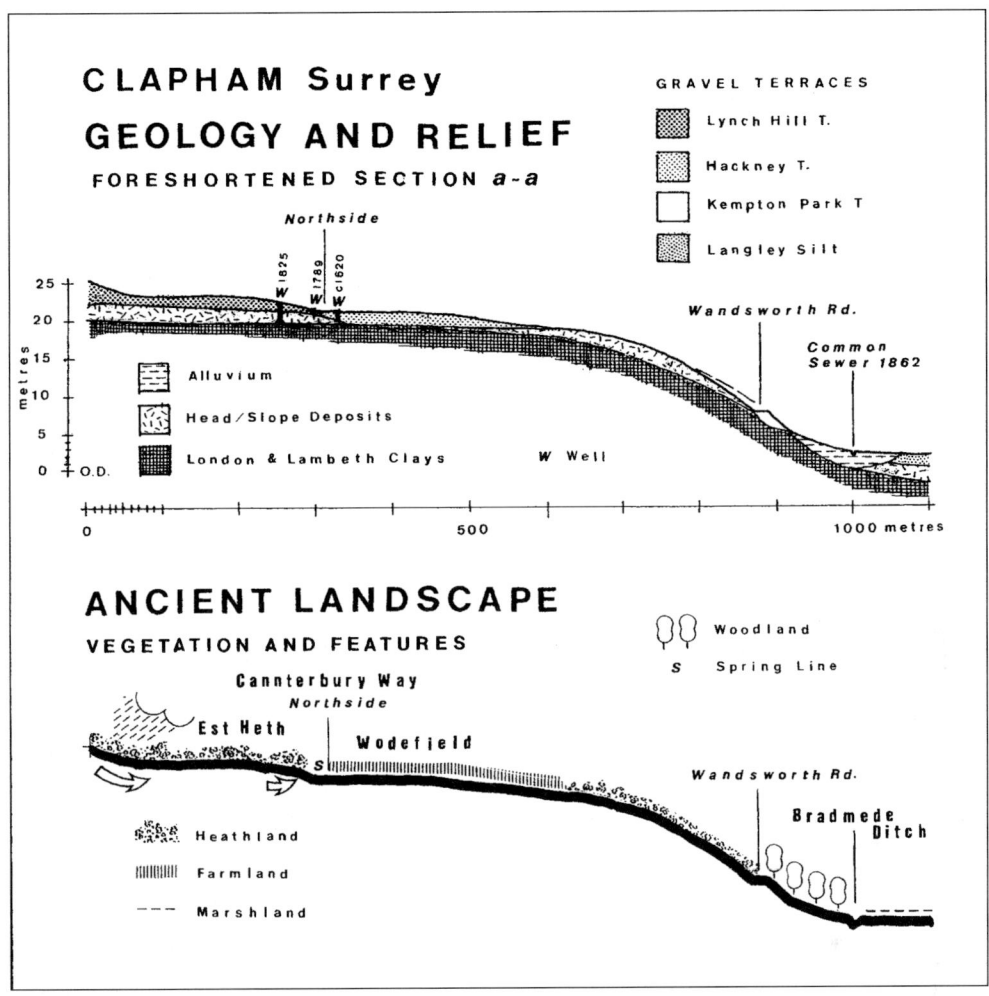

2 Geology and Relief. Foreshortened section A-A with Relief greatly exaggerated: ancient landscape of same section showing springline and medieval topographical features. *H.J.M. Green in part after L. Cundall*

east part of Clapham, this clayey landscape produces *pelo,* soils which are not only highly intractable in terms of agricultural working, but also acid and infertile. The baleful effect of the London Clay influenced the soil make-up of the overlying deposits, particularly, the periglacial material in front of the Anglian Ice Sheet which reached as far as north London; a process that began about 470,000 years ago.

The periglacial deposits washed down the slopes of valleys in front of the ice sheet and are termed *Head* deposits by geologists.

They formed principally beyond the ice limits during the glacial phases of the Pleistocene when erosion was accelerated because of the arctic climate and lack of vegetation. Debris of front-weathered material, which accumulated during the winters, formed a slurry when the snows melted in the spring. This gradually flowed down slopes, to form a poorly bedded deposit of very variable character.

Sumbler 1996, 123

The Head subsoils underlie most of the later agricultural land of eastern Clapham, and their poor quality was the subject of Mason's complaint in 1803. The heavy soil of the London Clay and Head deposits are likely to have been left as uncultivated *wildwood* until well into the prehistoric period and possibly later.

Overlying the Head deposits is the Pleistocene drift, which in the Clapham area occurs as terraces on the valley sides of the primeval Thames when it flowed about 25m above its present level. These terraces represent ancient floodplain deposits which became isolated as the river cut downwards to lower levels, reflecting the permutations of the glacial episodes when land and sea levels changed due to the weight of the ice sheets and amount of water trapped as ice. The highest terrace deposits are the oldest and are composed of a layer of sand and gravel (at Clapham about 7m thick) which originally would have been capped by a cover of silty loam (aka brickearth), formerly overbank mud of the river laid down during floods.

Although the effects of terrace formation have long been apparent to geologists, only in recent years have the various terrace deposits been thoroughly analysed in any detail in terms of their sequence and dating. This is thanks in part to the development of such diagnostic techniques as oxygen-isotope variation in the shells of *foraminifera* from deep sea sediments which have revealed the way in which global ice volume in temperature has fluctuated with time (Sumbler 1996, 110).

The local feature dating to this distant period called the 'Clapham plateau' consists basically of two successive terraces, now defined by north/south valleys formed by streams in the *Flandrian* or post-glacial phase, beginning about 10,000 years ago. To the west was the former Falcon Brook (previously the Hidaburn Stream) now buried beneath the Northcote Road and to the east the Hese Stream (Heath Wall Brook) which flowed down what is now Abbeville Road, then northwards to join the Thames at Vauxhall.

The upper and earlier of the two terraces, now Clapham Common, is classified as part of the Lynch Hill Gravels, deposited during the second of the four post-Anglian, interglacial periods, and correlates with Oxygen Isotope Stage 9 dating to between 325,000 and 300,000 years ago. It is probably related to the Hoxnian Interglacial, a temperate weather-phase when humans with an Acheulian hand-axe technology hunted in the middle Thames valley. A rough Palaeolithic instrument found in gravel is recorded from Clapham (Clinch 1902, 251). Probably a flint handaxe, it was reported as being exhibited at the Jermyn Street Museum, whose collections were transferred to the Geological Museum in 1934 and thence to the British Geological Survey collection at Keyworth. The BGS now has no record of the object, which may originally have been washed from a campsite on the riverbank into the gravels of one of the terraces at Clapham.

A.J. Stuart has described a similar ancient habitat revealed by excavations in 1974-8 at Hoxne, Suffolk:

> Temperate woodland is indicated by the remains of fallow deer, macaque monkey and extinct rhinoceros (*Dicerorhinus* sp) and less definitely by roe deer. At the same time, extensive areas of open vegetation are suggested by such animals as horse (the animal most abundantly represented) giant deer, lion, short-tailed vole and Norway lemming, ... red deer (in abundance second only to horse), bear and an unknown species of elephant.
>
> Stuart 1988, 29-30 (see *3a*)

It is difficult to convey a sense of the enormous time span that has passed between that distant period and now. The late eighteenth-century antiquary, John Frere, was aware of this when he spoke of hand axes from the Hoxne brickearths as being 'fabricated and used by people ... belonging to a very remote period indeed; even beyond that of the present world'. As early man moved along the hunting trails of the Thames riverbank

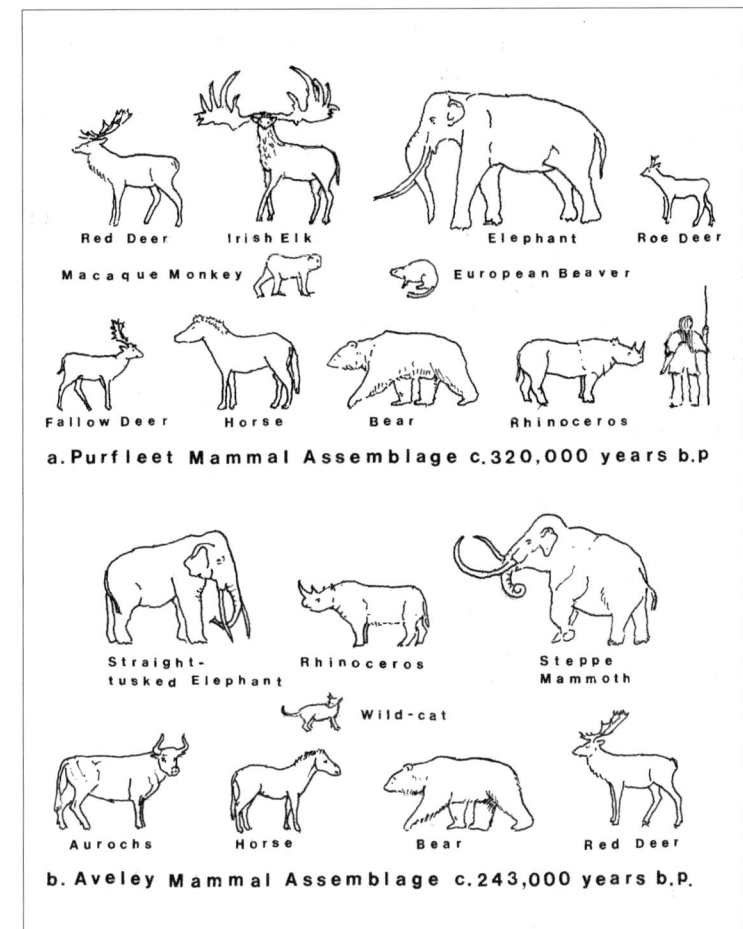

3 Typical palaeolithic animal assemblage zones associated with the Clapham Terraces:

3a Purfleet Interglacial group *c.*320,000 years BP found at Hoxne, Suffolk

3b Ilfordian Interglacial group *c.*243,000 years BP found at Aveley, Essex. *H.J.M. Green*

Red Deer   **Irish Elk**   **Elephant**   **Roe Deer**

Macaque Monkey   **European Beaver**

Fallow Deer   **Horse**   **Bear**   **Rhinoceros**

a. Purfleet Mammal Assemblage c.320,000 years b.p

Straight-tusked Elephant   **Rhinoceros**   **Steppe Mammoth**

Wild-cat

Aurochs   **Horse**   **Bear**   **Red Deer**

b. Aveley Mammal Assemblage c.243,000 years b.P.

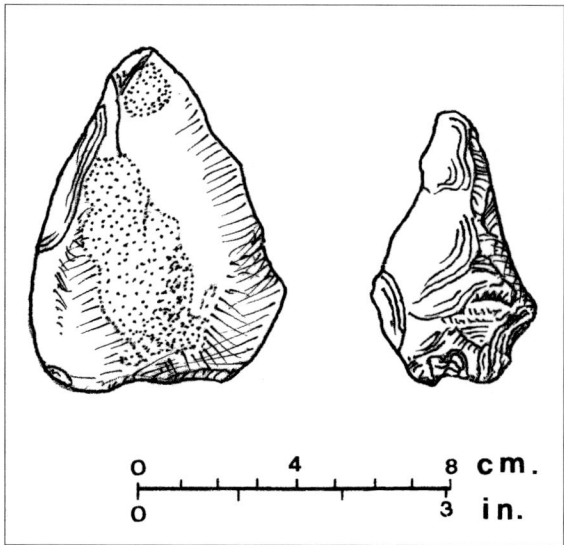

4 Neanderthal tools (*c.*243,000 years BP) derived from the 'brickheath' deposits over the Hackney Gravel Terrace (Ilfordian phase). Site L448/80 Rectory Grove, Clapham. Flint handaxe and blade of Prepared Core (Levallois) Technology. The brown (ferrous oxide) patinated surface of these tools distinguishes them from the grey flint blade assemblages of Neolithic date from the same site. *H.J.M. Green after Gower & Tyler 2003, 11*

while estuary birds piped in the marshes, they probably thought that their world would last for ever. Yet it did not, any more than ours will. In the following 300 millennia there were to be further ice ages and long cold spells when the landscape reverted to the steppe-tundra conditions of Siberia as the ice sheets crept southwards again.

The lower (and later) terrace to the north of Clapham Common is now designated as belonging to the 'Hackney Gravel' series, and survives as a belt of land approximately 1½ miles long, east-west, and varying between ¼ and ½ mile wide between the Wandsworth Road and Clapham Common Northside. The older name of the 'Hackney Gravel' is the 'Floodplain Terrace' (there are later terraces below the present floodplain level), which belongs to the third, post-Anglian interglacial period and correlates with Oxygen-Isotope Stage 7 dating to between 240,000-190,000 years ago. This has been equated to the Ilfordian phase (Sumbler 1996, 120) or Aveley Interglacial (Stringer 2006, 153) which at various sites has yielded evidence of estuarine conditions in a landscape frequented by woolly mammoth, straight-tusked elephant, extinct rhinoceros, lion, bear, giant deer, horse and, of course, man (*3b & 4; colour plate 2*). There is some debate in geological circles about the allocation of oxygen isotope stages in terms of their sequence in the British quaternary deposits, and more particularly the placing of certain Palaeolithic occupation sites in relation to both (for current, informed views on the subject see Barton 1997, 28; Ellison 2004, 53 & Stringer 2006, 85).

CLAPHAM HEATH (*colour plate 3*)

The differing geophysical character of the surface deposits in the Clapham area, and their detrimental effect on later agriculture, has already been noted in the case of the London Clay and Head deposits. The two terrace deposits of the Clapham Plateau are

5 The process of ridge-making with *lazybed* construction in nineteenth-century Ireland. 'The grassy strip which is to become the furrow is notched centrally down its length and the sods on each side are each undercut by two spade thrusts and levered over on to the beds, where they lie flat, grass to grass.' *Estyn Evans 1957, 145*

of greater importance in terms of the early settlement patterns of the Saxon vill and earlier occupation.

The key difference between the two interglacial terraces is that the Lynch Hill Gravel of Clapham Common has lost its original overlying alluvium (brickearth) cover through weathering and denudation, whereas the Hackney Gravel, further down the hill, did not. Indeed, it appears to have been enriched by the soil creep from the higher terrace, and emerged as the primary focus of arable agriculture and occupation from the Neolithic period onwards.

By the time early settlers began to cultivate the surrounding area some 5000 or more years ago, the surface soil of the Lynch Hill Gravel on the Common was Podzolic in character (i.e. raw humus surface and leached subsoil with black humus or 'iron pan') which was acid and infertile. This poorly-drained soil was effectively a heathland environment (the Common was called Clapham Heath before the eighteenth century) with its own characteristic microclimate and flora. The sterile, acid nature of the soil made it unsuitable for arable agriculture, which is demonstrated by the evidence from the aerial photographic coverage of 2003 (*colour plates 4 & 5*). There are no traces of conventional, prehistoric field systems, except for some small-scale *lazybed* workings (ridge and furrow spade agriculture) in the centre of the Common, but although this type of cultivation was used in the prehistoric, in this case the remaining traces probably date to the land hunger period in the thirteenth century (5). Until the nineteenth century, Clapham Common was, effectively, a 'morass' (Batten 1827, 33). Undrained, there were patches of surface peat and old gravel pits which later became ponds. The pits had their origins in providing gravel for repairing the 'impassable roads' which ran across the Common (1719 deposition by Robert Makepeace). The present park-like condition of the Common is completely different from its former state. The improvement owes its genesis to Christopher Baldwin who, in the later eighteenth century, was the moving force behind the reclamation, draining and planting of the Common.

Until the eighteenth century, the commonest flora on the Common were thorn bushes and brambles. In the 1719 deposition of Thomas Mattox, he remembered 'shrubbed oaks where he had seen gypsies resort to and lie'. The shrubbed oaks may well have included Pollard Oaks of the *pedunculate sp.* (*Quercus robur*) which are resistant to browsing by animals in a wood pasture environment. The last surviving remnant of the old heath is a small patch of thorn trees on rough, uneven ground near the Avenue. For the early inhabitants of Clapham, the most important use of the Common, apart from rough grazing by cattle and horses, was the provision of fuel and fresh water.

A SPRING OF SOFT WATER

As described earlier, the gravels of the Clapham Plateau (the Lynch Hill Gravels) overlie the glacial, clay Head deposits of the Anglian Ice Age, which slope gently from the south towards the Thames Valley. This geological structure provides a springline along the north side of Clapham Common which is shown by former streams, commercial wells and a general seepage of water collecting below the porous gravel levels on the impermeable surface of the Head deposits and flowing northwards (2). This geophysical feature, which was indeed a primary factor in the early settlement of Clapham in the prehistoric period, has been down the centuries both a blessing and a curse for the villagers. Between the valleys of the Falcon Brook to the west and the Hese Stream or Heath Wall Brook mentioned earlier, were at least three streams as indicated by the contours of their valleys (6).

The most important of these subsidiary streams was that which emerged from the area of the present Church of Holy Trinity. From there it ran along what is now Old Town, down a little valley between Rectory Grove and North Street following the line of Hazel Road and so to the Battersea marshes (6A). It was this stream which apparently determined the siting of the Saxon and earlier settlements on the eastern slope of the valley. The actual site of the springhead is uncertain, but in all likelihood lay in a patch of waste (and probably boggy) ground owned by the Lord of the Manor, which was donated by Mrs Penelope Pitt (the last of the Atkins family, to whom the Manor had descended) for building the new Church of Holy Trinity in 1774-6. The continual trouble with the foundations of the church for the following century was no doubt due to its unfortunate siting on wet, unstable ground (Smith 1976, 14).

The only documentary reference to this stream occurs in the 1326 Customal and Extent (cf. Chapter 8) which reads 'all customary [tenants] ought to repair suitably the walls about the said manor, to wit from a certain bank of the *water* on the south of the court to the churchyard ...' (*Calendar of Close Rolls* 19 Ed. II 1326 membrane 1d PRO 1898, 584). In the V.C.H. for Surrey, L.J. Redstone translates the relevant section as meaning '... and repair the wall of the *watercourse* as far as the churchyard' (Redstone 1967, 414), which perhaps makes better sense. This would imply that the

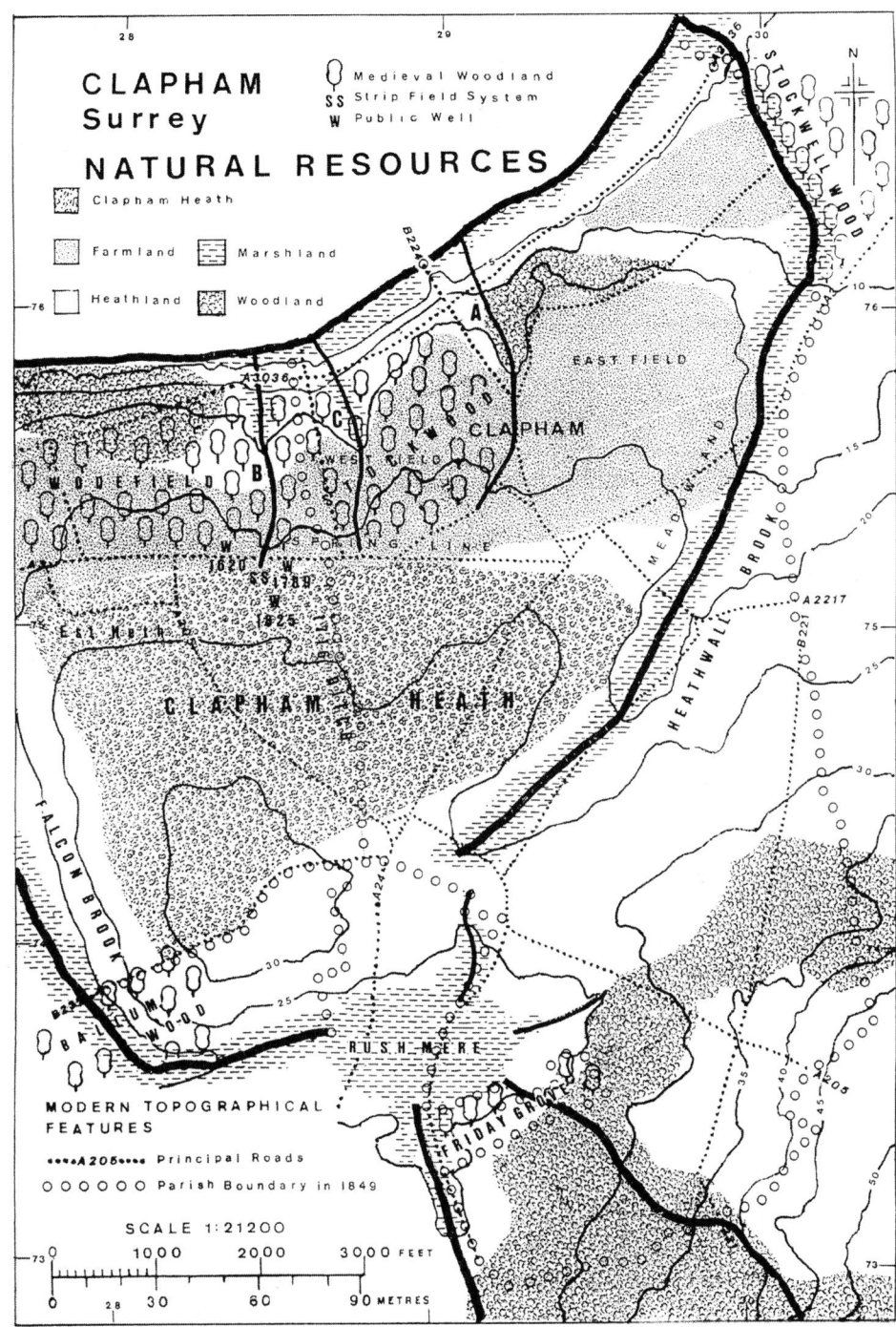

6 Geophysical map of ancient natural resources at Clapham showing contours, streams, marshland, heathland, woodland and farmland. Medieval woodland separately superimposed. *H.J.M. Green after A. and R. Bland 'Plan of the Parish of Clapham' (1849) and British Geological Survey England and Wales sheet 270. Solid and Drift Edition 1:50000 series published 1988. By permission of the B.G.S.*

7 Peasants carrying water in a lidded wooden tub and a pottery jug c.AD 1340. H.J.M. Green after Marginalia in the Luttrell Psalter (British Museum add. 42 130)

customary duties of the manorial tenants included the maintenance of the (earth/timber) revetments lining the bank of the stream to the point where it passed into the demesne and moat of the Lord of the Manor (which, as will be seen, included the glebe of the church).

During the medieval period and earlier, the water from this spring, flowing down the line of the village street, no doubt adequately served the needs of the community and filled the manor moat (7). However, between c.1617 and 1628, the new demesne Lord, Dr Henry Atkins, appears to have tapped the source and rerouted the water in 'pipes of leade' for watering the gardens of the Manor House (1628 'Extent' – *State Papers Domestic,* Charles I 154/93). From then on the villagers were obliged to obtain fresh water from other sources, principally from a spring half a mile distant to the west on the north side of the Common.

The spring of this new source of water was between Forthbridge Road and Jedburgh Street where they meet the Common, and served a little stream which had earlier run down the line of Taybridge Road towards Lavender Hill (6B). The first springhead was constructed on ground north of Northside, which later became the site of a house called Springwell, now Parkgate House School (Wilson 2000, 20). This 'fine spring of soft water of very superior quality' was, according to H.N. Batten writing in the early nineteenth century, in a reservoir of 'ancient construction' which had been repaired by the parish in 1717 (Batten 1829, 49).

8 The Village 'Pump Well' on Clapham Common Northside. In use *c.*1825-1885. *Lithograph by T.M. Baynes c.1826. Reproduced by permission of London Borough of Lambeth, Archives Department.*

In 1789, with a growing population (from 1625 in 1774 to 2477 in 1788) a new reservoir was opened on the opposite side of the road adjacent to Taybridge Road and closer to the village. The site is still marked by an old plane tree, the survivor of a spinney which surrounded the spring. This new reservoir continued to supply the neighbourhood until 1825, when due to a further increase in population (8588 in 1826: Batten 1827, 102) '... the consequent great demand for water, which the spring failed to supply, and the assemblage of the men with their carts waiting for their turn became a nuisance to the immediate inhabitants' (Batten 1827, 49). They therefore by subscription, opened a well still larger, about 100yds further into the Common, which produced sufficient to fill daily 150 butts (about 16,200 gallons) and was the source of employment and support to 18 families. A lithograph *c.*1826 of this new spring well shows an excavation taken down some 10ft through Lynch Hill Gravel drift material to, presumably, the top of the Head deposits (*8*). In the centre of the depression is a framed well-head from which water is being bucketed out and supplying water carts standing around. Although described on the 1869-70 OS survey as a 'Pump Well' there is no evidence of a pump in the 1826 lithograph. It appears that their new well did not rely on the catchment of water at the base of the gravel, as had been the case with the two previous springs, but was in effect an artesian well taken down to the junction of the Head deposit and the London Clay, a depth of some 10m. J.W. Grover, writing in 1887, describes the well as having been recently covered over by the Board of Works, presumably with the advent of piped water to the district. The capping of the well and the filling in of the depression was so efficient that no obvious trace of the site survives, even on the aerial photographs of 2003.

9 Ard Plough pulled by a team of two oxen. The wooden bent frame of the crook ard has an iron share tip for cutting through the topsoil. Although the illustration is of early medieval date, the ard plough is identical to those used in the prehistoric period. *II.J.M. Green after an illustration to Psalm 103 from the Harley Psalter of eleventh-century date, copying the Utrecht Psalter of c.820 AD (B.L. Harley MS 603 p. 516)*

The third stream which emerged from the Northside springline during the post-glacial period formed a valley in the area of Victoria Rise. The springhead was close to No. 42 Northside and the water was channelled through a series of ponds on the Gauden/Hewer Estate serving Clapham Place between 1660 and 1760. The stream then curved away down the slope probably following an old furlong boundary of the early medieval open field system and lasted until the 1850s when the farmland was developed as housing. It formerly crossed below the Wandsworth Road close to its junction with Cedars Road (6C).

EARLY SETTLEMENT

The discovery of flint tools of Palaeolithic date on the Clapham Plateau has already been noted. Our concern here is with settlement in Clapham in the post-glacial or Holocene period, beginning with the Mesolithic cultures at a time when Britain was still attached to the continent. Characteristic artefacts of this remote period some 8000 years ago, such as barbed points of antler for spear and *tranchet* type flint axeheads, have been dredged from the Thames at Wandsworth and Battersea (Sumbler 1996, 136). Patterns of settlement elsewhere in south London would suggest the presence of camp sites of hunters of red deer on islands and drier terraces alongside the river, including Clapham. Excavations when the Channel Tunnel Rail Terminal was built at Waterloo station revealed evidence of flint working for tools

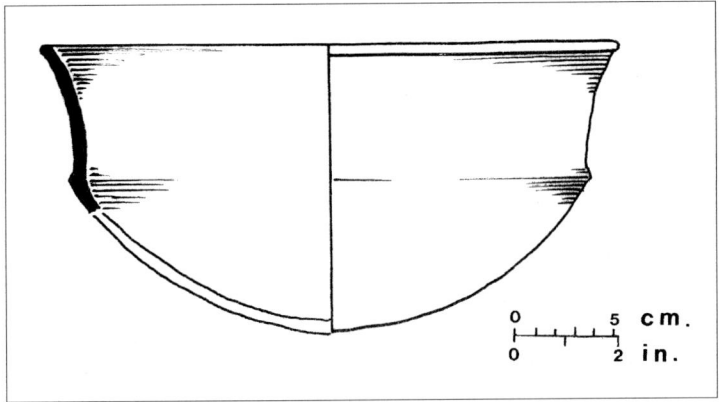

10a Neolithic wide-mouth, carinated bowl of clay tempered with crushed flint. This is a plain version of the Sussex, Whitehawk Hill style, *c.*3700-2900 BC (Malone 2001, 237). Site L448/80 Rectory Grove, Clapham. *H.J.M. Green after Densem and Seeley 1982, 184*

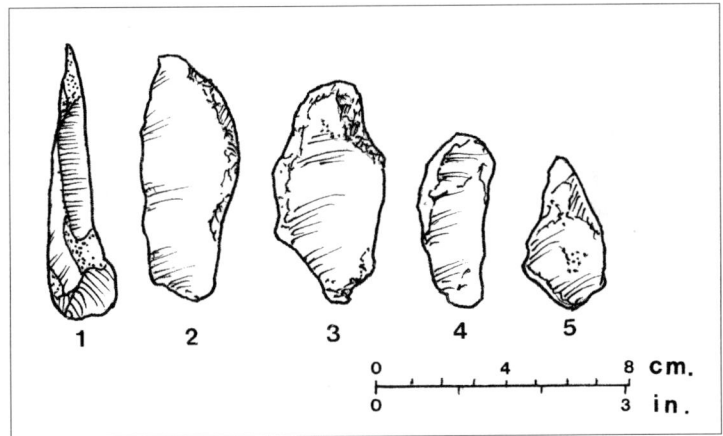

10b Neolithic and Bronze Age flint tools, *c.*3500-2500 BC. Dark grey flint. 1. Point. 2. Blunt-edged knife. 3. Multiple tool. 4. Plano-carvex scraper. 5. Awl, Site L448/80 Rectory Grove, Clapham. *H.J.M. Green after Gower and Tyler 2003, 11*

on what had formerly been an island which rose above the marsh (Gower & Tyler 2003, 9).

The warmer climate and the melting of the last of the glacial ice sheets resulted in a rise of sea levels with the result that the last land-link with the continent was severed by about 6500 BC. The era of the hunter-gatherers gradually drew to a close during the Neolithic and Early Bronze Age as people began to live in more permanent settlements. The advent of farming with the domestication of animals and the planting of crops on land cultivated with the use of the *Ard* plough, is a feature of these settlers from continental Europe (*9*). They also introduced the making of pottery, simple round-based bowls and storage jars; an example of the former was found overlying the 'natural' in Rectory Grove but was unassociated with any recognisable feature (*10a*). It dates to the early/middle Neolithic period, perhaps sometime around 3000 BC. In later features on the same site in 1980-1 flint tools and waste flakes dated to about 3500-2500 BC were found (*10b*). The attraction of Clapham for these early settlers were the springline streams along the north side of the Common and the relatively easily worked soils of the Floodplain Terrace, as indeed it was for later prehistoric peoples, since unstratified Bronze and Iron Age pottery has been found on the same site. No doubt the early settlers hunted deer

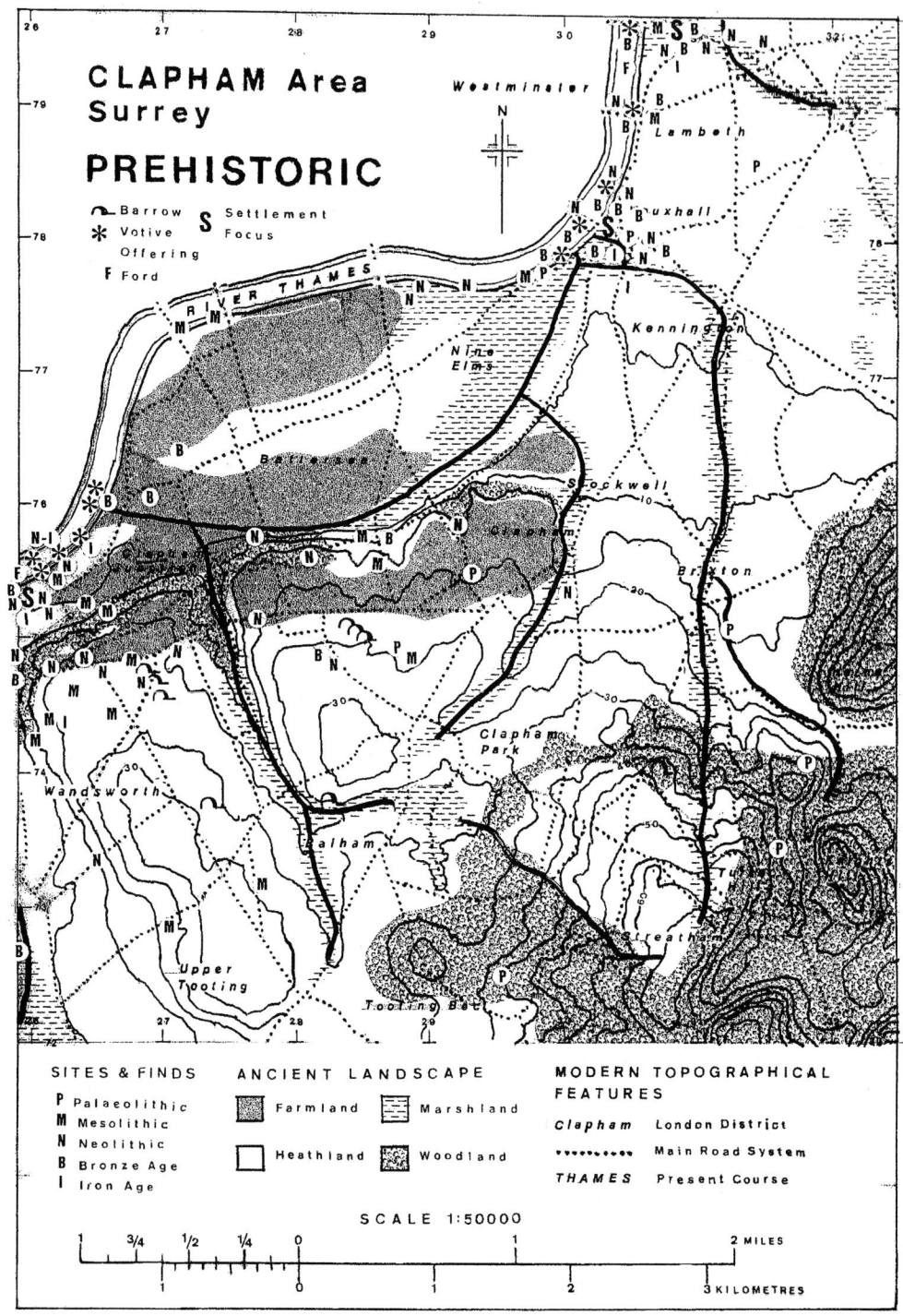

11 Prehistoric Distribution Map of the Clapham area based on the collected evidence of the National Monument Record for Lambeth and Wandsworth compiled by English Heritage. *H.J.M. Green Base Map after the British Geological Survey published 1998*

and boar on the heath and wildwood of the hinterland, as illustrated by the Neolithic polished flint knife found on Clapham Common during the 1930s (Gower & Tyler 2003, 11; Densley & Seeley 1987, 179). Other evidence for prehistoric activity comes in the shape of a group of ditched round barrows shown up by aerial photography in 2003 in the northwest corner of the Common, which may belong to a slightly later date. The barrows themselves, of course, have long been dug away and the sites flattened, but the positions of their surrounding ditches are evident, particularly on the south side where the water collected. The barrows themselves appear to have been between 20m and 40m in diameter (*colour plate 4*). This type of 'bell' barrow is conventionally dated to the third millennium BC (Pearson Parker 2005, 20).

The evidence for prehistoric settlement at Clapham needs to be seen in a broader context for proper evaluation. The prehistoric distribution map of the Clapham area (*11*) is based on the collected evidence of the National Monuments Record for Lambeth and Wandsworth compiled by English Heritage.

The older Palaeolithic material is widely spread over the whole area, probably the result of deposition due to the movement of the glacial Head deposits, and the same may also be true of the later formation of the drift terraces. The long span of time (c.8000–4000 BC) when the hunter-gatherers of the Mesolithic period were active in the area shows a pattern of occupation, probably seasonal camp sites, along the banks of the Thames. Away from the river, there is a scatter of finds stretching a couple of miles inland, perhaps representing material lost in the hunting runs of the heathland and wildwood.

The most surprising aspect from about 6000 b.p. for the next 4000 years, is the clear evidence for settlement nucleations at certain specific Thames-side locations within the study area. In every case along the south bank of the Thames, the settlement *foci* are set back along the banks of a major tributary stream: the east bank of the Wandle at Wandsworth, the north bank of the River Effra at Vauxhall, and the south bank of the early Neckinger Stream, evidenced as a relict waterway running northwards from its rising on Herne Hill (*12*). The evidence for occupation includes not only a concentration of find spots, but clear indications in every case of occupation at all these locations of floors, postholes of dwellings, and ditches. Once these settlements had been founded in the early Neolithic period (perhaps originating as Mesolithic camp sites) they continued on the same sites evidently for millennia. The developing technologies of the Neolithic, Bronze and Iron Ages may have come and gone but the same ancient communities remained – clear evidence for social continuity. The distribution pattern of isolated finds indicates use of the better soils of the Hackney Gravel Terrace from the Wandsworth settlement eastwards as far as Clapham. This evidence may indicate arable fields cultivated by the ard plough (*9*), the use of which in the locality is evidenced by marks cut into the subsoil at the Phoenix Wharf site at Southwark (Sidell, Cotton, Rayner & Wheeler 2002, 35). The isolated Neolithic sherd from Old Town, Clapham (*10a*) may suggest another use for the less fertile hinterland. A likely system of transhumance would have involved moving the flocks and herds of the community to spring and summer pastures on higher ground. This socio-economic activity would have entailed seasonal camps, but not settled communities, which may explain the Clapham find. Whatever the use of these lands, the distribution of finds of all periods suggests a clear boundary running across the top of the Wandsworth and Clapham heaths. It may be significant that the undated barrow fields identified in these locations (*11*) coincide with this boundary. The general absence of finds from the former heathland to the south in Tooting, Balham and Brixton, and less surprisingly the wildwood of Streatham and Tulse Hill, would suggest that these areas were primarily used for hunting. A skeleton of an *aurochs* (extinct wild cattle *3b*) found in a pit at Harmondsworth still had six Early Bronze Age arrowheads embedded in it (Hunt 2002, 45). Another unoccupied area appears to have been the marshland of Battersea, used perhaps only for fowling and fishing.

In connection with the Neolithic settlements it is worth mentioning here the numerous artefacts found in the Thames at Wandsworth, Battersea and Lambeth, which include some of the finest bronze work of Late Iron Age date ever recorded from Britain. The detailed NMR inventory brings into focus the sheer quantity of this high-class material, which from Wandsworth and Battersea alone covers a 4000 year span from the Mesolithic/Neolithic to the Roman Conquest, and possibly later.

Period	Date	Number of Artefacts
Mesolithic	10000–4000 BC	28
Neolithic	4000–2200 BC	54
Bronze Age	2200–700 BC	77
Iron Age	700 BC–AD 43	6

Although late nineteenth-century antiquarians and collectors tended to be deliberately vague about the exact source of most of this material, this period coincides with the erection of several London bridges in the study area: Wandsworth Bridge (1865-73), Battersea Railway Bridge (1883–1890) Albert Bridge (1870–1873) Chelsea Bridge (1846-1858) and Grosvenor Railway Bridge (1858–1866). Although some of these artefacts may have been found while dredging the river, the vast majority, I suspect, were found by workmen digging out the river mud in the caissons of the bridge pier-supports. The Wandsworth Bridge appears to have been a particularly prolific source of archaeological discoveries. Indeed, the few actual dates associated with this material would support such a theory. There are far too many objects over too long a period for them to have been derived solely in a battle context, as older antiquarians believed, and most of these artefacts are almost certainly ritual material deposited from certain specific locations by members of the local settlements.

The recent recognition of the existence of a ford 'slightly to the west of Wandsworth Bridge' (G.F. Lawrence, *Antiquities of the Middle Thames*: also NMR 031592/00/00) might provide a locational context, as indeed may the Horseferry ford at Lambeth (*11*). I would postulate that offerings were deposited in the river at the centre of such fords and allowed to float downstream. The heavier items would have sunk more or less straightaway and hence the concentration of such artefacts under Wandsworth Bridge. Other objects such as bronze axes with wooden shafts or cauldrons might have floated some distance before becoming waterlogged and sinking, a theory supported by the distribution of such finds downstream of Wandsworth Bridge (*11*). The background of such votive depositions in prehistoric Europe has been thoroughly covered in recent studies (Hutton 1991, 184).

Certain aspects of the deity to whom these ritual offerings were being dedicated can be established by the nature of the artefacts. Almost without exception, from the earliest period, these were weapons, particularly swords and axes. As is the case elsewhere in the Celtic west, this almost certainly reflects the worship of a tutelary, warlike deity, probably feminine. A candidate might be *Tamesa* mentioned by Tacitus, whose name is cognitive with the Indo-Aryan Sanskrit *Tamasa* (meaning dark) and the Old Welsh prefix *Tam-* (meaning fiery or fierce) i.e. 'the fierce, dark goddess' (cf. Ekwall 1947); from whom, of course, the name Thames is derived. Fords were particularly associated with such territorial goddesses (Proinsias MacCana 1979, 66). The subject is of great interest but strictly lies outside the scope of this study.

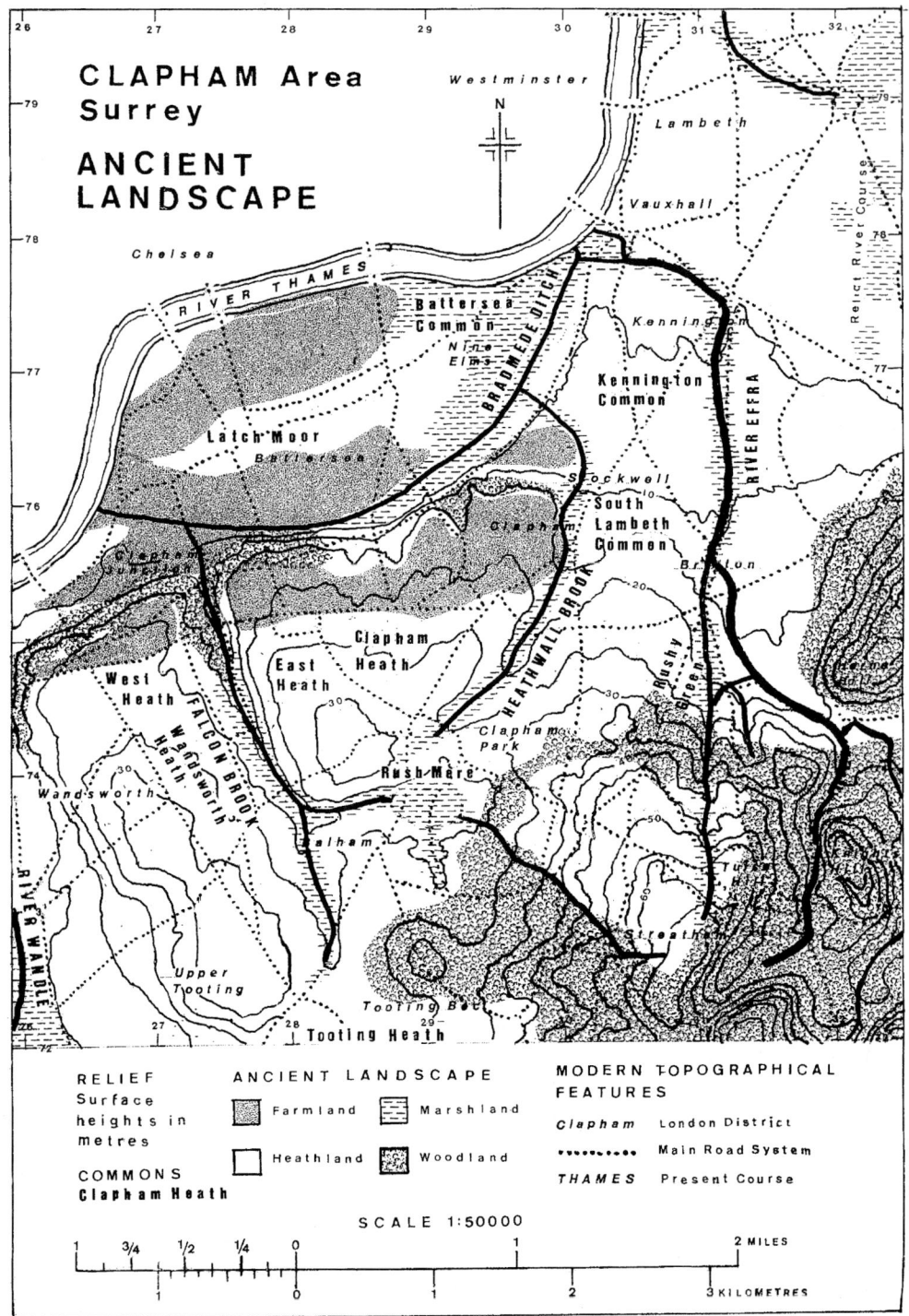

12 Geophysical map of the ancient landscape in the Clapham area showing contours, streams, marshland, heathland, woodland and farmland. *H.J.M. Green. Base Map after the British Geological Survey published 1998*

2

'CLAPHAM FIELD'

When the last of earth left to discover
Is that which was the beginning;
> T.S. Eliot, *Four Quartets*

THE AGRICULTURAL LANDS OF CLAPHAM (*12*)

There were five main subsoil types which were suitable for agricultural use down to the nineteenth century in Clapham. In ascending order in terms of their use and value:

1. The acrid, sterile gravels of Clapham Heath (the Lynch Hill Gravels) have already been considered. The heath was apparently only used for arable land in emergencies, but had valuable subsidiary uses for rough growing, fuel provision and access to fresh water.
2. The exposed areas of London Clay in south-east Clapham have poor, acid soils of *pelo-stagnogley* type classified as part of the 'Windsor Association' series. This soil is highly intractable for ploughing and has a wetness class III-IV (i.e. the soil profile is waterlogged within 70cm of depth for between 3 and 6 months or longer). Such soils coalesce into a sticky, intractable mess (Williamson 2003, 145) and can only be worked, if at all, by the heavy wheeled plough with coulter and mouldboard. Williamson has argued that such ploughs were in use during the Middle Saxon period, indeed at a time when Clapham was being settled (2003, 120; *13*).
3. The Head glacial deposits around the Common were almost as bad, since they contained washed-out sediment from the London Clay, but were intermixed with lenses of sand and gravel.
4. The Hackney Gravel drift deposits north of the Common broadly speaking retained an uneven level of alluvium (brick earth) subsoil. Where archaeological excavations took place in the area of Rectory Grove in the 1980s, the subsoil was found to be of variable consistency, mostly sandy loam but with lenses of sandy gravel and clay. The soils of this terrace would have been no easier to clear of the natural wildwood than the woods over the clays, but once cleared would have been infinitely easier to work with the primitive ard plough. Even here, however, the soils of what became effectively the East and West fields of the vill, differed in character. The great West field

13 Heavy wooden plough with iron fittings pulled by a team of four oxen. The earth slice is cut vertically by the coulter, undercut by the share and turned by the mould-board. Components of this type of plough were introduced as early as the Roman period. The example shown is of English fourteenth century date. *H.J.M. Green after the Luttrell Psalter (BL add. 42130 p.170, c.AD 1335-40)*

lay below the springline of Clapham Common. The principal springs and wells have already been discussed, but in addition, there was a steady seepage of water down the slope of the Hackney Gravel terrace, which, during wet seasons, must have rendered the land as intractable for arable agriculture as the London Clay and Head deposits.

5. The alluvial soils used for the hay meadows of the vill were the most valuable agricultural asset of the ancient community. Although the rough pasture north of the Wandsworth Road on the steep slope of the Thames Terrace was used as meadowland in the seventeenth century and later (it was unsuitable for the plough) the older meadows of the village were elsewhere. They appear to have been concentrated on the banks of the Heath Wall Brook tributary, where the valley opened out at the top of the Abbeville Road and across what are now housing estates to Clapham North Station, then along the north side of the Clapham Road to Union Road. This area of important hay meadows, which provided the winter fodder for the animals of the Clapham community, passed into the ownership of the church early in the medieval period (*14*; see Chapter 7).

The East and West fields of the Saxon vill were evidently the nucleus of the cultivated land during that period. It is not clear whether at the time they were identified as discrete units under these names.

It might be expected that the farming of these units of land in their later developed feudal state conformed to the classic open-field system where the standard villein holding comprised a *virgate* or *half-virgate* (at Clapham according to the 1326 Extent 16 and 8 acres respectively) divided into a large number of small, unhedged strips (*lands*) which were evenly scattered across the territory of the township. Because the soils were so heavy and badly drained, it was usual for each strip to be ploughed in ridges in order to facilitate the run-off of rainwater, thus producing the characteristic earthworks called 'ridge and furrow'. Strips were grouped into bundles called *furlongs*, which formed the basic unit for cropping, and these in turn were grouped into large blocks called fields, usually two or three in number, which formed the basic unit for fallowing: i.e. each year

14 'Haymaking in the manorial meadows.' The long-handled scythe has a straight bar-handle with a single handgrip. The iron blade is tanged and bound to the handle. A reaper is sharpening his blade with a sandstone rub; another is removing clods (which might damage the scythe) with a spade. A resting reaper on the right is drinking from a horn cup. *H.J.M. Green after the Cotton calendar for July (B.L. MS Julius A. VI). Eleventh century* AD

one field lay completely unsown (Williamson 2003, 65 quoting Hall 1982 and 1995). At Clapham any topographical evidence for the ridge and furrow system has long been destroyed by housing development over the last 150 years. However, archaeological evidence for this type of arable system has survived, remarkably, in one place. The aerial photographic coverage of Clapham Common in 2003 showed a pattern of such field strips faintly visible along the north margin of the Common opposite Taybridge Road, with slight evidence that it extended at least as far as Jedburgh Street on a slightly different alignment (*colour plate 4.7*). The system is set out at a slight angle to Northside which clearly truncates this early field layout. At least eight ridges and furrows can be seen running NW–SE about 100yds out onto the Common, with slight evidence of a headland at right angles marking its southern limit. As will be seen, the early medieval predecessor of Northside appears to have been laid out during the last quarter of the twelfth century (see Chapter 7) so this field or furlong system, part of Wodefield of Wassingham, must belong to an earlier period. In this locality, at least, the arable of the West field ran right up to the margin of the drift gravels on the Common.

A.R.H. Baker has suggested that the so-called 'Kentish field system' once prevailed in Surrey (and thus Clapham), a system with a mixture of open and enclosed fields:

> Within any individual township there might be many open and enclosed fields ... there was no evidence to suggest that they were grouped in any systematic fashion ... While many fields were explicitly called 'common fields' it is frequently the case that they were frequently small and that their unenclosed parcels were not shared among large numbers of tenants.
>
> Baker & Butlin 1873, 421

The 1326 Extent indicates that the East field (which stretched from Clapham Common Station almost as far as Stockwell) had already been broken up into some dozen or more smaller units, identified in the Extent as 'fields', 'lands' and 'crofts' (see Chapter 8). However, the evidence of the Extent indicates that the seigniorial holdings were fairly evenly distributed amongst these and many other units of land indicating that this was the standard type of land allotment at Clapham. This contradicts Baker's assessment of the Kentish/Surrey tradition where 'there was a tendency for the constituents of a holding to be clustered in one part of the township rather than to be regularly (or even randomly) distributed throughout it' (Baker & Butlin 1973, 421 quoting Gray 1915, 356-9).

One last aspect of the ploughlands of old Clapham needs to be discussed. During the archaeological excavations in the village centre in the 1980s there was discovered what Densem describes as a sandy loam (ploughsoil) which covered all the Saxon and Medieval features cut into the 'natural' (Densem & Seeley 1982, 179). This layer might be as much as 2ft 6in (0.75m) thick, but was usually less. Finds dated from the prehistoric through to the post-medieval period. This layer is not necessarily ploughsoil at all, but rather classic 'garden' earth heavily cultivated, usually by spade agriculture, for the last millennium or so. Its presence on most Clapham sites indicates the disturbed state of surface soil and subsoil deposits to a depth of ½m or more, effectively destroying all upper archaeological levels and slighter constructional features. Its presence, however, in the very centre of the old village is a reminder that, as Christopher Taylor's studies have shown, the planning of villages, their fields, house sites and road systems – even the position of the village itself – is subject to movement and change in response to economic and other factors (Taylor 1974, 150). The plan of the village centre of early Clapham was almost certainly very different from anything that we would recognise from the topographical layout of today.

A BUNDLE OF FAGGOTS

The furze (*Ulex Europaens*) from the Common was a valuable commodity as fuel 'to heat their ovens with all other uses' (1715 deposition of John Heather and Thomas Pearcey). The ovens in question were used for baking and required an intense heat for a short period to make the sides red hot, after which the ashes would be raked out and the bread inserted. However, furze or gorse did not have the long-burning, combustible properties of wood, thus rendering it uneconomical for open fires. The dry gorse would be cut on the Common, bundled up and tied with elm withes for carrying purposes. Two faggots were required for each bake which took place twice a week. Thus, 100 faggots a year was the usual estimate of fuel needed for a cottage or small farm house, allowing for a little extra for any special bakes (Ewart Evans 1956, 56, 59) (*15*).

By the seventeenth century, Clapham supported about 70 households, thus requiring in theory about 7000 faggots a year, a staggering quantity for the small area of Common available by that date, particularly if half the land had been appropriated by Battersea parish.

The friction between Clapham and Battersea went back a long way, indeed probably to the time of the Norman Conquest when Westminster annexed half the common land

15 Peasant carrying wood as part of his manorial duties. Although wood rather than furze is illustrated in this fifteenth-century scene from *Les Fables de Bidpois*, the back-breaking nature of the work is well demonstrated. *H.J.M. Green after MS 1389/680 Museé Condé a Chantilly*

of Saxon Clapham (see below). The exceptionally cold conditions which commenced in the early fourteenth century and lasted for 300 years (the so-called 'Little Ice Age') put a strain on this resource of free fuel for both communities. In 1578 a Clapham labourer was caught on the *Esteheath* mowing the fern and was sent packing by Battersea residents. The mowed fern was taken to Battersea Manor House by cart (Loobey 2002, 71). Battersea Manor was already rationing the amount of furze that could be gathered at any one time to that which could be carried away on a person's back (1719 deposition of William Noble of Battersea). Another severe winter in 1715 was probably the catalyst for Lord St John, Lord of the Manor of Battersea, sealing off the western side of the Common by erecting a ditch and bank in 1716 along the parish boundary, thereby denying Clapham of its commoner's rights, and, in particular, the right of gathering furze for fuel. As a consequence, Sir Henry Atkins, Lord of the Manor of Clapham, and other prominent citizens, brought an action for trespass against Henry Viscount St John. Clapham won its case in 1718, asserted its commoner's rights and the boundary works had to be removed. All of this was confirmed by a suit in chancery in 1719 (Dale 1927, 215-231). The traces of these works are visible on the 2003 aerial photographs of the Common in the area of the bandstand (*colour plates 4 & 5*). The value of this case for the historian is that the voices of Clapham villagers, normally so silent, came over loud and clear from 300 years ago!

THE WOODS OF CLAPHAM

Several parcels of woodland are mentioned in passing in the medieval and later records of Clapham, some of considerable acreage. No woodland is mentioned in the Domesday account of 1086, but references occur from the mid fourteenth century onwards and appear to be tied to geophysical and demographic disasters which reduced the capacity of the vill to work some of its more intractable land.

The adverse climatic changes between 1310 and 1320 heralded what has come to be known as the 'Little Ice Age', a devastating weather cycle which lingered, on and off, for 500 years (Fagan 2002, 39). It was marked in south-east England by unnatural spells of heavy and prolonged rain during the cool summers of 1315 and 1316. The winters were also cold and wet, the harshest being that of 1317-18. The folk memory of this dreadful time lingered on to be recorded in Shakespeare's 'With hey, ho, the wind and the rain … For the rain it raineth every day' (*Twelfth Night*). In an economy that was naturally fragile at the best of times, the consequences were predictable: widespread crop failure, ensuing hunger, famine-related epidemics and high rates of mortality. The period was known generically in historical studies as the 'Great Famine', its impact being worst between 1315 and 1318 (Jordan 1996, 18ff).

No chronicles recorded the plight of the people of Clapham, which has to be deduced indirectly from major changes in the management of the land and economy of the vill at this time. Two immediate consequences are evident: a fall in population numbers and consequent abandonment of agricultural land. This was due not only to the lack of field-hands, but to the poor condition of the soil, which was chronically affected by wet conditions and consequently impossible to work. Two years or more of almost continuous rain with a run-off down the slope from the springline of the Common over the Floodplain Terrace, reduced these base-poor, clayey soils to *puddle* conditions – that is a sticky mass which adheres to ploughs, harrows and other implements when wet, and which dries to a hard, brick-like mass (Williamson 2003, 143). By 1318 much of the heavy clay subsoils of Clapham were virtually unworkable and alternative uses had to be found for this land.

It may therefore be significant that the first mention of woodland occurs eight years later at Clapham. In 1326 at the Inquisition following the death of John de Fiennes, Lord of the Manor at Clapham, there is the first mention of 140 acres of *underwood* (*Chan. Inq.* PM 19 Edw. II 85). 'Underwood is a technical term indicating managed woodland regularly cropped by coppicing to produce poles for building and other purposes' (Rackham 1986, 65). The following year (1327) this woodland was described as being in two units of 70 acres (*Cal. Close* 1323-7, 583). These presumably are the 'two great woods' mentioned in the *1628 Extent* following the death of the Lord of Clapham Manor, Dr. Henry Atkins (*State papers Domestic,* Charles I 154/93, 1628) (*colour plate 7*).

Stockwood

One of the two woods was evidently the old West Field of the vill (although no contemporary records survive naming it as such). At the Inquisition held after the death of Sir Henry Atkins in 1639 (*Wandsworth LHS* MS 98 – item 29) this 70 acres of woodland 'lately converted into pasture and arable land' had formerly been known as 'Lord Montague's Wood', otherwise 'Stockwood'. The name 'Stockwood' is in itself significant, since *O.E. Stocc* means stock or tree stumps, a term which, when applied to woodland, implies that it was in the process of destruction. The 1639 Inquisition is of value since it indicates that this particular woodland was destroyed between 1628 and 1639, giving it a life of almost exactly 300 years.

This former woodland stretched from the western boundary of Clapham (now Wix's Lane) to the rear of the medieval *tofts* or tenements on the west side of North Street. The north and south boundaries were what is now the Wandsworth Road and Clapham Common Northside respectively. This discrete unit of land is exactly 70 acres and is of particular interest for this study, because in the mid seventeenth century it was to form the nucleus of the Gauden Estate. There survive faint echoes of this ancient woodland in old pollard trees still to be found in present garden boundaries in the area, which may date back in origin to this period. Another ghost of this lost woodland are the bluebells (*Endymion nonscriptus*) which grow naturally each spring in the gardens along Clapham Common Northside (*colour plate 6*). The Bluebell is a woodland plant which, once established, will survive for long periods, even though the previous land-use has long ceased (Rackham 1976, 126).

Stockwell Wood

In the Customal and Extent of 1326 following the death of Juliana Romayn, Lady of Clapham Manor, the two great woods of Clapham were divided between her daughter Margery de Weston, who inherited the Manor, and Roesia de Boreford (*Cal. Close* 1323-7, 583). The West Wood, which was attached to Clapham Manor, has already been covered. The description of the East Wood, describes it as a '*moiety*' (i.e. a half portion), and it is specified as being of 70 acres with a value of 66s. 8d. (the same as the west wood) lying on the east side 'toward Stockwell'. Both woods are described as being 'enclosed by boundaries', probably meaning that they had the traditional woodland boundary of a bank and a ditch, the bank being on the wood side (Rackham 1976, 115).

The difficulty here is finding a 70 acre parcel of land within the traditional boundaries of Clapham, since all the land holdings mentioned in the 1326 Extent can be accounted for (see Chapter 8). Evidently, Roesia and her husband John de Boreford inherited the Manor of Stockwell (*16*) which had also formed part of the Romayn Estate and had been acquired by Thomas and Juliana in 1294-5 (*Feet of F. Survey* Hil. 23 Ed. I). There are one or two possible locations for the East Wood. One in the London Road area, which formed a discrete block of land into the eighteenth century and was part of the Duke of Bedford's estates, can be ruled out. A primary feature of this parcel of land was a conduit (T.N.A. E/BER/S/L/16) and it is evident from the 1326 Extent that the land near the conduit was pasture in 1326 (*Cal. Close* 19 Edw. II 1326 1d).

The favoured location lies on the north-west side of Clapham Road SW9 and comprised a wedge-shaped unit of land between the old manorial boundaries of Clapham and Vauxhall (*6*). An estate map of 'Fauxhall Manour' from 1681 shows the southern boundary to have extended only as far as the present Lansdowne Way SW8 (copy of the Canterbury Cathedral Archive map in the Minet Library ref. AD 210/14/1681). The traditional Clapham boundary, on the other hand, followed the old

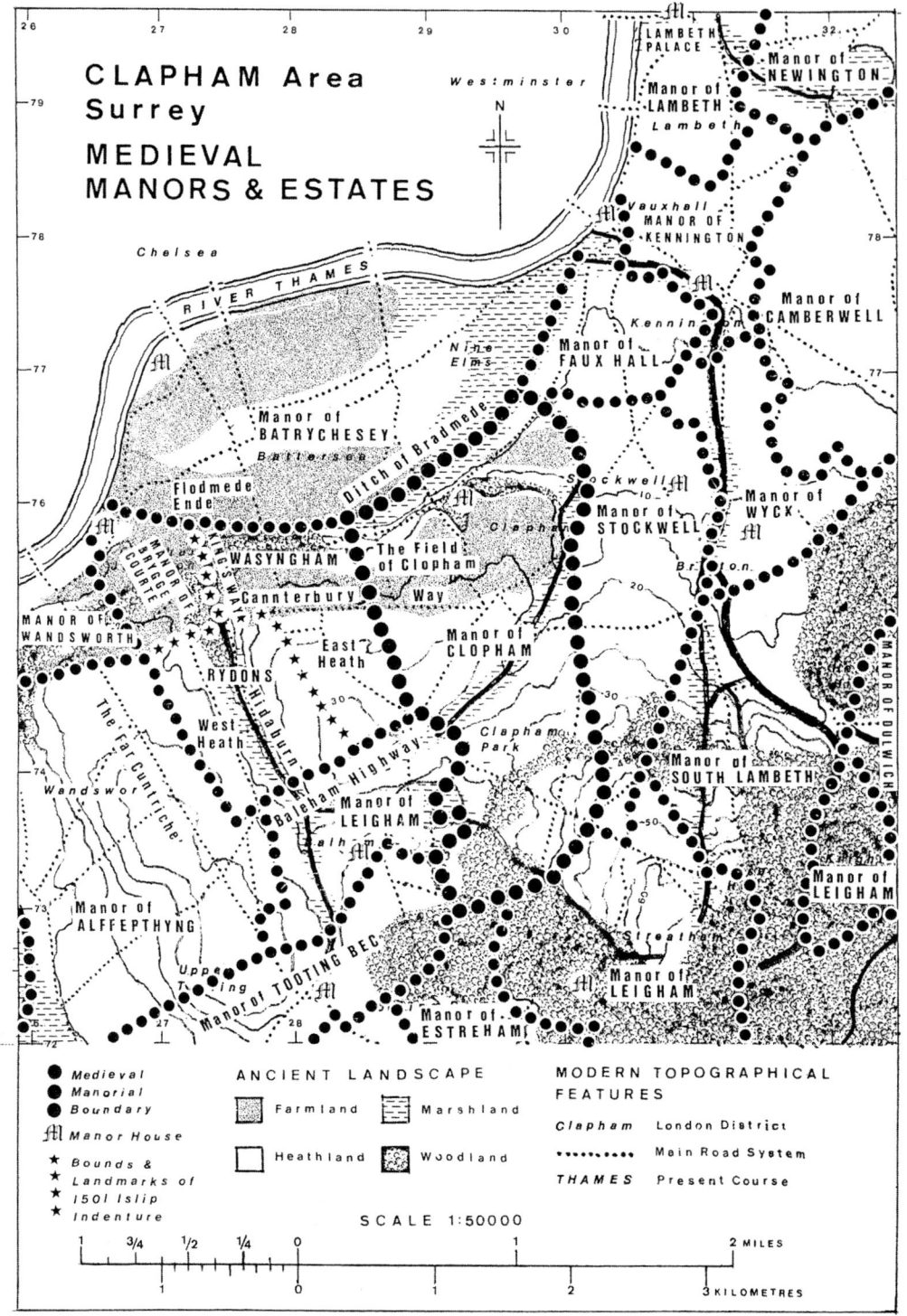

16 Map of medieval manors and estates in the Clapham area. *H.J.M. Green from various sources; Base Map based on the British Geological Survey published 1998. By permission of the B.G.S.*

course of the Heath Wall Brook further south, now marked by the southern boundaries of properties along Jeffreys Road SW4 and Southville SW8. The area between covers exactly 70 acres. A survey of lands of Stockwell Manor in 1551 (TNA E36/168 H138-40) held by Nicholas Brynisel does not mention this woodland.

It is evident that notwithstanding the bequest of Julian Romayn, the East Wood was still leased to Clapham Manor as late as 1628, when it is mentioned in the Extent following the death of Dr Henry Atkins (*State papers Domestic* Charles I 154/93, 1628). It is possible that the destruction of Stockwood which took place under Sir Henry Atkins between 1628 and 1639 also included the Stockwell Wood, which was subsequently lost to Clapham.

Wodefield

An even larger area of woodland associated with Clapham is that first mentioned in a Conveyance of 1437 (Dale 1927, 4) when Robert de Weston, Lord of Clapham Manor, conveyed *Wodefield* containing 300 acres to John Machon (6). There is no record of such a field in Clapham at any period, but in 1719, during the lawsuit between Clapham and Battersea, Robert Makepeace makes reference to *Woodfield* in the parish of Battersea, which lay to the west of Wix's Lane (T.N.A C24/1378 and C24/1379).

It is therefore significant that a large area of 75 acres comprising 6 parcels of land in 1787 was still being referred to in 1838 as *Oaken Stub Shott* (Battersea Tithe Assessment, 1839) in this locality. The significance of this field name with reference to former woodland is interesting. *Stub* refers to land covered with tree-stumps, indicating that this had formerly been an oak plantation. It would appear that this may have been the last area of this huge acreage of woodland to be cleared. Indeed, its location on the farmlands of Wassingham (see Chapter 4) would suggest that all the arable land here, as well as uncultivated land, had been turned over to woodland by the early fifteenth century. By my calculations, Wassingham had a total area (including the East Heath) of about 292 acres. Was this little hamlet (centred round St. Johns Road SW11) depopulated as a consequence of the demographic disasters of the early and mid fourteenth century?

Although it may have lost its villagers, the Estate still survived as a discrete unit into the sixteenth century and had a topographical identity into the eighteenth century. During the fifteenth century, Wassingham was customarily sublet by Westminster Abbey, the titular Lords of Battersea, to a succession of lessees, who included presumably Weston and Machon in 1437. How long this woodland remained part of the Clapham Estates is unclear, but by the middle of the fifteenth century it had been let to John Stanley, who also had Rights of Common on East Heath. His leasehold agreement was for 40 years, which may have been the standard fixed period of time for these contracts (Redstone 1967, 12). The medieval felling pattern was about 8 years (Rackham 1976, 72) so that a cycle of five felling rotations would have been achieved within the contractual period.

The South Clapham Woods (6)

There were other parcels of woodland on the heavy clays of south Clapham, whose history was closely tied up with the medieval Manor of Leigham in what is now

Balham, the Lordship of which was held by Bermondsey Abbey. The Estates of Bermondsey, which included Great Balams and Little Balams within Leigham Manor, drifted in and out of what are now the manorial boundaries of Clapham and Balham, according to the situation of the land market of the time and the financial pressures on the owners and manorial lords.

For example, in the early twelfth century, Leigham Manor was part of the land of the Mandeville family, who also owned Clapham. In 1103 the estate at Balham was given to Bermondsey Abbey by the Mandevilles (see Chapter 6). Land lost at this time to the old Saxo-Norman estate at Clapham was former woodland (amounting to 18 acres of land in the early nineteenth century) known under the Bermondsey Abbey ownership as *Friday Grove*. This parcel of land forms a re-entrant into Clapham parish in the area of Weir Road SW12. Friday comes from *Frigedaeg*, a Saxo-Norman personal name which occurs as a field name elsewhere in Clapham (see Chapter 8, *The Fields*). It was presumably these woods which were leased by Bermondsey in the earlier sixteenth century to one William Gardiner, a landowner living near the abbey, when the woodland was 27 acres in size (Gower 1996, 8). Friday Grove was arguably on the worst agricultural land in the vicinity, since the subsoil was London Clay. In the late Saxon period it was the site of Rush Mere, through which the Hidaburn Stream flowed (see Chapter 5). Even after the stream was drained and the Mere consequently disappeared, the area was unsuitable for anything except woodland in agricultural terms.

Cockinge's Wood lay in that part of the old parish termed 'Clapham Detached'. This seems to be because the wood was extensive and at one time included land outside the immediate area of Clapham, as is the case with many of the other woods reviewed here. During the medieval period, the western end of Clapham Detached was taken up by 20 acres of this woodland, as shown in a plan of Ballum Farm in 1622 (M.A E/DCA 257). William Cockinge was a tenant of the farm in the early seventeenth century. The wood evidently extended further to the west and south-west at an earlier period since Grubb Close (21 acres) is shown adjoining Cockinge's Wood. 'Grubb' in this connection refers to former woods which had been 'grubbed out' or cut down to provide arable land. The earlier name of this 40-acre woodland has not survived, but is perhaps to be identified with *Ballum Wood*. The location of this ancient woodland which covered the sloping ground from Ballum Wood Lane (Nightingale Lane) down to the former course of the Hidaburn Stream (later the York Sewer or Falcon Brook) is now the area of Fernside Road and east/west between the present Western Lane and Ravenslea Road SW12. In origin, Cockinge's Wood may belong to the same period (mid fourteenth century) as the two great woods of Clapham, and for the same reason of depopulation of the vill. In the mid seventeenth century the wood may have been acquired by Dennis Gauden when Clapham Place was built. On the estate map of Ballum Farm in 1800 (MA E/DCA 258) it is shown as 'Mr Hewer's Land', although the Hewer Estate had ceased to exist in the mid eighteenth century. William Hewer acquired Clapham Place in 1678 from Gauden. If so, Cockinge's Wood may have been cut down in the mid seventeenth century to provide timber building material for Clapham Place. Pepys' diary entry for 25 July 1663 mentions that Gauden was showing good husbandry in 'making his bricks and other things' (Latham 1986, 295) presumably from materials derived from his own estate. The trees from former Stockwood, on which Clapham Place was built, had all been cut down earlier in the seventeenth century, as we have seen.

Initially at least, these woods must have started life as *wood pastures*; that is without coppices (i.e. underwood) but with a reasonable quantity of herbage growing beneath the trees and with extensive open glades occupied by shrubs and rough vegetation (*colour plate 7*). Such areas were exploited for wood and timber, but they were not managed very intensively to this end (*17 & 18*). Sheep, cattle and goats were fed not only on the grass and herbage, but also on bushes and shrubs, and on the trees themselves, which might be eaten directly or cut and stored as *leafy hay* (Williamson 2003, 54). Later, as the trees of the two Great Woods of Clapham matured, more emphasis was put on husbandry of the wood resources. The 1326 Extent specifies 140 acres of underwood. Underwood as defined here is managed woodland (*19*) organised to produce coppice poles or suckers from low tree stumps (*stools*). A similar process, also for producing poles (but above the

17 Cutting tree foliage for leafy hay in the wood pasture using iron, long-bladed billhooks. *H.J.M. Green after the Cotton calendar for February (B.L. MS Julius A.VI). Eleventh century*

18 'Uses of managed woodland'. Left: hunting, the equipment should be compared with that used 500 years later for boar hunting (*colour plate 7*). Centre: the provision of pannage (acorns and beech-mast) for the manorial swine. Right: timber and wood products as indicated by a pollarded tree. *H.J.M. Green after the Cotton calendar for September (B.L. MS Tib. B5). Eleventh century*

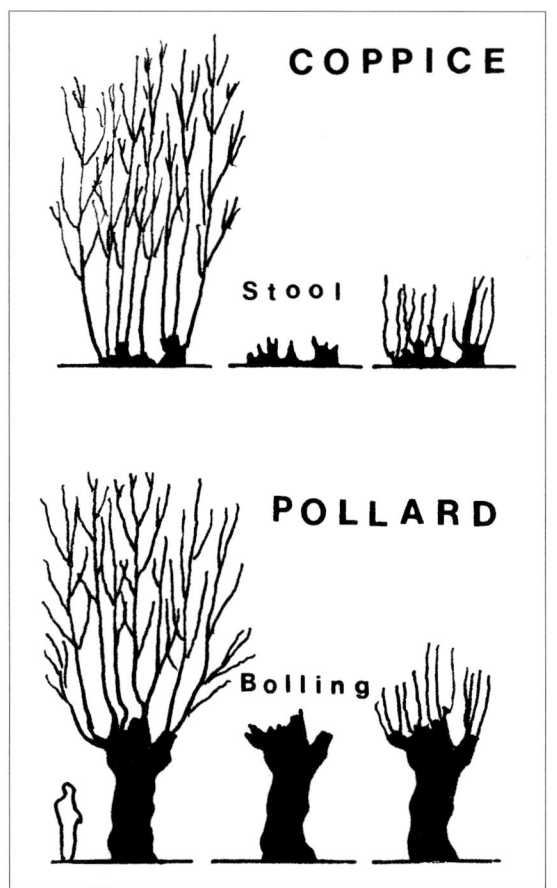

COPPICE

Stool

POLLARD

Bolling

19 Woodland management of coppice stool and pollard bolling. Each method is shown just before cutting, just after cutting and one year after cutting. *H.J.M. Green after O. Rackham (Rackham 1986, 66)*

reach of grazing animals) involves the *pollarding* of a tree crown whose trunk stands some 10ft above ground level. Underwood is traditionally cropped every seven or eight years. To produce a regular annual batch of poles, one seventh of the woodland would be cut. In the case of Stockwood (the West Wood) which had formerly been a common arable field, the old parcels of land (the furlongs) probably formed the basis of these forestry units. Each unit needed to be accessible to a trackway or *chase* used for cartage of the underwood poles. Remarkably, this roadway of Stockwood still survives running north–south across the former woodland, under the modern street name of *The Chase*. As late as the early nineteenth century, the positions of the seven *grove* subdivisions could be identified, used by then as parcels of land for arable and pasture (Clapham Tithe Map of 1838). In the case of pollarding from stools, the woodland would require careful hedging or fencing to protect the suckers from browsing animals (Rackham 1976, 60f.).

3

'MANY ROMAN ANTIQUITIES'

The Roman Road runs straight and bare
As the pale parting-line in hair
Across the Heath. And thoughtful men
Contrast its days of Now and Then,
And delve, and measure, and compare; …

Thomas Hardy, *Time's Laughingstocks*

STANE STREET

It was Pliny the Younger writing in the late first century AD who said that 'there is an enchantment in a change of air and landscape and even in merely journeying around …' (*E.P.* 3.19.4). It has been the fate of Clapham for most of its history to be largely a place through which people passed but did not linger, whether as a Roman merchant on his way to the south coast, a medieval pilgrim en route to St Thomas' shrine at Canterbury or the modern commuter to outer suburban London. It is therefore appropriate that the most lasting monuments of the Roman period are the roads which passed through Clapham, of which perhaps Stane Street was the most important (Margery route 15).

This ancient road was the main Roman feature of the area, running south-south-west across the eastern side of the present Common. The name is probably late Saxon (*O.E. stan*, meaning stone, is a reference to the metalled surface of the road) and occurs as Stonestret as early as 1177-86 at Ewell in a grant of land to Turbout by Merton Priory (Heales 1898, 29).

Archaeological evidence indicates that the road was built before AD 70, and may indeed have been laid out in the years following the Roman Conquest (AD 43), since it links *Londinium* with *Noviomagus* (Chichester) the cantonal capital of the *Regini* Tribe. Under its client king Tognidubnus, the tribe supported the Roman authority during the Boudiccan uprising of AD 60 and its aftermath (*20*). Tiberius Claudius Tognidubnus, *Rex* and *Legatus Augusti in Britannia*, 'who remained faithful down to this time' (Tacitus, *Agricola* 14 – writing *c.*AD 70) was rewarded with a great palace at Fishbourne, Sussex. He may have been a key figure in the rebuilding of London in the early AD 60s after its sack and burning by the *Iceni* tribe. The tribal woods and lands of the *Andred* forest of the

20 Fugitives from the sack of
Londinium *c.*AD 60 by Boudicca of the
Iceni. Stane Street through Clapham
was one of the main escape routes
to the south from the stricken town.
*H.J.M. Green after relief of conquered
German tribespeople on the sarcophagus of
Marcus Aurelius, Museo Nazionale, Rome*

Weald would have produced timber and iron ore in abundance for the reconstruction of
London, and most of it would have been carried along Stane Street.

The road took an almost direct route between London and Chichester, a tribute to the
surveying skills of the Roman *mensores*. It was set out in a series of long alignments, with,
however, some slight diversions to avoid awkward topographical features. Throughout
most of its course across outer London, including Clapham, the route has been followed
by later roads the history of which goes back to at least the early medieval period, and
it now constitutes the A24 (*21*).

SITE N.D.E 46

In the Clapham area, the present road makes a diversion to the west away from an
established alignment found at Stockwell and Brixton. The late I.D. Margery, who in the
1930s and 1940s was a leading authority on Roman roads, considered that the present
Clapham route was later and that the Roman road would have followed a direct alignment
between Stockwell and Brixton. In order to check this theory, in 1946 a watching brief was
carried out by C.T. Thomas in an area then being developed for housing in the Tableer
Avenue/Worsopp Drive area of the Notre Dame Estate. A deep trench 100yds long cut
across the possible line of the Roman route. It had 'completely negative results as far as
finding … traces of the road' (Wetherby 1946/7, 151). An area of gravel at the western end
of the trench was declared by Margery to be 'natural' (the margin of Clapham Common
drift deposit?). Some Roman and medieval pottery was found in the topsoil.

SITE CR71 (*22*)

Over 20 years later another attempt was made to establish the direct alignment of
Stane Street through Clapham in three excavations carried out by the Southwark and

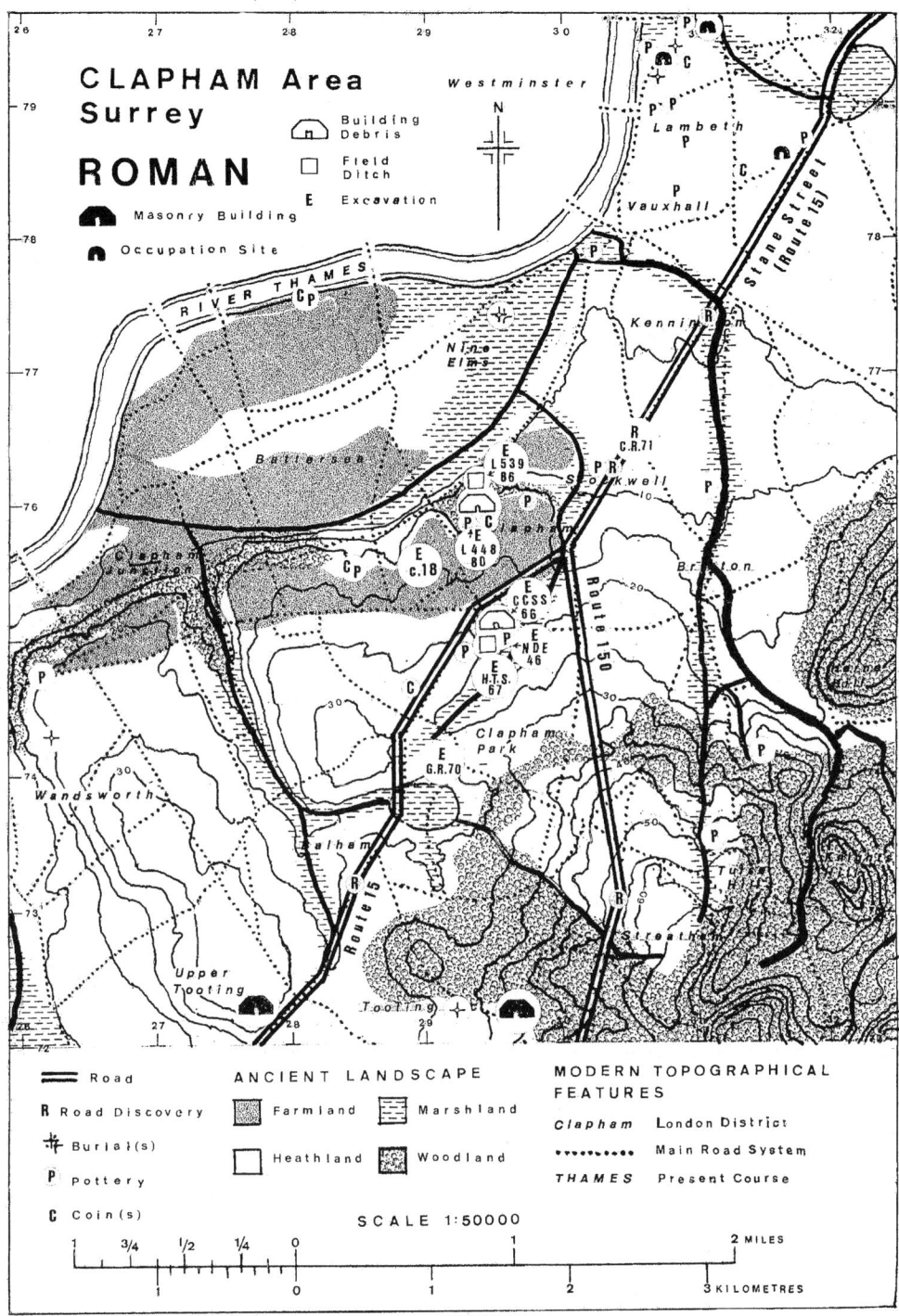

21 Roman distribution map of the Clapham area based on the collected evidence of the National Monuments Record for Lambeth and Wandsworth compiled by English Heritage. *H.J.M. Green. Base Map after the British Geological Survey published 1998*

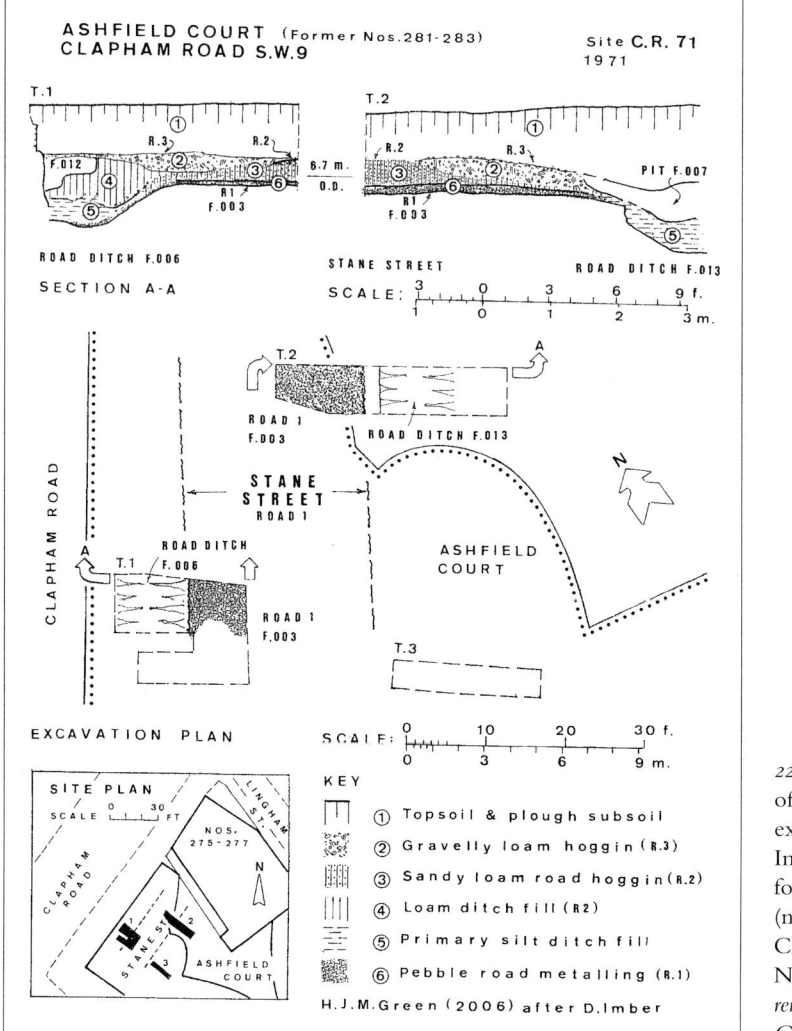

22 Plan and sections of site CR71 (1971) excavated by D. Imber on the site of former Nos 281-283 (now Ashfield Court) Clapham Road NW8. *Redrawn and reinterpreted by H.J.M. Green after D. Imber*

Lambeth Archaeological Society under the direction of Donald Imber (Imber 1968, 12–15: 1974, 235–50).

The most important of the three sites tested as part of this exercise were the excavations in 1971 in the front gardens of Nos 281–283 Clapham Road, Stockwell (now part of the site of Ashfield Court). This excavation was on an alignment of Stane Street which is not in dispute and produced structural evidence of the road together with Roman dating material. It showed the likely nature and condition of the highway if it is ever to be located in Clapham. The careful excavation by Donald Imber revealed a complex stratification as illustrated in the published report (Imber 1974, 235-250). However, his findings require re-evaluation in the light of more recent work which has demonstrated the problems of interpreting the structure of a complex road system subject to multiple phases of wear and resurfacing.

Imber correctly identified the earliest road system as F.003 (here designated as layer 6, road 1) which had been constructed on cleared and levelled areas of natural. The sandy subsoil here has lenses of gravelly clay characteristic of the Hackney Gravel Series. On this surface was laid pebbly-gravel road metalling, approximately 7m wide (23ft to 25ft), but due to heavy wear of the road surface, it had lost all but 0.03-0.13m (3in approximately) of the original hoggin.

The Roman road to the east of Clapham (Margery route 150) sometimes called the 'London-Brighton road' since it ran through Streatham to the South Coast, was found in better condition in Telford Avenue, SW2, in 1967 (Imber 1974, 239). Here the gravel hoggin had a cambered surface of varied flint metalling with an overall thickness of 0.43 m (1.5 Roman ft). The road was flanked by substantial drainage ditches. The western ditch at Clapham (F. 006) had a silty primary fill (layer 5) into which had washed some of the road metalling. F. 006 was probably 2.5m wide. The eastern road ditch (F. 013), some 2m wide, also contained spreads of silt and stones from the road metalling. There was no closely datable material from these deposits.

However, this was not the only Roman road level found in 1971. Problems of flooding in this low-lying area led to the next road system, (road 2) being constructed on a raised *agger* of the sandy-loam hoggin (layer 3) of which traces of the gravel road metalling survived at the margins. The western road ditch (F. 006) may have been recut. Its secondary sandy loam filling contained Samian ware pottery datable to *c.*AD 70-100. The western edge of this ditch was disturbed by F. 012, possibly a footing trench associated with medieval road-side settlement. It was probably this or an associated feature which produced a sherd of late medieval Surrey ware. The upper levels of the eastern road ditch (F. 013) were cut by a medieval pond or pit (F. 007) containing sherds of Surrey ware and red ware in its primary and secondary fills respectively.

A third phase of road use (road 3) is characterised by a mixed deposit of gravel grit and loam (layer 2) almost certainly a deposit disturbed by heavy road traffic. Imber was inclined to date this phase to post-Roman use of Stane Street.

The Roman dating evidence, based on the Samian ware from this excavation, appears to be confined to the Flavian period or, at the latest, early Trajanic. However, there is no evidence elsewhere that Stane Street was abandoned, rather it continued in use throughout the Roman period (25) and later as a major highway. The reason for this apparent anomaly is almost certainly the problem identified on other Roman sites, where intensive late Saxon and medieval agriculture has taken place, resulting in the total ploughing out and removal of the upper levels of the site, including any subsequent road surfaces. The upper levels of other Clapham sites, particularly in the village centre, had similarly been destroyed by later agriculture.

One last feature requires comment, namely the medieval realignment of the road to the west of its original course. The site lies on the northern margin of the medieval village of Stockwell, on a main road with a frontage which would have been built-up from an early period (indeed, evidence of such activity has already been noted above). A primary concern of such occupation would have been to find dry foundations for the buildings. Hence the appropriation of the raised gravel *agger* of the old Roman road for building on.

SITES H.T.S. 67 AND GR70 (*21*)

Extensive excavations were undertaken in 1967 in the grounds of what is now Lambeth College to check the theoretical line of Stane Street. Only one group of trenches (B and C) produced any features which might be interpreted as a gravel road. One feature, 6.7m wide (nearly 22ft) ran nearly the full length of the trench (F3). At the south-east end, and apparently sealed by F3, was F12, a shallow ditch running NE-SW. No Roman artefacts were found. In the eighteenth and nineteenth centuries this locality was developed as an elaborate landscape project for Eldon House with a complex pattern of gravel paths bordering lawns, flowerbeds, kitchen gardens and boundary features at the bottom of the grounds (Smith 1976, 71). An unusual feature of this layout, and noted at the time, was that the gravel walks ran round the whole estate and 'encompassed several meadows' (Edwards 1801, 11). A watercolour by H. Hopley White from 1863 shows the neatly cambered gravel walks of this garden (Smith 1976, pl.80).

When the excavation trenches are carefully plotted on O.S. maps, and as transparencies are overlain on large-scale C19 maps, problems arise in the interpretation of these road features as being of Roman date. Trenches B and C are in a slightly skewed alignment with a paddock boundary, presumably bordered by a gravel path, shown on maps of 1838 and 1849. The ditch F12 is evidently an earlier estate boundary of Eldon House, shown on the 1746 Rocque map, where it meets the former common fields of the village. It would appear that the gravel feature F3 turned at this point to run alongside the boundary.

To the south of H.T.S. 67 is another site, G.R. 70, where a further attempt was made in 1970 to intercept the projected course of Stane Street in properties on the north side of Gaskarth Road, SW12. Although patches of pebble and gravel, together with a ditch, were found, there was again the same failure to check the archaeological findings against old topographical features, such as boundaries, shown on early O.S. maps before the existing street pattern was formed. The 1874, 25in to a mile O.S. map shows that Trenches 1, 4 and 5 lie along the north boundary of a large, late eighteenth-century villa fronting Balham Hill. A gravel path evidently running alongside the boundary was followed for much of its length (some 12.5m) in trenches 2 and 3, and was interpreted as being a section across Stane Street by the excavators (F3). The ditch (F7) is exactly on the line of an old medieval field boundary of the Little Balam's Estate. No Roman artefacts were found on this site.

In the light of this evidence, I believe that the case for maintaining the direct alignment hypothesis, along the line tested by the 1946, 1967 and 1970 excavations, has not been convincingly made. Moreover, there is an important topographical reason for abandoning this theory. The projected, direct alignment would have taken Stane Street along 2 miles of boggy ground, conditions that Roman road engineers had been careful to avoid elsewhere along its route (Merrifield 1969, 58). Although the Heath Wall Brook is now canalised by sewers below Abbeville Road, the water table is still high in the vicinity, as the archaeologists of both the 1967 and 1970 excavations noted at the time.

Faced with two miles of marsh culminating in a 7 acre lake, the Roman *viatores* probably made a diversion which would have taken the route about 1000ft to the west on higher ground, a course it has followed ever since. The diversion starts at Clapham North, where the road would have crossed the Heath Wall Brook by a ford, up Clapham High Street, changes course to run parallel with the main alignment along the south side of Clapham Common, then from Clapham South veers slightly to the east avoiding Rushmere to join up with the main alignment again at Balham.

However, a recent find which may support the traditional alignment of Stane Street across Clapham Common is the discovery of Roman coins by a treasure hunter some years ago when the area around the Eagle Pond (alongside the A24) was landscaped (OS grid ref. 290.740). Mr Wilf White, in a private communication to me in 2006, mentioned that he had seen a *denarius*, indecipherable but probably of second-century date, and some bronze coins. The treasure hunter also mentioned the discovery of a coin of Helena, presumably the wife of Constantine I, dating to the earlier fourth century.

OTHER ROMAN ROADS (*21*)

Some attention has necessarily been paid to the matter of establishing the correct route of Stane Street at Clapham. It is not a mere academic quibble, but vitally affects our understanding of other Roman discoveries in the vicinity, as well as the course of two other Roman roads which joined Stane Street here.

Another important north-south road mentioned earlier, the so-called London-Brighton way (Margery route 150), may also be associated with Clapham. This Roman road has been traced with some certainty through Streatham to the eastern end of Telford Avenue where the section of the road, previously described, was seen in 1967. Northwards from here the course is uncertain. The traditional view is that it ran through Brixton to join up with Stane Street at Kennington Park (Merrifield 1969, 59-60). However, the fourth edition of the *Ordnance Survey Map of Roman Britain* (1994) postulates another hypothetical line to meet Stane Street further south in the Clapham area. The eastern boundary of the Clapham manorial demesne, dating to at least as early as the Middle Saxon period (and subsequently followed by the parochial boundary) was a straight trackway now followed in part by the Lyham and Bedford Roads emerging at Clapham North. A copy of a mid thirteenth century charter purporting to date to 1062 (see Chapter 5 for its significance in regards to the Saxo-Norman Clapham boundary) describes this road as the *est* or eastern street, to distinguish it presumably from the western route of Stane Street (Mon. Angl. VI 61-2, No. 1). This projected route is in direct alignment with the Telford Road discovery.

If these two roads ran north-south, there may have been another route, east-west, passing along the edge of the flood-plain terrace to join up with Stane Street in the Clapham area. Excavation of the Roman settlement at Putney in the early 1970s revealed evidence of a substantial gravel road, flanked by ditches running parallel with and slightly south of the Upper Richmond Road (Farrant 1972, 369; 1974, 214). It was postulated that it might connect with Stane Street via Clapham Common Northside, described as an ancient causeway. This trackway was later promoted by Merton Priory as a pilgrimage route ('Canterbury Way') in the late twelfth century (Chapter 7). It is possible that the plough headlands in the south side of the great west field of medieval Clapham were formed out of the agger of this road.

ROMAN OCCUPATION SITES

The watching brief in 1952 on the Notre Dame Estate near Crescent Lane produced Roman material in the ploughsoil overlying the natural, described in the report as miscellaneous pottery, some Roman and some early medieval (Site CCSS 52; Wetherby 1946-7, 152). Close by, on the other side of Crescent Lane, in the former garden of No. 31 Clapham Common Southside, similar finds were discovered. In the summer of 1966, two local youths approached the writer, then living in Clapham, with a small group of Roman pottery and a Ptolemaic coin which they claimed to have found when digging a small (unauthorised) hole in the abandoned garden of No. 31, then awaiting development. There was certainly a small trench taken down to natural, but no obvious traces of Roman features. A sub-committee meeting of the Southwark Archaeological Excavation Committee shortly afterwards, as I recollect, expressed great interest in the finds and site, which they said should be the subject of further work and publication. In due course, a small excavation was carried out in the winter of 1966 for the *Clapham Antiquarian Society* and reported on by the author (Site CCSS 66/70; Green 1969, 27-32).

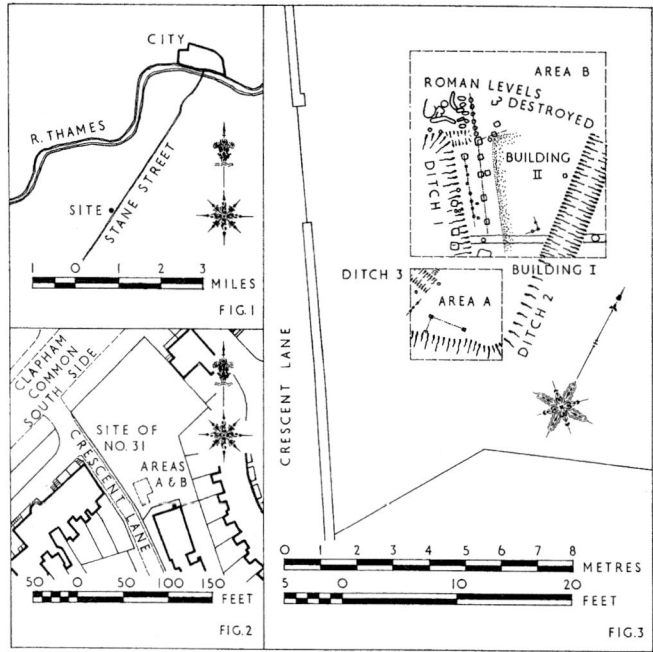

23 Plan of site CCSS 66/70 (1970) excavated by H.J.M. Green on the site of former No. 31 Clapham Common Southside (now Nos 30-31 Clapham Common Southside). The line of Stane Street on the location map is shown as following the 'Margery direct alignment', now discredited (see above). The site actually lay just south-east of the Roman road. *H.J.M. Green, published in LAMAS 22 pl. 2. (1969) p.28*

There was nearly 2m of post-medieval garden soil covering the site which contained neither Roman material nor any substantive indications of Roman features below, as was made clear in the report. However, careful cleaning down of the natural showed soil stains (i.e. features that had been backfilled with the same subsoil material, but showed themselves as a change of colour and texture). There were traces of a wall slot, stake and posthole settings cut by two shallow ditches representing, it was believed at the time, at least 3 phases of occupation. Ditch 2, area A, produced a sherd of Samian form 37 of Antonine date, together with two tesserae and a piece of grey Purbeck wall veneer. A residual handmade sherd of probably prehistoric date was also found in this feature. A similar handmade sherd was found in the wall slot. Fragments of Roman roofing tiles (*tegulae* and *imbrices*) and another piece of Purbeck marble were discovered in old ploughsoil immediately overlying these features. The finds were stored in a locked, former garden shed on the site, but as soon as the excavations were completed, the shed was broken into, all the Roman and earlier material (such as it was) stolen and the rest of the finds destroyed. The material found by the two youths had earlier been returned to them at their request.

As soon as the report was published, a follow-up excavation adjacent to the 1966 trenches was carried out by members of the Southwark Archaeological Excavation Committee in 1970. This too produced no Roman features, but because the excavations failed to clean down the natural (as was noted by this writer at the time) neither soil stains nor underlying features were discovered. The subsequent report of the 1970 excavations was highly critical of the 1966 work: 'all the features excavated in 1970 appeared to be of seventeenth century or later date, and none of those dug in 1966 can definitely be assigned to an earlier period' (Sheldon 1973, 151-4).

With hindsight after nearly 40 years, the peculiar sequence of events surrounding these excavations seems extremely suspicious. At the time the late Ralph Merrifield, then Assistant Director of the London Museum, told me that he believed that the whole business was a hoax aimed at discrediting the excavator and that the Roman material ostensibly found by the two youths had in fact come from other unrelated sites in the area. He also said that the two youths were known volunteer diggers on London archaeological sites. If Merrifield suspected that there were more extensive ramifications to this 'sting', he did not say so. It would be interesting to know whether, in the highly competitive professional world of London archaeology at that time, there were other cases of this nature. It is perhaps ironic that what may have started off as a 'joke' at the expense of the excavator eventually backfired on the perpetrators when a possible Roman site was discovered.

Site CCSS 66 needs to be seen in the context of the 1980s excavations on various nearly sites in Rectory Grove (Site L448/80). With the suggested re-alignment of Stane Street on its old, traditional route along Clapham Common Southside (see above) both CCSS 52 and 66/70 may now be seen to have added relevance as indicating a possible small settlement straddling Stane Street at the junction of a possible east-west road from Putney.

All the archaeological sites at Clapham in the old village centre suffered, as did site CCSS 66, from having a considerable overburden of garden and ploughsoil to a depth

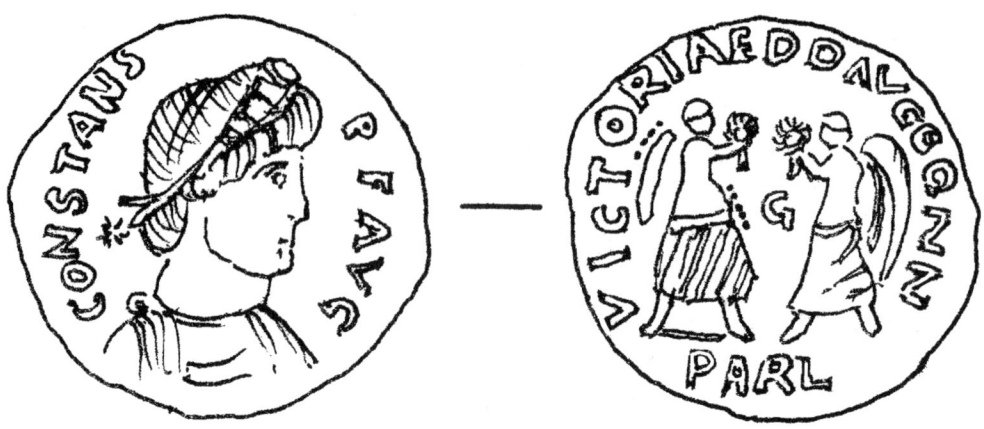

24 Bronze (AE3) coin of the Emperor Constans I issued at the Arles mint AD 341-46 of the type that was found on site L448/80. The reverse celebrates military victories of the joint Emperors Constans and Constantius II. *H.J.M. Green, scale 2:1*

of nearly 2m in places. These deposits and the underlying natural had been seriously disturbed further by eighteenth century and later features. Most medieval and earlier levels have consequently been almost completely removed, leaving only the very bottom of early features such as pits and postholes intact. Certainly, this was the case of the 1966 excavations. Another characteristic of these sites, perhaps for the above reason, appears to be that the Roman material has all occurred redeposited in secondary contexts of Saxon or medieval date. The slight traces of structures discovered in 1966 may indeed have all belonged to later periods. Certainly there was not enough associated Roman material to be certain that they were contemporaneous.

In the interim report on the archaeological excavations carried out in Rectory Grove, 1980-82, 1984 and 1986 (Densen & Seeley provisional summary report & *LAM* 448 level 3 report) the Roman discoveries were summarised as follows:

> No Roman features were found. A Roman coin [AD 340-6] Roman [roofing] tile fragments and less than 40 Roman pot-sherds were recovered as residual finds from Saxon and later features and from the grey-brown earth [interpreted as 'ploughsoil']. Saxon pit 4 contained some 10 large fragments of unabraided Roman tile, which may have been robbed from a building, perhaps nearby (see *24*).

The statement that 'no features were found' requires re-examination. Stake-hole alignments, usually indicative of wattle and daub buildings, were found cut by the Saxon pits and show on photographs of the site (Densem & Seeley 1982, 177 fig. 1) but were not picked up by the excavators.

Excavations on both sides of Stane Street therefore suggest that there was a Roman masonry building (or buildings) with tiled roofs, tessellated floors and other structural

25 'Packhorse traffic on Roman Stane Street'. *H.J.M. Green after a relief sculpture on the Igel Column; the funerary monument of the Secundinii family at Trier, Germany (late second or early third century AD)*

features in the immediate vicinity. The nature of these structures must remain speculative until they can be located. One possibility is that it is not a roadside building at all, but a farming establishment taking advantage of the Clapham Common springline and the light soils of the 'Floodplain' terrace. Such *villa*-farmsteads are beginning to be located in the area of outer London where they had previously been thought to be non-existent (Merrifield 1969, 142). Examples may be quoted from Beddington near the River Wandle (*Recent Archaeological Excavations in greater London 1990*) and Carshalton at Sutton (*London Region Archaeology* 2003, 6). One thing that can be stated with some certainty, however, is that the Clapham building was not a *mansio* or state staging-post as originally suggested in the 1969 report. It is too close to *Londinium*. The Roman site at Ewell on Stane Street (12 miles distant from the City) is a more likely candidate for this type of establishment (Merrifield 1969, 145).

THE EIGHTEENTH-CENTURY DISCOVERIES

The discoveries in Rectory Grove and nearby are not the only archaeological finds at Clapham which may relate to this period. In the manuscript minute book of the Society of Antiquaries of London is recorded the proceedings of a meeting on the 26 May 1757 at which a presentation was made by a certain Mr Dacosta. These include the following notes:

> That at the Village of Clapham many Roman Antiquities were found in Digging for Gravel, which in the year 1708 were in the possession of Mrs Edgehill [probably Mrs Edgeley Hewer] of that Place; so that by proper Enquiries after that family it is likely he thinks many curious things might be recovered from oblivion.

This report probably concerns the same site, the subject of a communication by the 'ingenious' Mr John Bagford in 1715 to the editor of John Leland's *De Rebus Britannicus Collecteanea,* where it was there printed in due course (Vol. 1, 1774 edition, p.59):

> To these must be added a great many roman antiquities that [have been] found in the grounds of Mr Ewer [William Hewer] at Clapham in digging for gravel. They are still in being, and have been viewed by Mr John Kemp, who as he is a great Judge in these Affairs, so, he owns that some of them are extraordinary and such as he had not seen before.

The nature of this discovery, its location in Clapham and the present whereabouts of this material has been a mystery, indeed a source of concern, to local historians ever since (*Clapham Antiquarian Society News Sheet* 1962, No. 177). However, something more can be added to the bare details that have survived from the eighteenth century, although after this long lapse of time, any theorising must necessarily be somewhat speculative.

Digging for gravel at Clapham in the early eighteenth century was almost wholly concerned with the provision of road metalling, as can be seen from the deposition of Robert Makepeace, roadmaker, in the Chancery Suit of 1719 concerning Clapham Common (Dale 1927, 217). It is unlikely that the work of gravel extraction was being carried out for the public highways by William Hewer, who lived at Clapham Place, sited in the middle of the present Chase, from 1688 to his death in 1715 (he had owned the property since 1678). The reference to the grounds of the Estate suggests that the gravel was required for the resurfacing of an approach road to the house. The condition of the lane known as Back Chase, giving access to the north front of the property, was giving concern to the owners at this time and indeed in 1716 was entirely reconstructed by Samuel Edgeley Hewer. This date is too late for the earlier discoveries (before 1708) but may refer to gravel extraction alongside the road for an earlier resurfacing. Indeed there is only one suitable location for this pit which evidently later became a field pond. The estate maps of the Edgeley Hewer property of *c.*1728 (see Chapter 9) has a large pond shown beside the Back Chase, clearly marked as such, and with access to the main avenue. The same rectilinear pond, 50 x 70ft is shown on the 1838 Tithe Maps, from which it can be estimated that the site (now of course, filled in) lies beneath the present back gardens of Nos 57 and 59, The Chase.

The gravel working must have revealed striking archaeological remains to have been noticed by the workmen and indeed Hewer. I would tentatively suggest a cremation cemetery with complete pots and possibly accompanying grave goods, which might represent a discrete family burial ground on the margins of the Roman settlement. However, it does not necessarily have to be Roman material. The ordinary classes of Romano-British pottery were already familiar to 'ingenious' scholars at this time. The fact that Kemp, a specialist in this field, found the material 'extraordinary' suggests that there were problems with its identification and it may well have dated to the Saxon period with finds perhaps akin to the 'barrow field' of Warriors' burials on Wandsworth Heath (see Chapter 5).

26 Oolite statue base of Titus Licinius
Ascanius. Late first- or early second-
century AD. In the forecourt of the
Clapham Public Library. *After R.P. Wright,*
The Roman Inscriptions of Britain Vol. 1 (1965)

The discovery of 'many Roman Antiquities' constitutes unfinished archaeological
business in Clapham studies. Where are the objects? If they were that important they
are hardly likely to have been destroyed in the eighteenth century or later. When the
Edgeley Hewer connection with Clapham ended in the mid eighteenth century, the
collection may have passed to one of the branches of the family. Alternatively, it may have
been donated by one such connection to a national or regional museum, where it may
still be in existence accessed under 'Clapham, Surrey'. This is the best hope. The worst
scenario is that it was sold and dispersed. There is also the enduring hope that there are
further Roman remains waiting to be discovered in The Chase area.

TITUS LICINIUS ASCANIUS (*26*)

The inscribed statue base now standing in the forecourt of the Clapham Public Library
is included here for two reasons. Firstly, it has been in Clapham probably for the best part
of 200 years and, secondly, it is the only Roman object that can be seen locally, even if
in antiquity it had no connection with the place.

The base was originally found in 1777 in the foundations of the Ordnance Office at
the Tower of London when it was rebuilt in 1777-80. The object had evidently been
reused in the foundations of the earlier medieval and Tudor palace which lay underneath
the site. In origin, it probably came from a Roman tomb in the east cemetery outside
the walls of *Londinium*. By 1873, the object had disappeared, but was rediscovered in 1911

in the grounds of Cavendish House when the site was redeveloped. It would appear to have been used as a nineteenth-century garden ornament. Some knowledge of the circumstances of its disappearance seems to have been common knowledge amongst local historians at Clapham, since a diary entry from 16 February 1919 of John Burns (the social reformer and local antiquarian) mentions that 'Cavendish' was responsible for the removal of the stone and that he (John Burns) had chided him for not returning it to the Tower of London (Kent 1948, No. 11).

Of Barnack, Oolitic limestone, the statue base measures 24 x 33 x 17in and has a socket on the top. The inscription reads:

Dis/Manib(us)/T(iti) Licini/
Ascani/U(iuus) s(ibi) f(ecit)

To the spirits of the departed and of Titus Licinius
Ascanius; he made this for himself in his lifetime

There has been a considerable literature about the inscription since the late eighteenth century (Collingwood and Wright 1965, 7) and a local account of its discovery and loss was reported by F.A.J. Cole in 1971 (Cole 1971, No. 202).

The opening formula 'Dis Manibus' has not been abbreviated to D.M. which indicates a date in the first or early second century AD. The dedicatee has three names: a *praenomen* or forename abbreviated to the first letter only, T; a *nomen gentilicum*, a family surname, Licinius; and a *cognomen* or sobriquet, Ascanius. The use of the *Tria nomina* indicates that Licinius was a Roman citizen.

Ascanius (Julus) was a legendary son of Aeneas, and reputedly founded *Alba Longa* in Italy. The Roman senatorial family, the *Julii Caesares* claimed to have descended from Julius. The use of this cognomen, therefore, suggests that Licinius was either a freedman or client of this powerful family. Alternatively, he may have been a citizen of Alba Longa. One might speculate that Licinius was a Roman trader or government official without family or connections in *Londinium*, who took the precaution of having a memorial made *ante mortem*, possibly to save his staff or burial club these particular funeral expenses.

4

LADY EALHTHRYTH'S INHERITANCE

My father was well known among the nations,
a nobly born man of foremost rank.
Surely every wise man far and wide remembers him readily?

Beowulf

EALDORMAN ALFRED

The earliest historical reference to *Cloppaham* occurs in a will of Ealdorman Alfred drawn up between 871 and 888 (*Stowe Charter* XX):

> I grant my inheritance and bookland ... 30 hides in Cloppaham to Waerburgh and Ealhthryth, child of us both. And whatever man it may be who shall have the use of the land at Cloppaham after my death, let him pay 200 pence every year to Chertsey (abbey) as a help to their provisions for the sake of Alfred's soul.
>
> Translation by Whitelocke (1979, 97)

The ealdorman was a powerful landowner, probably in charge of Surrey, with land elsewhere in the county. The term 'bookland' in the will indicates that the land was held by title from the Crown. The name of the Saxon vill, which only assumed its present form by the early sixteenth century, is derived from two elements, the Old English term *clop* meaning hill and *ham* with the connotation of village, manor, or most likely in this instance, estate (Erkwall 1947, 104). The reference to *clop* probably refers to the higher ground (now Clapham Common) rising to 25m above the Thames floodplain between the valleys of the former Heath Wall (earlier Hese) and Falcon (earlier Hidaburn) streams. The association of the estate boundaries with the ecclesiastical parish was a later, medieval development.

THE FOUNDING OF CLOPPAHAM

Between the end of the Roman period in the early fifth century and the emergence of Ealdorman Alfred in the late ninth century, some 350 years had elapsed; a period of

27 Relief of Dark Age warriors which catches the ferocity of the Viking marauders who ravaged the outlands of Lundenwic in the ninth century AD. *H.J.M. Green after the Lindisfarne Stone, Northumberland (ninth to tenth centuries AD)*

time as long as that from the age of Cromwell in the seventeenth century to the present day. Much may have happened in the Clapham area during the early Saxon period, which by the end of the fifth century was under Anglo-Saxon control. The hinterland of Londinium does not appear to have been densely settled in the Roman period, and small family and clan groups of the migration period evidently occupied both new and older settlement sites. Did incoming Saxon migrants settle alongside the existing Romano-British or was there conflict? We simply do not know.

This area of Surrey was known as *Sutherge* (the southern district) of the kingdom of the East Saxons centred on Essex and Middlesex. Recent research in connection with the excavation of Middle Saxon *Lundenwic* (Leary 2004, 4) would suggest that this market settlement centred on the Aldwych dates to the seventh century, the same period that saw the founding of Cloppaham (see below). Local farming settlements are likely to have been revived by the opportunity of selling foodstuffs to the burgeoning markets of the new *emporium*.

The ferocious Viking sack of London in 842 and again in 851, and the occupation of *Lundenwic* by the 'Great Army' of the Danes over the winter of 871-2 (*27*) brought to an end for all practical purposes the earlier Anglo-Saxon occupation of the area. Like the Normans two centuries later, Viking marauders would have effectively destroyed any outlying settlements, including Cloppaham. The restoration of London and pacification of its hinterland was left to the Wessex king, Alfred, who after hard fighting in 878 formally refounded London in 886, moving it back into the old walled area of the former Roman city. At the same time, it is likely that Alfred refortified Southwark so that both settlements, in combination, would block off the Thames route into central England to the longboats of any Viking raiders.

An important surviving document of this period, the *Burghal Hidage*, provides a list of fortified sites which formed the defensive network against the Vikings in Alfred's time, together with an assessment of how much land was attached to each fort or town to provide its garrison and support (Wood 2005, 84). Southwark is specifically mentioned as having 1800 hides. On Wood's estimation, this would provide some 1800 men defending 2475yds of defensive works around Southwark. Now in the claylands of Sutherge, the hide appears to have had an area of some 64 acres (see below), i.e. the total acreage within the bailiwick or district of Southwark was some 115,200 acres. This substantial area of land, carefully assessed by the surveyors of the new Lord of London, the Mercian Ealdorman Ethelred (King Alfred's son-in-law) lay in the Surrey hinterland of Southwark. Indeed, the old Burghal Hidage name for Southwark, *Supriganaweorc* means 'the fort of the Surrey people', *Suprige* being a derivative of Surrey. The area concerned comprised much of the Hundred of Brixton, with its meeting place at *Beorghtsig's stone* (cf. Chapter 5) and will have included the Cloppaham Estate. The figure of 30 hides for this estate, in the Alfred will, based on similar *Burghal Hidage* figures, would indicate that the vill was theoretically supplying 30 able-bodied men for the defence of Southwark, if called upon. If these were the heads of households (although it probably included some older sons) then a maximum population for Cloppaham will have been some 135 souls (according to the Rogers demographic calculation – see Chapter 6) most of whom will have probably lived in the vill itself. This figure should be compared with the estimated population calculation in 1086 of 310 persons, almost exactly double the earlier figure (see Chapter 6).

As Wood states, the royal official who drew up the *Burghal Hidage* was 'in possession of a detailed knowledge of what we would call the logistics of the areas dependent on each borough' (Wood 2005, *loc. cit.*) and this evidently included reasonably accurate surveys of the lands concerned. If I am correct in my surmise that the territory in the immediate hinterland of *Lundenwic* had to be virtually resettled after the Viking (Dane) interregnum, then it is to this period *c.*AD 880 that the basic territorial divisions of the Clapham area belong, and have lasted in all essentials down to the present day.

This is particularly evident from the plan of the medieval manor and estate layout (*16*). In the Clapham area, the Black Dyke (later the Ditch of Bradmede) appears to have functioned as a base-line from which strips of land a mile wide were set out extending southwards some 2 miles to take in a share of pasture, arable, woodland and heathland. The outline of the Clapham Estate followed by late parochial and borough boundaries is still fairly clear, as indeed is that of the Wasyingham/Hidaburna (Rydons) Estate to the west, with beyond it the former manors of Wandsworth/Alffephyng. To the east of Clapham, a group of former manors – Kennington, Vauxhall, Stockwell and Wych appear to form the nucleus of another estate. Landmarks included natural features but also Roman roads and perhaps older burial mounds.

Ealdorman Alfred belongs to the first generation of the new estate owners holding their lands (bookland) by title from the Crown, and it is perhaps no accident, therefore, that he is named after his royal namesake and benefactor.

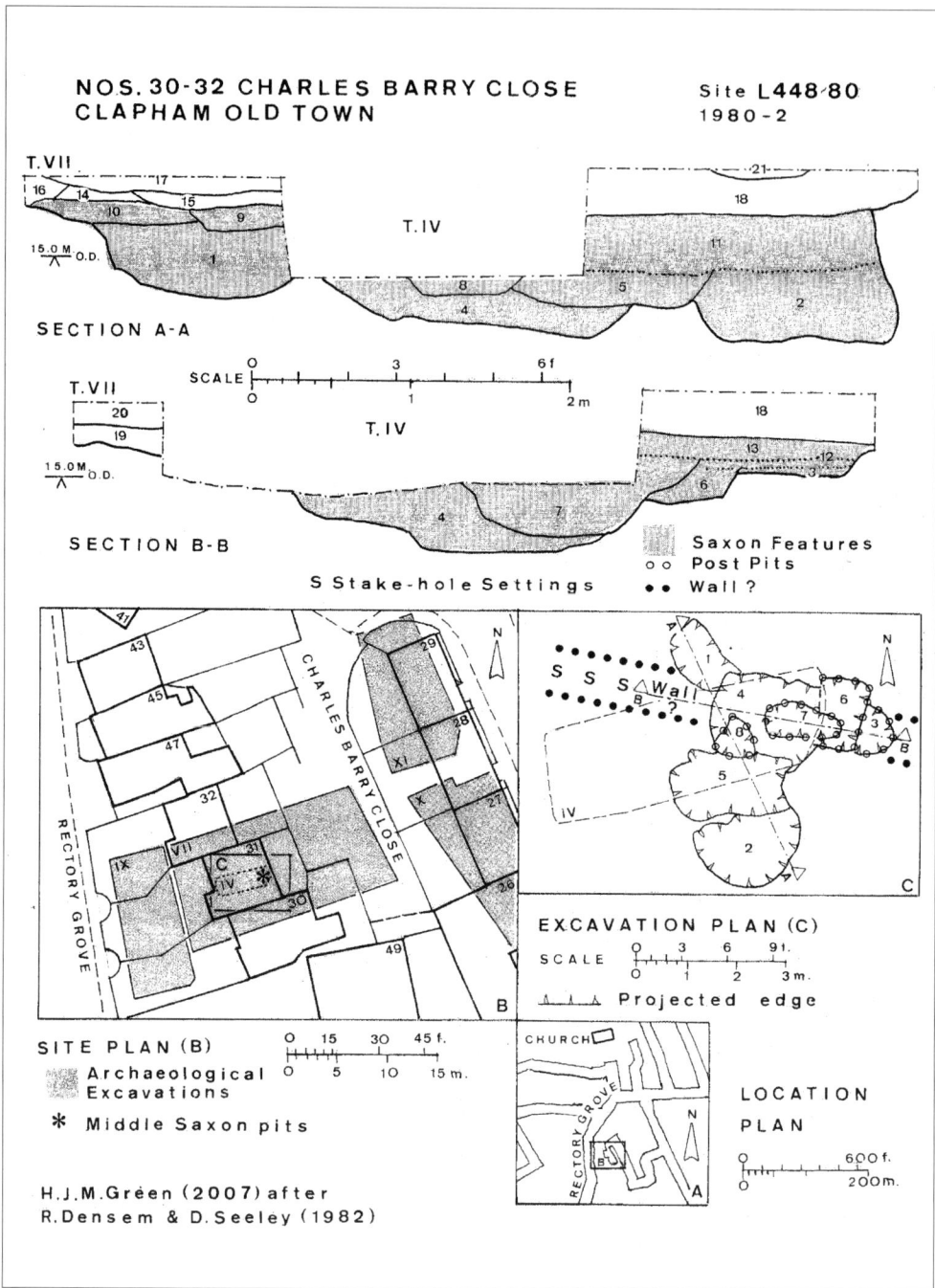

28 Plans and sections of site L448/80 (1980-82) excavated by R. Densen and D. Seeley on the site of what is now Nos 30-32 Charles Barry Close, Clapham Old Town, showing the location of Nos 1-8 of the Saxon pits and post holes. *Redrawn by H.J.M. Green after Densen and Seeley (1982) 1-8, fig. 2 & 182-3, fig. 4). Base plan © Crown copyright. All rights reserved. Licence number 100047602*

THE SAXON SETTLEMENT

Evidence for a late, Early Saxon settlement was discovered from excavations in 1980-81 on a site between Nos 47 and 49 Rectory Grove (now Nos 30-32 Charles Barry Close) (*28*). The site evidently lay at the rear of former messuages lining the east side of the old village street, and produced 10 Saxon pits. Although there was evidence for occupation nearby, no traces of buildings or hearths were recognised at the time. Re-examination of the evidence since 1982 suggests that the small pits (successively 3, 6, 7 and 8) may be post-pits for a major building (or reconstructions of the same) rather than rubbish pits. Similar post-pits were found during the excavation of a Royal hall of Middle Saxon date (part of the *Lundenwic* settlement) by the writer in 1961-3 (Cowie 2004, 201-9). This would explain the absence of animal bones from these features, since structural pits associated with buildings were not used for rubbish disposal. Whether these features were part of Ealdorman Alfred's hall is, of course, entirely another matter. A recent assessment of the pottery by Lynn Blackmore suggests a general date of *c.*575-625 for the group, but the presence of Stamped and Coarse Slipped Ware may indicate occupation prior to 550 (*29*) (Densem & Seeley 177-184, Cowie and Blackmore 2002, 44). Two spindle whorls indicate local spinning of flax or wool (*30*).

Agricultural activity (*31*) was evidenced by carbonised grains of hulled 6-row barley and oats (Densem & Seeley 1982, 179). Many impressions of these cereals were recognised on the Saxon pottery. Ears of corn were roasted before threshing, prevented sprouting and killing off pests, as well as making the hulls brittle so that the grain could be released by pounding. Barley bread was heavy with a greyish tinge and soon

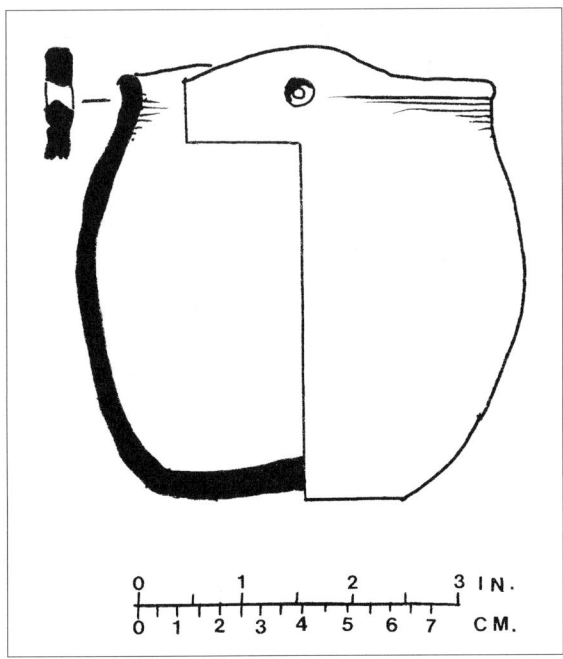

29 Saxon handmade pottery pipkin with pierced lugs for suspension over an open fire. Site LA48/80. Late sixth or early seventh century AD. *H.J.M. Green after Densen & Seeley (1982) 184, fig. 5.2*

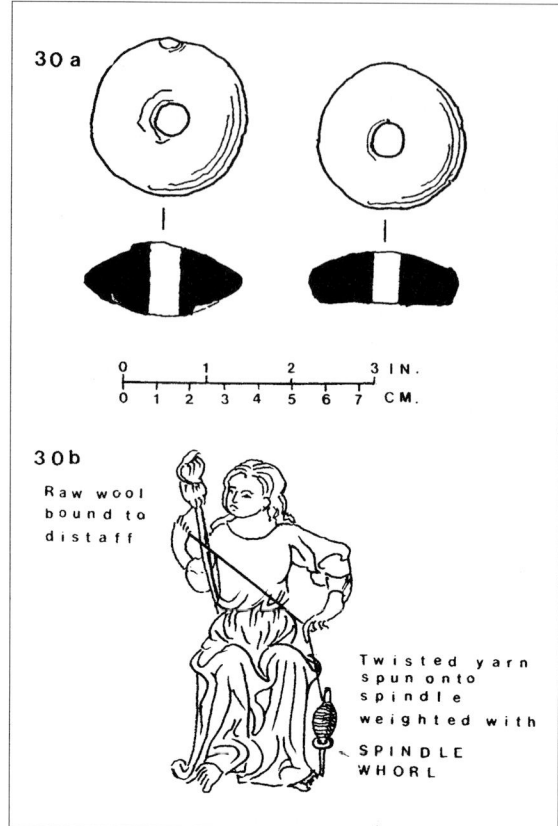

30a Saxon pottery spindle whorls indicative of local spinning of flax or wool at Cloppaham. Site L448/80. Late sixth or early seventh century AD. *H.J.M. Green after Denson and Seeley (1982), 184, fig. 5.27*

30b The spinning process where a bunch of raw wool loosely tied to a wooden distaff stick is teased out to make twisted yarn spun on a wood spindle. The pottery spindle whorl fixed to the spindle provides weight and centrifugal momentum. *H.J.M. Green after 'medieval seasonal activities'. B.L. MS Add. 47682 p.6*

became impalatable and mouldy. However, this coarse-grained, sticky crumb bread is very nutritious and suitable for a high fibre diet. Equally, the carbonised grains may be the result of roasting for the malting process of beer production. Like barley, oats was an excellent fodder crop for animals, but in this context was perhaps more likely to have been used for making pottage for human consumption. Oatmeal formed the basis of numerous cakes, as well as oatcakes. A staple peasant diet of bread, pottage and broth (composed of vegetables and a small amount of salted pork or beef for taste) must have lasted well into the post-medieval period at Clapham, as elsewhere in Britain. A curiosity of the site was the lack of animal bones, normally prolific in such contexts. Domestic animals must have been kept and slaughtered. Poor survival conditions do not seem to be an adequate explanation (see above).

In the absence of any structural remains, the appearance of the buildings of the vill is necessarily conjectural (*colour plates 8 & 9*). However, they are likely to have been timber-framed structures with thatched roofs similar to those found at *Lundenwic* (Horsman 1988, 71ff). The choice of site for the settlement nucleus of Cloppaham, as in earlier periods, appears to have been determined by the presence of a stream running north, one of several that emerged from the springline along the northern gravel edge of the Common.

31 Spring agricultural activities. L to R: Breaking up the ground with an iron mattock. Spade agriculture using the Gaelic Cas Chrom spade type with an iron tip for turning the sods. Hand-sowing using the rolled-up kirtle-garment as a basket. Raking the sown ground and covering the seeds with a wooden *Racan*. H.J.M. Green after the Cotton calendar for March (B.L. MS Julius Al. VI.). Eleventh-century AD

By the time the settlement was founded it had established a course still evident in old street plans north of Old Town, with presumably an adjoining trackway and village buildings on both banks.

THE ALFRED ESTATE (*32*)

Returning to the village and estate in the Alfred Will of the late ninth century, the striking feature is the statement that the 'bookland' was of 30 hides. This Saxon term of land measurement, the hide, represented the amount of ground which could be ploughed in a year using one plough and support a family. Theoretically, it could vary in area according to soil quality, generally between 60 and 180 acres (J. Richardson, *The Local Historian's Encyclopaedia* 1974, A21). Fortunately, at Clapham one such unit of land survived into the medieval period in the shape of an open field named *La Hidehalle* in the 1327 Extent and was still known as Hyde Farm in the nineteenth century. When measured by the 1838 Tithe Assessors, this compact parcel of land was approximately 63 acres. Furthermore this estimated size of the hide land unit at Clapham is confirmed by the Western Inquisition of the demesne of 1326 (see Chapter 8). Not only is each bondman assessed in terms of his holding of *virgates* or *half-virgates* of land (4 virgates = 1 hide) but the acreage is also given. This amounts to 16 acres per virgate or 64 acres per hide. This figure seems about right in terms of the heavy clay conditions in Clapham.

On the basis of these figures it can be estimated that the Alfred Estate of 30 hides comprised some 1920 acres, if the 64 acre to a hide figure is followed. According to the 1838 Tithe Schedule, the Clapham parish area amounted to 1170 acres. Even allowing for changes in the parish boundary during this thousand year interval, it is evident that a substantial area of land had been lost since the late ninth century. Where was it?

In pursuit of this missing land, it is necessary to consider a much later topographical situation with identifiable landmarks, in connection with the mysterious lost estates of Rydons and Wassingham (*32*).

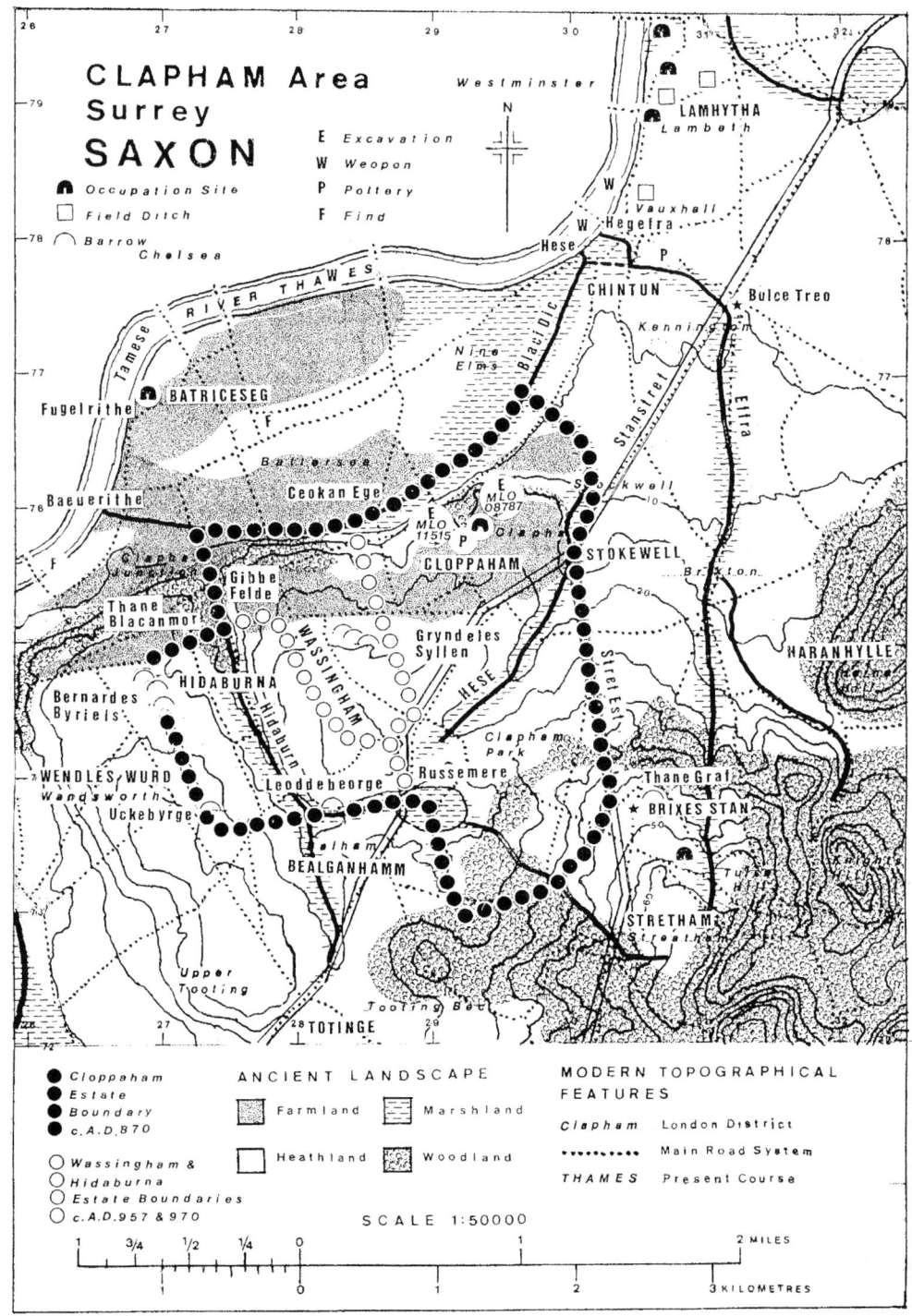

32 Saxon Distribution Map of the Clapham area based on the collected evidence of the National Monuments Record for Lambeth and Wandsworth compiled by English Heritage. *H.J.M. Green. Base Map based on the British Geological Survey published 1998. By permission of B.G.S.*

33 'Dinner at the high table of Ealdorman Alfred's hall'. Bread loaves, rectangular wooden trenchers, a skillet and wine bowl, and iron scramasaxe knives are on the long table. The page holds a horn beaker which will be shared by the guests. *H.J.M. Green after a Cotton M.S. (B.L. MS. Claud. B.V.). Eleventh-century AD*

In 1501, John Islip, Abbot of Westminster, conveyed certain property in Battersea to Thomas Savage, Archbishop of York, including the lands called Rydons, 'sometime parcel of the manor of Brygge Court within the Domaine of Batrichesey' (*Westminster Register*, Book 1, folio 135). The Roydon family had been connected with Battersea and Wandsworth from at least the fourteenth century and the name occurs frequently in the accounts and rolls of Down in Wandsworth and of the Battersea manors (Redstone 1967, 8 fu. 12).

The 'vill called Watsingaham' (Wassingham) first appears in the Erconwold Charter of 693, (see Chapter 5) as does an estate called *Hidabuna* (named after the stream) whose title was changed to Rydons in the fourteenth century. Amongst the thirteenth century list of Westminster Abbey tenants, there occurs the name of Osbert of Wassyngham who was a free tenant of Wassyngham. Edward IV (1461-83) made a grant of tenements and lands in 'Batrichesey, Wannesworth and Wassyngham "to Lawrence Booth, Bishop of Durham; and another in Batessey and Wannesworth" to the King's aunt, Anne, Duchess of Buckingham, together with pasture in the common called Est Heth' (i.e. Clapham Common) and 'in the common call West Heth [i.e. Wandsworth Common] from Wassyngham, Rydon and Wandesworth to Totyng' (Taylor 1925, 11). Within the material of the 1501 Islip Indenture are set out the late medieval boundaries of both Rydons and Wassingham whose topographical locations can now be established with some confidence (Taylor 1925, 11-13). The salient features and landmarks are shown on the maps of Saxon and Medieval Clapham (*32* & *78*).

WASSINGHAM

Wassingham comprised an L-shaped estate, whose eastern arm consisted of the common called 'East Heath' in the fifteenth-century Buckingham grant and later known as Washingham Common in the eighteenth century. It now forms the west side of Clapham Common. The boundaries of the northern arm defined a long, rectilinear plan. The northern limits were marked by the 'ditch of Bradmede', still in evidence as the 'Common Sewer' in the mid nineteenth century. Now lost, the stream ran parallel with Lavender Hill and Wandsworth Road, on the north side at the bottom of the slope. The present Robertson Street follows part of the line. The southern boundary was 'the Cannterbury Way' (now Battersea Rise and Clapham Common Northside). This was the old, medieval pilgrim route to the shrine of St Thomas at Canterbury, which was carefully directed by Merton Priory to take this lucrative travel business through the village, past the church and along what is now Larkhall Rise. The eastern extent was 'as far as the ancient boundaries marking the Field of Clopham' (now Wix's Lane). The western boundary was the highway 'near Flodmede Ende, leading from Batrichesey to Wassyngham' (Taylor 1925, 11). This road, now St John's Road and Falcon Road, bordered the Hidaburn Stream which flowed on its western side. The site of the hamlet has not been identified, but the Old English name derivative is *waese* = swamp and *ham* = settlement, this suggests that it was low-lying, possibly in the area of St John's Road. The Rocque map of 1746 shows that this locality was even then swampy, with big pools and ponds.

RYDONS (FORMER *HIDABURNA*)

Rydons was situated to the south and west of Wassingham. In the 1501 Indenture, the northern boundary is Canterbury Way, the eastern is 'the common pasture of Batrichesey called Estheth' and the southern, 'the King's highway next Legham and called Baleham' on the south (now Nightingale Lane). The western boundary is undefined, but may be that mentioned under the section of Wassingham in the Indenture (whose actual western bounds were in fact fixed as Falcon Road – see above) 'as far as the open *cuntriche* on the West'. For the tired monkish land surveyor (*agrimensor*) from Westminster, having to face the prospect of fixing landmarks on the featureless heath that is now Wandsworth after a day of pacing out the bounds of the estate over rough ground, may have left him with a weary feeling of 'over the hills and far away'! However, the boundary had actually been fixed centuries before in relation to the position of ancient barrows and is still marked by the existing borough boundary.

SAXON MENSURATION

In addition to the delineation of the boundaries particular topographical landmarks are mentioned in the 1501 Indenture where the bounds changed direction. The significance of these landmarks for Clapham will be discussed under 'the Saxo-Norman land charters' (see Chapter 5). The importance of the Islip Indenture is that it establishes clearly the boundaries of these estates, and from this their area (64 acres to a hide) *c.*1500 can be calculated:

Batrychesey	28.2 hides	= 1522.8 acres
Wasyngham	5.4 hides	= 291.6 acres
Rydons	5.4 hides	= 291.6 acres

The discrepancies between these figures and those quoted by J.G. Taylor in 1925 (and subsequently copied by every local historian since then) lies in his failure to get the acreage of the old hide land unit even approximately correct. His figure of 120 acres to the hide (Taylor 1925, 17) is almost exactly double the true figure. Since the accurate measurement of these ancient estates is critical, both in terms of their boundaries, landmarks and indeed history, his subsequent topographical exegesis is hopelessly flawed, since the greater area implied led him to include Wandsworth and territories even further afield within the territory of Battersea.

There are problems even when using the established figure of 64 acres to 1 hide. First, the actual acreage area, and hence the size of the hide, was almost certainly slightly different from what it became with standardisation in later centuries. Indeed, the figure was probably closer to 63 acres as established with the post-medieval Hyde Farm Estate. Secondly, there has been a tendency in the past to accept too readily the figures handed out by the monkish surveyors. These late Saxon land surveys were not instrument-based, but used pacing to a standard unit of length, usually the standard unit of English long measure, the yard. At nearby Merton Priory, for example, a survey of land between the 'two woods of Kingeswode' (which included a marsh) was carried out *c.*1180 by Robert the Prior and one of the brothers, 'who had computed its area on perambulating it' (Heales 1898, 29). In calculating the area of land units, a form of primitive triangulation may have been employed using internal trackways across the estate. The sketch field plans and tabulated columns of measurements would then be taken back to Westminster to be drawn up geometrically. The resulting figures for the land areas could only be approximations. Indeed, the figures for Battersea in the tenth and eleventh centuries in three separate documents varied between 68 and 72 hides.

SAXO-NORMAN CLAPHAM

With these caveats in mind, let us look again at the 30 hides of the Alfred Estate of *c.*AD 880 at Clapham as now established by calculation:

Clapham	–	20.15 hides
Wassingham	–	5.4 hides
Rydons	–	5.4 hides
Total	–	30.23 hides

This is so close to the Saxon figure that it may be assumed with reasonable confidence that the question of the location of the missing lands of Clapham, with which this study opened, can now be answered. In the ninth century the Clapham Estate of Alfred extended as far west as the Wandsworth border and incorporated land known as Wassingham, which was later subdivided to include an estate called *Hidaburna* (which subsequently became Rydons).

The Wassingham Estate appears to have reverted to the Crown at some point after Ealdorman Alfred's death, since it was held by Harold II in 1066 and was assessed as part of Battersea in William I's grant to Westminster Abbey of 1085-9 (Taylor 1925, 15-16). Here, Wassingham was described as an appanage of Battersea, together with Rigedure (Rydons?) and the berewick named Wandleswurthe. The additional land is reflected in the enlarged holding of 61½ hides, 'of which aforesaid hides forsooth the smaller number is counted on the western side of the stream which is called Hydeburna' (Taylor 1925, 16). The later history of Wassingham and Rydons, already touched on earlier, need not concern us further at this point.

5

'THE OPEN COUNTRY'

An uncharted territory ... the perilous waterways of a swamp.
Above it the rime-encrusted thickets overshadow the water ...
it is not a pleasant place.

Beowulf

THE SAXO-NORMAN, WESTMINSTER CHARTERS

There are three charters originating from Westminster, and purporting to be of Saxon date, which are of the greatest interest in the study of ancient Clapham, not so much as legal indentures, but because two of the charters include land surveys which provide vital topographical information about the character of the countryside in the late Saxon period. These documents are discussed in detail by J.G. Taylor (Taylor 1925, 1).

1. THE 'AGELRIC' CHARTER OF 693 (34)

A grant of 68 hides in Battersea (*Batrice ege* – 28 hides; *Watsingham* – 20 hides; *Hidaburna* – 20 hides) from King Ceduuala (Caedwall) who reigned 685-688 as King of the West Saxons, and confirmed by Athelred of Mercia (675-704). The main text is in Latin in eleventh-century hand, but the land survey of the designated territory is expressed in Old English. The name(s) of the recipient of the grant has been deliberately erased. A fifteenth-century endorsement of this grant describes it as a record of 'lands at Baterseye, Wassingham and Hideborne granted to the church of Westminster by Agelric, Bishop of Dorchester in 693'.

2. THE 'ERCONWOLD' CHARTER OF 693 OR 695 (35)

This charter is of uncertain date because the essential numbering at the time of Taylor's examination was indecipherable (Taylor 1925, 4). Erconwold died in 693. This charter, related to 1 above, survives as a very late copy (probably seventeenth century). It claims

Above: 34 'The Agelric Charter of AD 693'. Westminster cartulary MS of eleventh-century date with fifteenth-century endorsement of the grant of lands at Baterseye, Wassingham and Hideborne to the Church of Westminster. *Taylor 1925, pl. 2a*

Left: 35 'The Erconwold Charter of AD 693 or 695' (BK. MS f. 112) mentioning '70 hides of lands bordering upon Hydaburn … called Badoricesheah'. *Taylor 1925, pl. 3*

to be a grant by Bishop Erconwold (Bishop of London 675–693) to the monastery of Barking (built by Erconwold before 674 for his sister Ethelberga, its first abbess). Among the lands bestowed on Erconwold 'by kings' for the endowment of the said monastery and which he handed over to it, 'the fifth bordering upon Hydaburn, given by King Ceduulla, of 70 hides, is called Badorices-heah'. There is no survey attached to this grant.

3. THE EADWIG CHARTER OF 957 (36)

A second list of 'landmarks at Batriceseie' is attached to a charter of King Eadwig granting lands in Lockersley and Tunworth to Lyfing in 957. It is couched in Early English in a similar hand to that of the previous list of landmarks.

Great play was made by medieval Westminster using these documents to prove that the Abbey was a foundation of the seventh century. However, Dorothy Whitelock considered the Erconwold material to be a forgery (although containing genuine elements from old land grants) and excluded it from her magisterial *English Historical Documents* (Whitelock 1979, 486 especially No. 60, fns 8 & 9). So we are left with a fraudulent Saxon charter into which has been copied a genuine list of landmarks (1) and a genuine charter to which has been wrongly attached again a genuine topographical list (3). Neither list appears to have been copied from the other, and although there are common elements, each list contains some different landmarks. The feeling is that we are looking at two different surveys made within a short time of each other but covering exactly the same area of land. The boundary of this territory can be established with some accuracy, and when the area is measured gives:

Battersea	–	28.2 hides
Wassingham	–	5.4 hides
Hydeborne or 'bordering upon Hydaburna' (presumably the earlier name of the Rydons Estate)	–	5.4 hides

A total of 39 hides in no way agrees with the claims of the Erconwold material whether 68 or 70 hides (1 and 2). So what has happened?

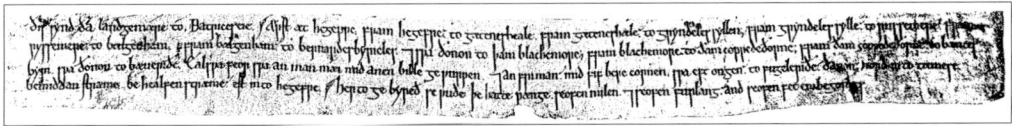

36 'The Eadwig Charter of AD 957'. Westminster cartulary MS of Battersea lands appended to a charter of King Eadwig. Text of landmarks list of eleventh-century date. *Taylor 1925, pl. 2b*

THE POLITICS OF LAND OWNERSHIP

A clue may lie in the unauthorised appropriations of land around the time of the Conquest by various secular and ecclesiastical authorities. The Domesday Book states that under Harold, Westminster held 72 hides in 1066 which subsequently dropped to 18 hides. Westminster badly needed to re-establish its claim to this lost land, and the best way to go about this was to make a case for its earlier possession in the Saxon period. Hence the production of the Erconwold forgery, into which was copied a land survey from a previous period, of territory held by Battersea before 'the berewick adjoining it named Wandleswithe' had been added to the manor. The scribe drawing up the bogus charter was probably unaware that the survey details which he was copying into the document actually covered a smaller area of land than they claimed.

However, in the event, the first and second grants of William I in 1067 and 1085-7, respectively, of lands 'on both sides of Hideburna stream' to Westminster appears to have accepted these claims and allocated 61½ hides to 'Batricesye' and its appanages including Hyse (Nine elms area), Rigedune (Rydons), Wassingham, Giufeld (Gibbefeld?) and 'the berewick named Wendleswrithe'. As Taylor shows, the difference between the figures of 61½ and 72 hides was made up of land which at that stage could not be prised away from the new owners (1925, 18).

So what caused the two land surveys to be made in the first place, and when? A church establishment, possibly intended as a monastery, was established by King Offa in the eighth century at Westminster. The grant, purportedly of 785, is bogus, but may reflect a genuine tradition (Brooke 1975, 295). If there was a church it was probably destroyed by the Viking raids of 842 and 851. The great prelate, Dunstan, was Bishop of London in the late 950s and it was under his auspices that a small monastic house was re-established *c.*958-9 under its first abbot, Wulfsige. The exact date is uncertain and it may well be that the Eadwig charter could push the founding date back a year earlier to 957, which conforms with the earlier dating bracket given by Dan Knowles (Knowles 1949, 49 fn.2). As the *Anglo-Saxon Chronicle* relates 'Dunstan … came to King Edgar and asked that he be given all the monasteries the heathen men had destroyed, because he wishes to rebuild them, and the king gladly granted it' (Savage, 1983, 128). One of the first things that would have had to be sorted out was to ensure that the monastery was adequately endowed with land, if necessary by using local courts to claim back long lost property owned by the earlier monastic house. Surveys of the disputed land would be critical evidence if presented in court. It was said of Bishop Aethelwold, a contemporary and colleague of Dunstan, that 'He never forgot a possible claim at law, and was prepared to plead in local courts far from his own diocese' (Stenton 1950, 446) (37).

It may well be that the lands known as Wassingham and Hydeborne (later Rydons) which were held at some point between 871 and 888 by Ealdorman Alfred, fell exactly into this category of property acquired through unauthorised appropriation from the earlier minster at Westminster, after its destruction by the Vikings a generation earlier.

37 King Edgar seated between Ss Ethelwold (L) and Dunstan (R) at the meeting of the *Regularis Concordia* at Winchester *c.*AD 970. These appear to be portraits which (inadvertently) bring out the respective characters of these two great churchmen. *H.J.M. Green after the Cotton MS. Tiberius A. III. Second half of the eleventh century* AD

Indeed, the third quarter of the tenth century may possibly be the period at which these lands were claimed back by Westminster as part of the property of the manor of Battersea, and were subsequently lost by the Clapham Estate.

There are, however, two surveys to be accounted for. As we have seen, the earlier was probably made *c.*957 or slightly after. The second occurred, I believe, between 969 and 971 which regularised the earlier grant arrangements (Birch 1893, 1264). When the two surveys are closely compared, it can be seen that the one of *c.*957 ('Eadwig', No. 3) tended to be vaguer about topographical details than that of *c.*970 ('Erconwold/Agelric', nos 1 & 2). A general reference to Grendel's bog (Clapham Common) in 957 is replaced by a specific landmark, 'Grendel's alders' in the second survey; again, the Baelgenham (Balham) Estate reference is replaced by two local landmarks, both barrows — and so on. In the sharply litigious atmosphere at that time, precise topographical landmarks were probably felt to be obligatory, necessitating a resurvey of the Battersea manor Estate some 13 years after the initial perambulation.

Westminster Abbey has had an unfortunate reputation for promoting a virtual industry of forged charters which emerged from the *scriptorium* in the eleventh and twelfth centuries (Brooke 1975, 295). This has added greatly to the difficulties in tracing the history of the Battersea charters and their associated surveys. After the two surveys had been completed, the survey documents would have been stored in the Westminster cartulary. The '957' survey appears to have mistakenly (?) attached to an unassociated charter of the same date. A century later it would seem that the '970' survey was fished out and copied on to the 'Agelric' charter. It may be significant that several of the landmarks of this survey appear in the Westminster charter of William I in 1085-7 (W.A.M. *Domes. Chart.* f.46b).

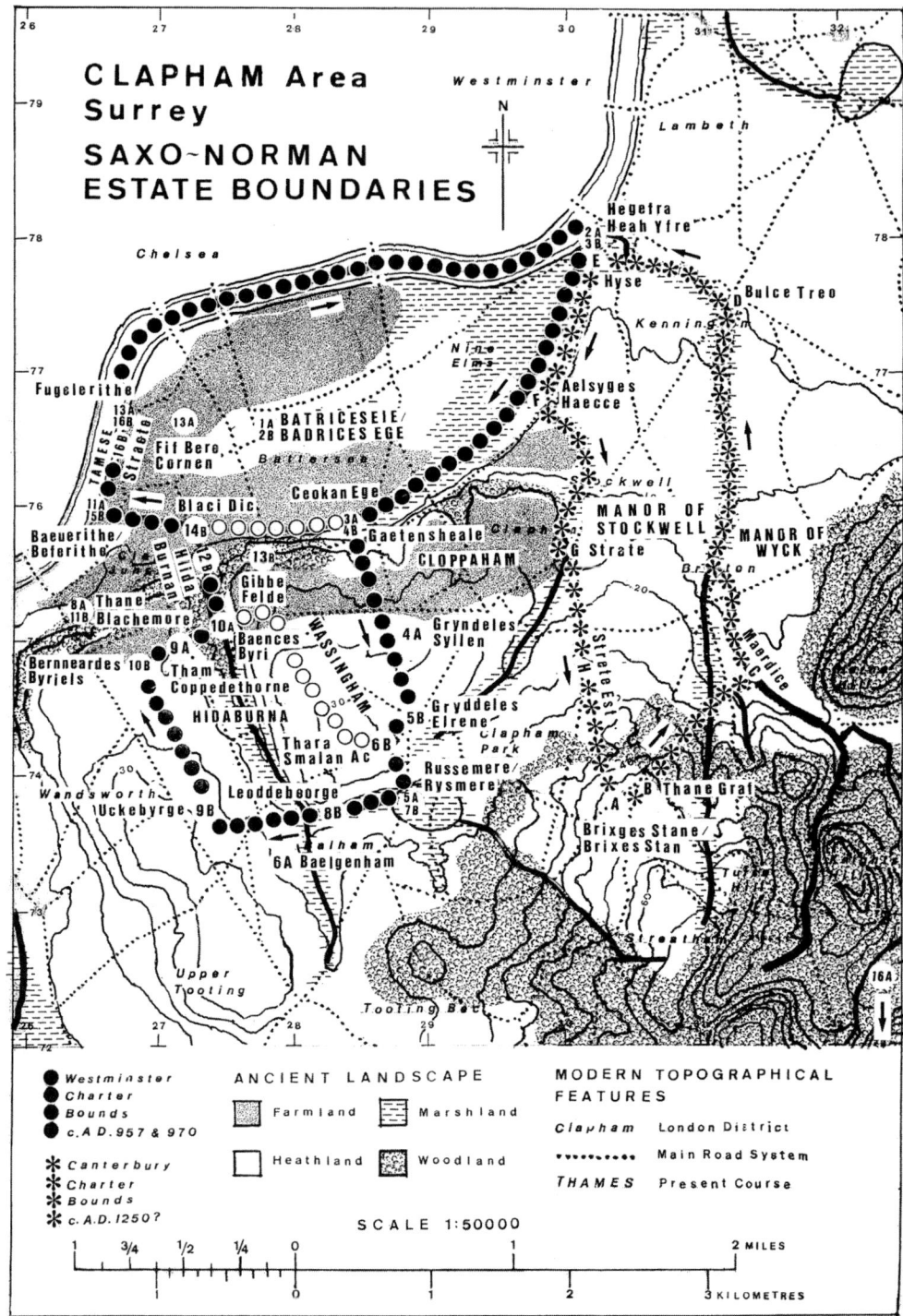

38 Map of Saxo-Norman estate boundaries of the Clapham area based on the land survey of the Westminster and Lambeth Charters. *H.J.M. Green. Base Map after the British Geological Survey published 1998*

The two surveys detailed here are provided with an approximate translation of the Old English syntax. For ease of reference, each clause is sequentially numbered and provided with a letter 'A' or 'B' for the '957' or '970' survey respectively. Each boundary location marks a point where the line changes direction.

As already set out, the general limits of the Battersea Estate have already been deduced from later evidence, as indeed have some of the landmarks. Putting these strands of topographical evidence together provides a fairly clear overall framework for the Saxon survey, into which some of the more obscure boundary features can now be fitted (*38*).

THE FIRST SURVEY (*c.957*)

1A THIS SYND THAT LANDGEMAERE TO BATRICESEIE
These are the landmarks for Battersea.

2A A'RST AET HEGEFRE
That is from the boundary of the High Effra
The survey is from east to west, as stated in 2B, and begins with the outlet of the River Effra into the Thames in what is now Vauxhall. Rising in Norwood, the Effra was some 12ft wide and 6ft deep at its main outfall into the Thames near the old Cox's bridge just upstream of the present Vauxhall Bridge (Barton 1962, 43). The epithet 'High' may refer either to flood banks at the outlet, or, more likely, to the fact that this was the larger of the two streams which had an outfall here (*32*). This second branch of the Effra (the Hese) lay to the southwest where it joined with a long drainage ditch (probably the Black Dyke, cf. 14B) which collected the water from the higher ground adjoining the floodplain of the Battersea fields. The drainage ditch line still marks the Battersea Borough boundary running beneath the New Covent Garden Market. See also 15A and 3B.

3A FROM HEGEFRE TO GAETENSEHEALE
From the Effra to Goat Hall (O.S. Get = goat − Heall = hall)
This landmark formed the ancient corner of the Wassingham Estate and probably lay in the present vicinity of Bassett Close. The entry is probably a contemporary ironic reference to a goat-herdsman's hut (*39*). Up to this point the boundary had followed the drainage ditch, the Black Dyke (cf. 14B).

4A FROM GAETENSHAELE TO GRYNDELES SYLLEN
From Goat Hall to Grendel's bog (Sylv = Miry Place)
From Goat Hall the boundary appears to have followed the old Clapham parish boundary down Wix's Lane southwards across Clapham Common, of which *Gryndeles Syllen* appears to have been an early generic name. See 5B below.

5A FROM GRYNDELES SYLLE TO RUSSEMERE
From Grendel's Bog to Rush Mere

39 Goat-herdsmen with goats (*Capra Aegagrus Hircus*). Although of Romano–British date (fourth century AD) the Riseley Park *lanx* (silver dish) shows a timeless pastoral scene. *H.J.M. Green after BM photograph (Henig 1995, pl. 96)*

Southwards went the boundary to the bottom of the present Balham Hill. Here the Hidaburn Stream ran westwards along what is now Oldridge Road. In this boggy area was another landmark, Rush Mere, marking the southeast corner of the old Ryden Estate, where the boundary turned west following the stream.

A low lying exposed patch of London Clay at the bottom of Balham Hill appears to have underlain the site of Rush Mere (British Geological Survey of South London, 1:50000 series, sheet 270, 1998). The relief structure indicates an elliptical dip, probably the site of the Mere, extending east-west from Sanderstead Close in Atkins Road to just west of Balham Hill and north-south from Weir Road to Balham New road, an area of some 30 acres. The 25m O.S. contour in this vicinity indicates that a number of small streams formerly flowed into Rush Mere, whose outfall to the west was a branch of the Hidaburn Stream(*32*).

6A FROM RYSSEMERE TO BAELGENHAM

From Rush Mere to Balham
The Saxon Estate of Baelgenham extended all along the southern boundary of Rydens. As a boundary marker it is therefore very indeterminate (see above).

7A FROM BAELGENHAM TO BERNARDES BYRIELS

(*O.E. Beorn* = *warrior; Byrgen* = *burials*)
From Balham to the Warriors' graves
A line of Anglo-Saxon or earlier barrows lying along the old Wandsworth boundary marks the western edge of this survey. At least three mounds are shown on the 1746 map of outer London by Rocque (*40*) straddling what is now the railway line in the vicinity of Emmanuel School. The northernmost of the mounds marks the northwest corner of Rydens where the boundary turns east.

8A AND SWA THONON TO THAM BLACHEMORE

And thus through to Thane Blach's moor
The eastern turn involved crossing a patch of moorland at the northern end of

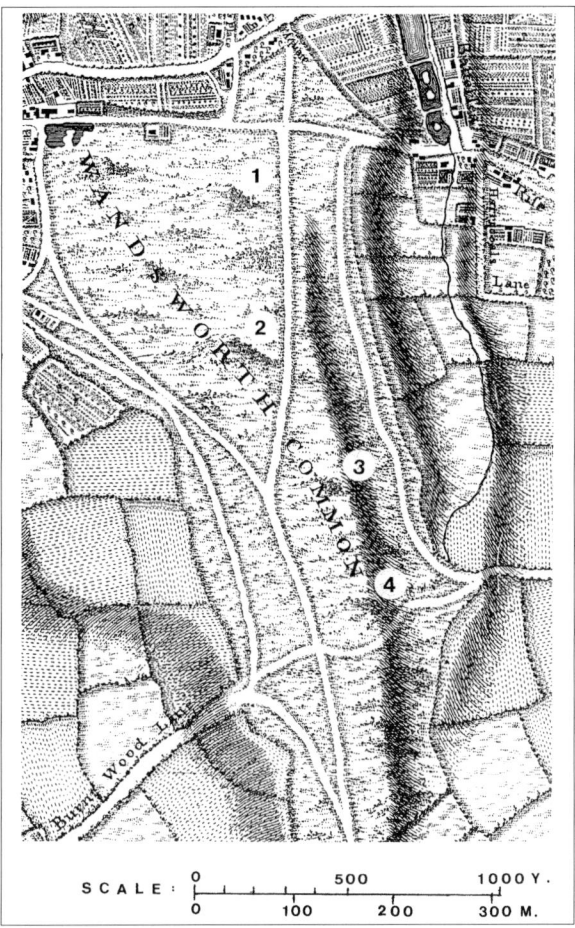

40 Barrow field with extant mounds nos 1-4 of Saxon or earlier date marking the boundary between Wandsworth and Battersea on Wandsworth Common. Recorded by John Rocque *c.*1741-5 and published in his cartographic survey of London and adjacent countryside 'ten miles round' in 1746. *Courtesy of the City of London, London Metropolitan Archives*

Wandsworth Common, now Spencer Park. A Thane was a member of a king or lord's household. *Blach* appears to be a personal name cognitive with *Blac* or *Blaec*.

9A FROM BLACHEMORE TO THAM COPPEDETHORNE

From Blach's moor to the Thane's coppiced thorn (bush)

Following a line still marked by hedges in the nineteenth century to the south of the present Battersea Rise, the next boundary point was the Thane's coppiced thorn bush which marked the eastern edge of Blach's Moor. A coppiced tree or bush was one which had been cut to near ground level every few years and allowed to grow again from the stool for coppicing as underwood.

10A FRAM THAM COPPEDETHORNE TO BAENCES BYRI

From the Thane's coppiced thorn to Baence's cowhouse

Baence appears to be a personal name cognate with O.E. Baecqa. The next landmark at the bottom of the hill in the vicinity of the present Cairn's Road was Baence's byre or cowhouse (*41*). Situated in the pasture land alongside the Hidaburn Stream (Hida

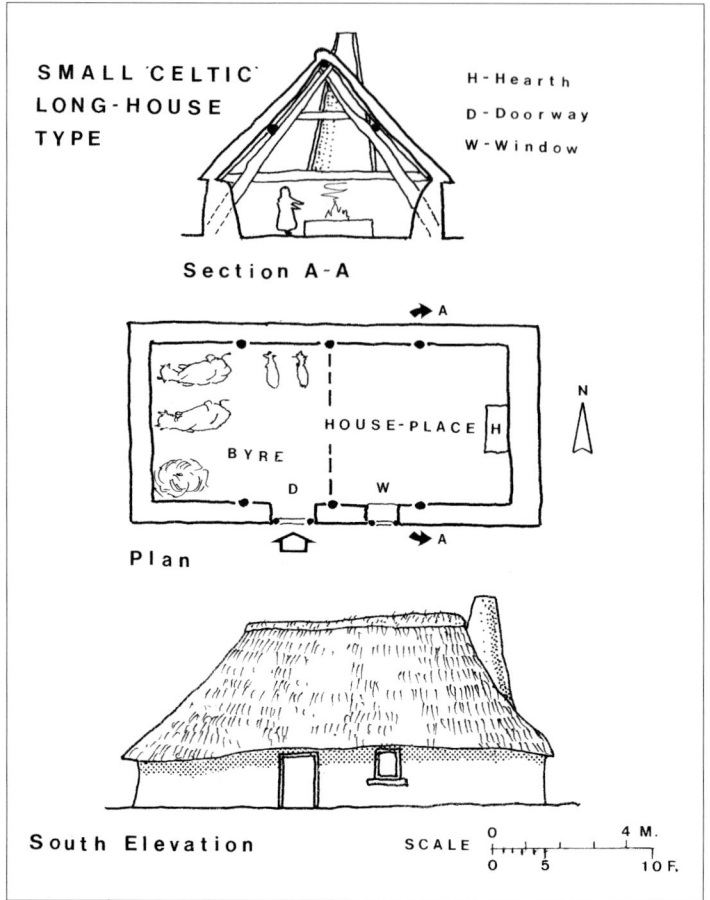

SMALL 'CELTIC'
LONG-HOUSE
TYPE

H - Hearth
D - Doorway
W - Window

Section A-A

Plan

HOUSE-PLACE
BYRE

South Elevation

SCALE

41 Small 'Celtic' long-house type. Traditional peasant cot combining the byre and house-place as a single unit. 'Baence's byre' was probably of this type as indeed was most of the housing at Cloppaham during the Saxon and Medieval periods. *H.J.M. Green after* Enquête sur l'architecture rurale, *doc. 44. 215.7; Archives du Museé Nationale des Arts et Traditions Populaires, Paris*

Burnan) this structure may have been part of the lost hamlet of Hydeborne (named after the stream) the predecessor of Rydens, which may have clustered round the junction of the present Northcote Road and Battersea Rise, the latter becoming the Canterbury Way in the medieval period.

11A SWA THONON TO BAEUERITHE
Thus through to the 'pasture' hythe
The Hidaburn Stream appears to have been followed (not evident in this account but clarified in the second survey) through to its outlet on the Thames described as 'Baeuerithe' (O.E. Hyp = landing place. O.E. Baer = pasture, but may be a personal name cf. 15B) now Battersea Creek.

12A EALSWA FEOR SWA AN MAN MAE I MID ANEN BILLE GE WURDEN
'Just as far out at it pleases a person to stretch out his sword' (Bill = sword)
One of the more enigmatic phrases in the survey. The hythe appears to have been a board-walk on timber trestles stretching out a short way into the river. The meaning may

indicate that ownership extended along the hythe for a sword's length (i.e. to include the immediate foreshore, but not out to the centre of the river as in the case of the Fugel Rithe (16B)). These restrictions probably have to do with fishing rights.

13A AND AN FRIMAN MID FIF BERE CORNEN SWA EST ONGEN. TO FUGELERITHE THANON NORD

And one advances amid five barley corn (fields) thus east again. To Fugelrithe, then north.

The boundary then turns northwards along the old foreshore road, passing five barley corn fields for half a mile until it reached Fugelrithe, or 'Bird' stream (*42*) an inlet just south of St Mary's parish church, Battersea. The Fugelrithe itself had, as in the likely case of the Baeurithe, a light pier stretching into the river from the foreshore, presumably for access to beached boats. The boundary turned west (not north as in the survey) to run out along the pier and on a projected line to the centre of the Thames.

14A THANON NORD INTO TAMESE BE MIDDAN STRAEME

Then north into the Thames to the middle of the stream. See 13A above.

15A BE HEALFEN STRAEME. EST INTO HEGEFRE

Following the stream halfway across to Hegefre

The survey has thus been brought back to its starting place, the River Effra. There is, however, one additional asset of Battersea which the surveyor is careful to note.

42 Fugelrithe or 'bird stream' near St Mary's Church, Battersea. *H.J.M. Green after Cotton MS (B.L. Claud. B. IV)*

16A HERTO GE BYRETH SE WUDE THE HATTE PAENGE. SEOPEN MILEN
AND SEOPEN FURLANG AND SEOPEN FET EMBEGANCIES

*Formerly this brought you to the wood called 'Penge'. Seven miles, seven furlongs and seven feet
in circumference*

At some point during the late Saxon period, Battersea had acquired timber rights for
the estate from this source, since the Thames floodplain evidently did not provide such
timber at this period. Taylor has traced the history of this connection which lasted to
the nineteenth century (1925, 5).

THE SECOND SURVEY (*c.*970)

1B HEC SUNT TERMINA HUT TELLURIS

Here are the boundary points of the land (or estate)

Note that the survey description starts in Latin but quickly reverts to Old English.

2B THIS SYNDON THAT LANDGEMAERA TO BADRICES EGE AND TO
WENDLESWURTHE

These are the landmarks from Battersea (the island of Badric) to Wandsworth

This is an improvement on 1A since it indicates that the survey route moves from
east to west up to the boundaries of Wandsworth, which was not included at that stage.

3B THAET IS AEREST HEAH YFRE

That is originally from High Effra –

The description of the River Effra outfall is covered in 2A.

4B OF HEAH YFRE INTO CEOKAN EGE

From High Effra to Ceacca's Island

Ceacca's island, or possibly promontory, has replaced 'Goat Hall' as a landmark. Since
these always mark a change of direction, the same locality as 3A must be indicated, the
ephemeral 'hall' having presumably disappeared. As before, the old boundary watercourse
has been followed up to this point (cf. 3A & 14B).

5B OF CEOKAN EGE INTO GRYDDELES ELRENE

From Ceacca's Island to Grendel's Alders

Following the old boundary southwards, as in 4A, the rather vague 'Grendel's bog' has
been replaced by a specific landmark, 'Grendel's alders'. The location and subsequent
history of this site is of the greatest interest. The precise spot appears to have been north
of Clapham South Underground Station roughly where the present Avenue meets
Clapham Common Southside, a point where the old boundary turned south-west.
Gryddel (43) is the Norse Grendel, the monster who features in the ancient Saxon saga
of *Beowulf* (Cotton Vitellius A XV). This locality at the southern tip of the Common

appears to have retained its mythological connection as the 'Dragon's Pond', from which Dragmire Lane (now Cavendish Road) was named (Gower 1990, 5). The clue to why the ancient Clapham community might have thought that something nasty might be lurking at the bottom of the Dragon's mere or pool is a passage in *Beowulf* describing the lair of Grendel:

> …an uncharted territory … the perilous waterways of a swamp. Above it the rime-encrusted thickets, the firmly rooted trees overshadow the water. *There each night is to be seen a sinister spectacle: fire on the pool* [my italics] … it is not a pleasant place. When the wind whips up foul weather … the air grows thick with muck and the skies weep'.
>
> Translation by Bradley 1982, 447

The key phrase is the 'fire on the pool', in other words, marsh-fire or marsh-lights caused by self-igniting gases from decaying plants, an association with Grendel which would not have escaped the Anglo-Saxon mind in Clapham. This must have been a common enough phenomenon on the desolate pools and bogs of Clapham Heath a thousand years ago, and would have added to the sinister reputation of the place. In wet winters there is still a damp rectangular area visible, 250ft by 180ft, set back about 40ft from the margin of Clapham Common South Side, and parallel with the road. If a small spinney of alders was situated at the south-west corner of this former pond, the trees would line up with Nightingale Lane, the old medieval estate boundary of Rydons. Indeed, it is possible that the origins of this ancient pond, 'home of Grendel' lay in the Roman period when a gravel pit may have been dug alongside Stane Street to provide metalling for its surface. By the late Saxon period, this pit had become an overgrown and fetid pool – the source of the marsh lights.

6B OF GRYDDELES ELRENE. INTO THARA SMALAN AC
From Grendel's alders to Thara's small oak
This landmark has been interposed in this second survey between the Grendel features and Rush Mere (7B). The reason for this is that the boundary does a dog-leg in this

43 'Gryddel', a demonic ghoul believed by the Anglo-Saxons to haunt the swamps and pools of what is now Clapham Common. *H.J.M. Green after the Macclesfield Psalter marginalia (c.AD 1330). Left-hand figure, MS 1-2005 f. 140 r; right-hand figure, MS 1-2005 f. 10v*

vicinity. From Grendel's alder the route evidently followed a trackway, the predecessor of Nightingale Lane, some 300yds southwest to the 'small oak', whence it turned south along the old parish boundary in the vicinity of what is now St Francis's College.

7B OF THARA SMALAN AC. INTO RYSMERE
From Thara's small oak to Rushmere
The southern course of the boundary, its junction with Rushmere and westward course along the Hidaburn Stream are described under 5A.

8B OF RYSMERE INTO LEODDEBEORGE
From Rushmere to Leodde's mount (or monument)
The next landmark, again at a slight angle of the boundary line, was the first of a series of burial mounds used as markers across what is now Wandsworth Common. This mound would appear to be on the eastern edge of the Common near what is now Wandsworth Common Station. *Leodde* is almost certainly a personal name, but O.E. *Leode* also means 'people', with perhaps the connotation of a 'folk' mound – a meeting place or moot of earlier Saxon settlers.

9B OF LEODDEBYRGE. INTO UCKEBYRGE
From Leodde's mound to Ucca's mound
The boundary crosses the southern end of Wandsworth Common to another barrow, Ucca's mound (another O.E. personal name) at the eastern end of what is now Routh Road. This boundary point still marks the old parish boundary between Wandsworth and Battersea. It will be noted how the use of these barrow landmarks by the second group of surveyors gave a far better definition of the boundary than the earlier exercise.

10B OF UCCEBYRGE. INTO BERNNEARDES BYRIELS
From Ucca's mound to the 'Warrior's burials'
For a description of this site, see 7A. The distinction between 'Beorge' and 'Byriels' may lie in the latter being regarded as a burial field (Byrgen) or place, as opposed to a lone barrow. In both cases, burial mounds appear to be meant (*40*).

11B OF BYNRAERDES BYRIELS. INNE THANE BLACANMOR
From the Warrior Burials into Thane Blacs' moor
The boundary turned east at the 'Warrior's burials' as described in 8A.

12B OF THAN BALCANMORE. OTH MIDDAN HLIDABURNAN
From thane Blac's Moor up to the middle of the Hiddaburna (Hidaburn) Stream
Two landmarks have been omitted in the new survey, the 'Thane's coppiced thorn' (9A) and 'Baences cowhouse' (10A). The second group of surveyors seem to have been uneasy using buildings as landmarks, in view perhaps of their temporary nature (cf. omission of 'Goat Hall' – 3A). The Hidaburn Stream is not mentioned in the first survey, although it is implicit when the general course of the boundary is followed.

13B OF HLIDA BURNAN. IN GIBBE FELDE

From the Hiddaburna stream to Gibbe Field

The boundary then proceeded due north following the course of the Hidaburn Stream along what is now St John's road through Gibbe Field. Gibbe is related to Guppa, Gyppi or Gypla, all personal names. Giufeld appears in William I's Charter of 1085-9 and is probably the same. This was evidently a large common field of Wassingham through which the Hidaburn Stream flowed.

14B OF GIBBE FELDE. IN THA BLACI DIC

From Gibbe Field into the Black Dyke

The Black Dyke is the watercourse identified in the Islip (1501) indenture as the Ditch of Bradmede, and was still extant as the 'Common Sewer' into the nineteenth century. Its long curving course from Battersea Creek to Vauxhall represented a major drainage programme possibly dating as far back as the Roman period. The black colouring would have been due to the surface loam washed down into it from the higher ground (cf. 2A).

15B ANDLANG BLACI DIC. INTO BEFERITHI

Along the Black Dyke to Beffra's Stream

The boundary turns west at the confluence of the two streams and is followed to the outlet at Battersea Creek. The term 'Pasture' (O.E. Baer) as rendered in 11A looks more like a personal name, O.E. 'Beffa' as used here.

16B OF BEFERITHE. ANDLANG STRAETE INTO FUGEL RITHE

From Beffa's Stream along the street to Fugel Rythe

The boundary turned north along the foreshore road (cf. 13A) which here is described as a 'straete' (if this is indeed the correct rendering). Normally, this term is reserved for Roman roads, but in this context meant that it had a metalled surface. For Fugel Rythe, see 13A.

17B ANDLANG FUGEL RITHE. INTO THAERE TAEMESE OTH MIDNE STREAM

Along the Fugel Rythe into the Thames there, up to the middle of the stream

For the significance of this statement, see 13A and p.86.

18B ANDLANG STREAMES EST INTO HEAHEFRE

Along the stream east to High Effra.

See 2A.

THE LAMBETH CHARTER

The Westminster surveys are not the only source of topographical information of this type about the landscape of Clapham in the early medieval period. The late tenth-century surveys covered the western boundary of the Clapham Estate and its extended area to the west under Ealdorman Alfred in the late ninth century. Another, purportedly contemporary survey, connected with a different charter, fills in the details of the eastern boundary of the Clapham manor.

The survey of this charter survives as a thirteenth-century copy (*c*.1250), with an original supposed to date to 1062. However, as is the case of the 'Algeric' Charter, it is generally considered to be a forgery, although the landmarks (as in their case) seem to be genuine enough (RHS 1968, 307).

The material is treated here in the same way as the two Westminster surveys, i.e. broken down into lettered clauses identifiable on the Saxo-Norman Clapham map (*38*). As in the other two surveys, each boundary location marks a point where the line changed direction.

THIS SYND THAT LANDGEMAERE INTO LAMBEHYTH
These are the landmarks of Lambeth

The area enclosed would appear to equate mainly with the manor of Stockwell, which formed part of South Lambeth in the thirteenth century (16). This devolved into the manors of Stockwell and Vauxhall soon after 1293 as we have seen (Chapter 2). Stockwell Manor became part of the holdings of the Thomas Romeyn Estate (Lord of Clapham Manor) in 1294-5 (Hawtrey 1967, 56).

A. AEREST AET BRIXGES STANE
That is from Brixge's Stone

The topographical name Brixton is rendered Brixistane in 1067 (EPNS survey 1934, 11), *Brixiestan* in 1086, *Brissistan* in 1230 and also '*Beorghtsig's stone*' (Ekwall 1947, 63). The fact that this particular stone gave its name to the Brixton Hundred (a territorial sub-unit of Surrey) suggests that it was the site of the Saxo-Norman court (*44*). This met at regular intervals and was presided over by the Hundred Reeve (acting as Royal authority) and attended by freeholders. It dealt with such matters as criminal offences, minor ecclesiastical matters and private pleas. It also levied taxes. Hundred courts met in the open air at some distinctive landmark, in this case possibly a prehistoric monument. The identification of this site is critical since the survey began and ended at this spot.

Authorities are agreed that the stone stood on Brixton Hill, but there is no tradition as regards its historical site, which has to be deduced from other evidence. The likelihood is that the Hundred-mote met, as elsewhere, at a boundary junction or 'point-landmark' (Rackham 1986, 19). There is one such place on Brixton Hill where the four ancient manorial estates converged: Clapham, Wyck, Leigham and Dulwich. It was situated at the southernmost point of the former Rushey Green (Brixton Causeway Common) opposite where Morrish Road SW2 meets Brixton Hill, and is still marked by the junction of parish boundaries. This is the highest point of the hill, and in the absence of any other evidence, is the strongest contender for the former location of the *Brixges Stane* (*38*). G. Gower independently reached a

44 'A Hundred Court session at Brixges Stane'. *H.J.M. Green after scene* 'By the Waters of Babylon' *Triple Psalter, with Glossa ordinaria (the Eadwine Psalter). Mid twelfth-century (Trinity College MS R. 17.1 p. 243v)*

similar conclusion about the location of the meeting place of the Brixton Hundred (Gower 1995).

B. AND SWA FORD THURWH THANE GRAF TO THAM MAERCDICE
And thus forth by the Thane's grave to the boundary dyke (or watercourse)
The eastern boundary appears to be the first to be followed, and at the time this was indicated by passing the Thane's grave which was situated nearby to the east of the road. The 'grave', presumably a barrow like those on Wandsworth Common (see 7A) has long disappeared, like the Brixges Stone itself.

The perambulation proceeds north-east along the old manorial boundary between Wick and Dulwich, and down the upper end of the former Water Lane (now Brixton Water Lane). Here there is a change of direction where it meets up with the 'boundary dyke' later known as the Effra River. The Effra long functioned as a boundary line, and at its northern end, divided the manors of Kennington and Vauxhall (Barton 1962, 63). At this point it separated the manors of Wyck and Camberwell, close to what is now Effra Road.

C. AND SWA TO BULCE TREO
And thus to Bulce's Tree
The Effra stream is followed northwards along the Brixton Road to a point where the boundary changes direction to run north-westward. The tree (O.E. *treo*) is the second element of the landmark, the first probably being a personal name *Bulce*. 'In such a case the tree marks a [communal] meeting place, the first element being that of a lawman' (Ekwall 1947, 458). It is of interest that this particular location is the

45 'Bulce's Tree'. The place of execution
for the County of Surrey. *H.J.M. Green
after vignette from the medieval bible of Alba
51 r; the story of Joseph in which the baker
was hanged on the gallows and the birds ate
his flesh*

south-west corner of what was formerly Kennington Common (now the site of St
Mark's Church by the Oval station) which was the traditional place of execution for
the county of Surrey, and was still being used as such as late as the mid eighteenth
century (45).

D. AND FRAM BULCE TREO TO HYSE

And from Bulce's Tree to (the) Hese

The topographical location of *Hese* is in the Nine Elms area at Vauxhall. It occurs as
'Hyse' in William I's charter of 1067 to Westminster (see p.70), 'Hese' in 1134 (Cott.
Claud A XIII), it had become 'Hesefeld' by 1456 and 'Hesewall' by 1474 (Westminster
Abbey Muniments). The later name of the Heath Wall Brook (or sewer) was a garbled
version where *Hese* had been transmuted to *Heath*.

In origin therefore, the term Hese refers to a stream, which also gave its name
to a small estate around its mouth on to the Thames, and also the river wall or
embankment in that area. The exact relationship between the Hese and the Effra is
unclear, since their courses have been lost in this area. The Hese may have flowed
into the Effra, but the surviving evidence suggests that they were in fact two separate
streams whose outfalls lay close together in Vauxhall near the New Covent Garden
Market (Barton 1962, 43). The *Black Dyke* (see item 14B) an apparently artificial
drainage system, flowed into the Hese near its mouth. Hese (O.E.) means youth, or
possibly in this context 'little one' in comparison with the larger Effra stream (the
name Effra may possibly be derived from the Old Welsh *yfrid* meaning a torrent).
The meaning in the context of this charter survey is clear. When the boundary line
following the Effra met the outfall of the Hese, the boundary turned southwards

to follow the Hese stream, which at this point coincides with the line of the Black Dyke (*32*).

E. AND FRAM HYSE TO AELSYGES HAECCE
And from Hyse to Aelsyge's 'corner'
In the area of Brookland's Road, SW8, there was a sharp turn in the direction of the boundary to the south-east to follow the Hese Stream on its course above the Thames floodplain. The place where this took place has a personal name *Aelsge* with second element (O.E. *Hac*) meaning in this context 'a bend' or 'corner'.

F. AND SWA EST TO THAARE STRATE
And thus east to the street there
The course of the Hese Stream is followed to the junction of Stane Street and the so-called Roman 'London-Brighton' road where it passes through Streatham to Clapham North (see Chapter 3). There is a dog-leg at Stane Street eastwards to join the line of the 'London-Brighton' road. From Aelsyge's corner all the way down south, back to Brixges Stone, the boundary separates the two manors of Clapham (west) and Stockwell (east).

G. AND SWA ANDLANG STRETE EST TO BRIXES STAN
And thus along the eastern street to Brixes Stan
It is made clear that the eastern of the two Roman roads is followed, i.e. the London-Brighton route. Starting at Clapham North, the boundary follows Bedford Road and then Lyham road to its junction with New Park Road, SW2. From there, the course of the road is lost, but is in direct alignment with the postulated site of the Brixes Stan (see item A above).

The area of the survey thus delineated covers exactly the land of the Manor of Stockwell. However there is a problem here with a charter purporting to date to 1062. This manor as a discrete unit was not formed out of the manor of South Lambeth territory until the thirteenth century. The lands that were to become the future Stockwell Manor were in fee (i.e. inheritable land) to the Redvers family. In 1258 these landowners were involved in a scheme to make the South Lambeth manor a separate hundred, with all the financial advantages that accrued from this arrangement. In 1262, Baldwin de Redvers died and his widow Margaret held it in dower (i.e. the widow was a beneficiary of the estate) as she did the Manor of Vauxhall. Now the Lord of Vauxhall and also the adjoining Manor of Wyck was the archbishop and chapter of Canterbury. Canterbury also had designs on Stockwell, another lay manorial unit in south Lambeth and part of the Vauxhall Hundred. King Henry III also had an interest in the Vauxhall Hundred, which he wished should revert to the royal Hundred of Brixton (Hawtrey 1967, 55). At this critical moment in the middle of the thirteenth century, Canterbury suddenly remembered that it had a charter purporting to date to before the conquest proving that Stockwell was actually a part of Wyck Manor all along! The suspicion that this was a timely forgery is almost irresistible, but, as we have seen before, the landmarks are genuine.

THE SAXO–NORMAN LANDSCAPE

There are parts of Britain today, even in the Home Counties, which still retain something of the character of the countryside as it was a thousand or more years ago. However, in Clapham, and indeed in most of London suburbia, this ancient world is wholly lost. Today, the former fields and woodland groan under the weight of tarmac, brick and concrete. In Clapham, apart from the generalised shape of the Common and the surrounding network of roads, nothing at all survives of this old landscape. The place today would be unrecognisable to any of its former inhabitants.

In these thousand-year old land surveys, it was a landscape almost without figures. Even traces of agricultural and pastoral use of the land are sparse. There are the five fields of barley corn at Battersea ('On either side the river lie/Long fields of barley and of rye') where now are *bijou* condominiums. Goat Hall, the hut of the herdsman surrounded by his flock, was where the flower shop stands on Lavender Hill. Baence's cowhouse in the meadows beside the Hidaburn Stream was in the centre of the fashionable winebar and restaurant district along Northcote Road. Away from the stream on the uplands were lonely moors crowned by barrows of long-forgotten warriors, marking territorial boundaries which still survive to this day. Where footballers play on manicured pitches of Clapham Common was a bog with marsh lights haunting the pools where it was believed lurked the dreadful monster Grendel. Perhaps only the mewing of the gulls along the Battersea foreshore at low tide is a faint echo of their ancestors who gave their name to the 'Fugelerithe' there a thousand years ago (*fugel* = Old English for bird or fowl, rīp pronounced 'rithe' = small stream in Old English, i.e. 'stream frequented by birds'. The stream would have flowed from the Battersea marshes to the tidal inlet south of St Mary's church).

6

'WITH SAKE AND WITH SOKE'

Only the wind moves
Over the empty fields, untilled
Where the plough rests at an angle
To the furrow

T.S. Eliot, *The Rock*

THE DOMESDAY BOOK AT CLOPHAM

The curious legal expression of this chapter heading reads in full 'With Sake and with Soke, with Toll and with Team and with Infangenetheof'. First appearing in the late Saxon period, it became under the Normans the accepted formula for the description of a lord's judicial rights. The words 'sake and soke' can be broadly rendered 'by cause and suit', or perhaps, in modern parlance, 'by due legal process'. 'Toll' and 'team' assert the lord's right to receive tolls on merchandise and hold a market. 'Infangenetheof' declares the lord's duty to execute justice on any criminal apprehended in the area of his domain (Stenton 1947, 490). This alliterative phrase neatly conveys the overwhelming and oppressive legal powers of seigniorial authority under the feudal system in the medieval period, now to be examined at Clapham. Nowhere is this more clearly demonstrated than in the dry terminology of the Domesday Book commissioned by King William I in 1086 as a record of land ownership over the whole of England.

XXV the land of Geoffrey de Mandeville
IN BRIXTON HUNDRED
GEOFFREY de Mandeville holds CLOPHAM.
Thorbiorn held it of King Edward. It was
then assessed at 10 hides: now at 3 hides.
There is land for 7 ploughs. In demesne
is 1 plough: and 8 villans and 3 bordars
with 5 ploughs. There are 5 acres of
meadows. In the time of King Edward
(TRE) it was worth £10: afterwards

46 'Unfree Clopham villagers working their lord's land.' Vignette of *c.*AD 1330 (Psalm 96) which catches the grinding toil required of the *villan* and *bordar*. *H.J.M. Green after marginalia in the Luttnell Psalter BL f. 171 v*

the same: now £ 7 10.

The men say that Geoffrey has this manor

wrongfully, because it does not belong

to Esger's land. What Geoffrey gave

in alms from this manor is worth 20s.

Translation from Williams & Martin (2003, 85)

This unique assessment for the periods immediately before and after the Conquest in 1066 is the subject of this chapter. Since, however, the primary concern here is to identify changes in use of different classes of land at Clapham, some initial consideration must be paid to the status and consequent likely land ownership of the two types of villager identified: the *villan* and *bordar*. Although villans (L. *villani* = villagers) were of a higher status than bordars (O.E. *bordarii* = hut-dwellers) both were unfree in the sense that they were both subject to the manorial court and thus were an essential part of the domanial economy (*46*). In Middlesex the villan's holding was a standard unit of land, usually a virgate or half-virgate, while bordars had smaller holdings (Erskine & Williams 2003, 57–8).

Possibly a clearer definition between these two classes of unfree peasants is to be found for Clapham in the 1326 Extent despite the 240-year interval. At this later date (apart from the free tenants) there were 31 *bondmen* and 4 *cottars* (O.E. *cottager*). By 1326 the cottars were not a viable economic group in terms of land holdings, so that the two effective subdivisions are likely to have been between the two types of *bondmen* or *virgators* identified in 1326: those holding 1 virgate (16 acres) and those with a half-virgate (8 acres), to be probably equalled with the Domesday villans and bordars respectively. In his study of the conditions in 1086 at Hampstead, Sullivan reached much the same conclusions in connection with the land holdings of villans and bordars (Sullivan 1994, 118).

On the basis of this projection, the amount of common arable land parcelled out in 1086 at Clapham between the villans would have amounted to 128 acres and that for the bordars would have been some 24 acres, a total of 152 acres. From the Domesday Book we know that Clapham comprised 3 hides of arable land, some 189 acres, if the 63 acres to a hide figure is followed (see Chapter 4). The balance of 37 acres must therefore have been farmed by the demesne. So where were these lands and what had happened to the 7 hides (371 acres) apparently lost between the time of King Edward and William I (see p.87)?

ARABLE AND MEADOWLAND (47)

The formation and break-up of the Middle Saxon Alfred Estate, traced in Chapter 4, is a classic example of a large dispersed territory being subsequently fragmented and taken over by the new class of independent local lords who emerged in the tenth and eleventh centuries. It appears to be not so much a case of fission into discrete areas of arable, woodland and grazing, but the result of the sheer physical impossibility of managing a large estate from a single centre (cf. recent studies discussed by Williamson 2003, 15).

Unlike other late Saxon estates in the vicinity, such as Wandsworth and Battersea, the estate centre or *caput* (47 manor: 1★) was not alongside the Thames, but situated some distance inland. The choice of Clapham (Clopeham or Cloppeham as it was known between the ninth and thirteenth centuries; Redstone 1967, 36) was determined by two factors: easy access to fresh water and the availability of fertile soil along the Hackney Gravel Drift Terrace (see Chapter 1). This land appears to have been used for pastoralism or agriculture since the Neolithic period. The Lynch Hill Gravels of Clapham Common have an acid subsoil unsuitable for arable farming (see p.29). Aerial photography in September 2003 of Clapham Common (*colour plate 4*) did not reveal any ancient field systems there, except along the northern perimeter where the southern edge of strip systems of one of the open fields of the former Wassingham Estate still survived as crop marks (*colour plate 4:7*). Elsewhere on Clapham Common there are traces of lazy-bed agriculture (*colour plate 4:1*), but these could be of any period, the strongest likelihood being the time of land hunger during the thirteenth century (see Chapter 8).

The background to the alienation of the Wassingham and Hidaburn (Rydon) Estates from Clapham has already been discussed (see Chapter 4). If the Erconwold material is to be dated to the mid tenth century, these land units must have already been in the possession of manors and holdings in Battersea and Wandsworth, possibly through sale by Ealdorman Alfred's legatees. One hundred years later, at the time of the Norman Conquest, Clapham was held by Thorbiorn and was assessed at 10 hides (Williams and Martin 1992, 85). Using the standard hide unit of measurement established for Clapham (see Chapter 4) the amount of arable land involved would have been in the region of 630 acres.

By 1086, the Domesday account records that the amount of arable land had fallen to 3 hides (192 acres) with 5 acres of meadow. It was also stated that there was land for 7 ploughs, but only 6 ploughs were in use (including one on the demesne lands). In other words, the arable potential was underused. The number of ploughs in a community, according to Williamson, was more a measure of the vill's capacity to farm its lands rather than an indication of the extent of its holdings (Williamson 2003, 155). The community would have needed to organise its plough teams on the basis of co-operation or joint ploughing. At Clapham with its heavy clay subsoils (even in part on the Hackney Gravel Drift Terrace) there would have to have been quick mobilisation for a brief burst of activity with the spring ploughing involving every plough that was available. The plough equipment, of course, was only part of the resources needed. On this type of land, a full team of 8 oxen would have been required to pull the plough (*13*). Upwards of 50 beasts with additional animals for breeding purposes may have required pasturing in the townlands and stabling in the winter. The 5 acres of hay meadows were of critical importance in this process, since they would have provided the bulk of the fodder for the winter feeds. In summer, the animals would have browsed on the common heathland.

The likely location of the Saxo-Norman arable can be postulated on the basis of various topographical features: soil fertility, easy access to the vill, later land divisions and field names, particularly those of the 1326 Extent. Of the 192 acres, 70 are accounted for by possibly the oldest of the townlands, which is termed here the 'West Field' (*47*). Its original name has not survived, but may simply have been 'Clapham Field', as occurs in some post-medieval records. The remaining 122 acres of farmland in all probability lay along the Hackney Gravel Drift Terrace to the east of the vill, and has been given the generic title of 'East Field'. This may have been taken in later than the West Field. Indeed, one of the larger parcels of land in 1326 was called Firse (Furze) Field, indicating that it had formerly been part of the surrounding heathland. There is a long, continuous eastern boundary flanking what was called in 1326 *Hemereshull* (*47*A) (i.e. Border Hill) now marked by Albion Avenue and Sibella Road. The various parcels of land in 1326 likely to have formed the Saxo-Norman East Field lay on both sides of the present Clapham High Street:

La Breche	36 acres in 1086 (*47 B*)
Richemanneslond / Firsefeld	40 acres (*47* C)
La Batteslond	30 acres (*47* D)
Cherchehull	10 acres (*47* E)
La Pende	4 acres (*47* F)
Total arable land in the East Field:	120 acres

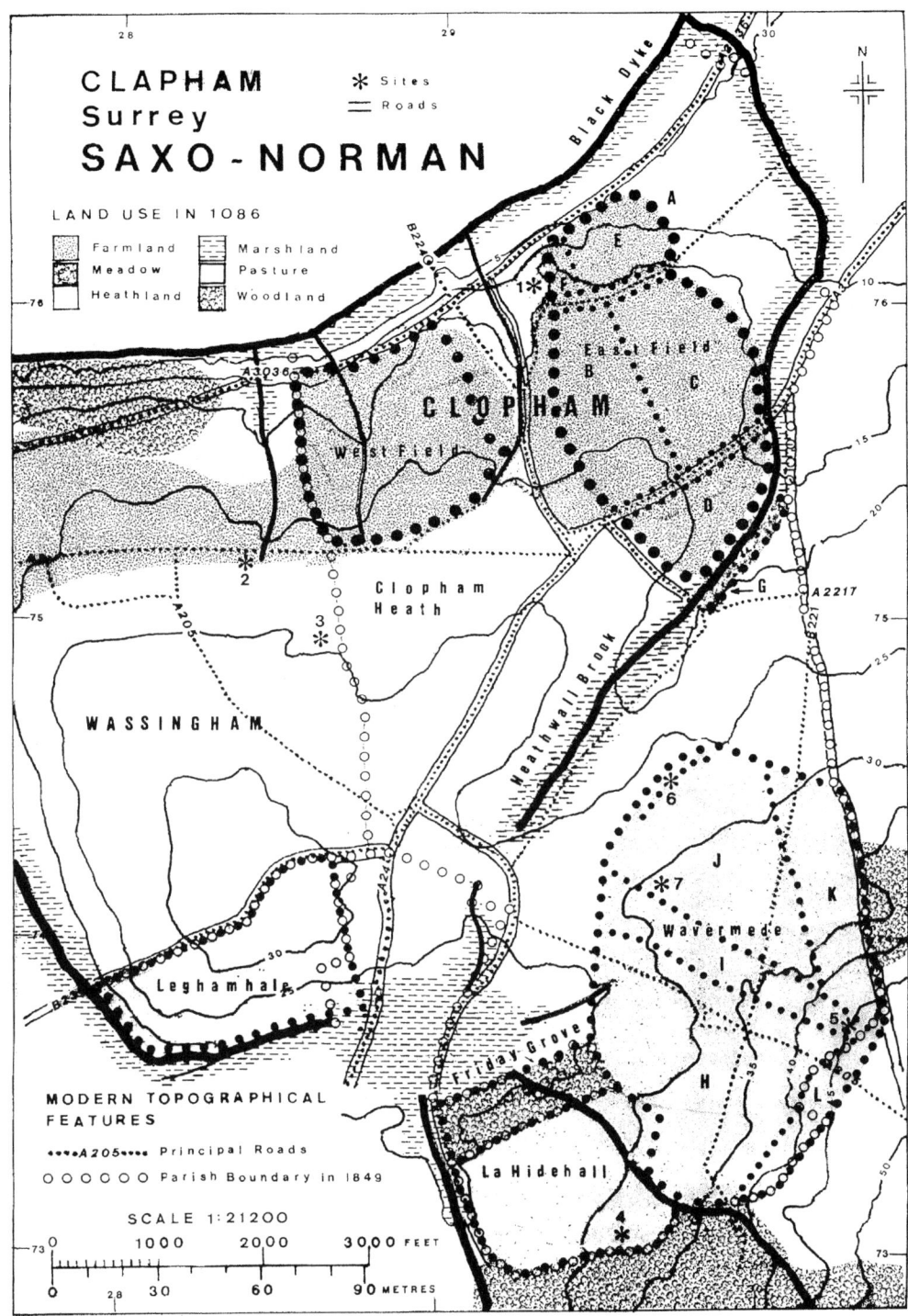

47 Map of Saxo-Norman land use in the Clapham area based on various sources of topographical and historical evidence. *H.J.M. Green. Base Map after the British Geological Survey published 1990.* By permission of the B.G.S.

With the 70 acres in the West Field this gives a total manorial arable of 190 acres compared with the 192 acres in Domesday. This land, together with the 5 acres of meadows, constitute the core agricultural land of the manorial estate. The 371 acres of other land, effectively outlying dependencies or berewicks, are characteristic of Late Saxon estate fragmentation (Erskine and Williams 2003, 56). The Norman hay meadows were some of the most valuable lands in the Clapham Manor and were of necessity sited as close as possible to the vill, both for access during the crucial hay-making season and for supervision (*14*). The principal meadowland of the community appears to have lain alongside the Heathwall Brook, which formed a valley (now centred, in part, on Abbeville Road) and eventually ran through to the Black Dyke, marking the north-eastern boundary of the Clapham Estate. The pelocalcareous alluvial clay soil of the valley bottom, seasonally waterlogged, was ideal for meadowland. Access to the 5 acres of Domesday meadowland was provided by an early predecessor of Clapham Park Road from the village centre. Later the hay meadows moved downstream where the ribbon of meadowland was wider. In 1326 a narrow parcel of meadows alongside the brook was called *La Groveshotte* and amounted to 9 acres by that time (*47G*).

The later medieval meadowland north of the Wandsworth road was on a steep slope and does not appear to have been used for either arable or pasture in the eleventh century. An old field name, 'Peddar's Chase', might suggest that at some early period it had been woodland, sited on the heavy subsoils of the Head clay deposits.

ASSARTING AND PASTORALISM

During the Late Saxon period, there are indications that in addition to the east and west fields of the vill, there was considerable *assarting* (enclosure or taking-in of uncultivated land for agricultural purposes) at the southern end and along the eastern side of the estate. As the land-use map (*6*) indicates, this land had previously been heathland in earlier periods. However, patches of some old wildwood may still have survived in the vicinity, although it is more likely to have been ancient agricultural land that had reverted or, in arboreal parlance, been allowed to 'tumble-down' to woodland (*48*).

There were three areas in this part of the Clapham Estate which appear to have been assarted at this time:

Leghamhale	–	62 acres
La Hidehall	–	63 acres, which may initially have included
Friday Grove	–	21 acres
Wavermede	–	222 acres

These units of land have been given the 1326 Extent field names, which include various subdivisions by this period and parcels of land no longer owned by the manor.

The *Leghamhale* land was originally part of the ninth-century Alfred estate of *Cloppaham*, surviving as an outfield of the manor when the lands to the north were

48 Woodland clearance for agriculture (assarting) using two-handled, iron 'Danish' axes and an open-sided pole-cart for the removal of tree trunks, dragged by oxen. *H.J.M. Green after the Cotton Calendar for June (BL MS Julius A. VI eleventh century)*

ceded to Battersea as the Wassingham Estate. It was probably lost to the Clapham manor in 1103 when the De Mandevilles gave Balham to Bermondsey Abbey (Gower 1996, 6). Leghamhale was subsequently acquired by the Streatham Manor of Leigham Court. The western end (18 acres) was apparently put down to woodland in the earlier fourteenth century as *Ballum Wood*. In the post-medieval period the land was designated as the parochial unit of Clapham Detached.

La Hidehall was another assart on the margins of the Clapham Estate, later known as the Hyde or Hydefield after the unit of land measurement, the hide. The parcel of land adjoining to the north, *Friday Grove*, may also have formed part of the Hyde in 1086. Friday Grove appears to have been another casualty of 1103 and was lost to Clapham at this time. Hydefield itself also went in the later medieval period and passed eventually to Merton Priory, perhaps in 1392 when John Queshm of Clapham granted 30 acres and 2 roods of pasture land to Merton Priory (P. Hopkins, Merton Historical Society, *pers. comm.*). After the Reformation it was eventually sold to Emmanuel College, Cambridge in 1587, who still hold the title (Emmanuel College, Cambridge: Hyde Farm Estate Papers, Box 28, A7). Hydehall Estate was farmed from a hall or farmstead, evidently the predecessor of the late sixteenth- or early seventeenth-century farmhouse which survived into the early twentieth century on the site of what is now Glenfield Road (Gower 1996, 29f.; *colour plate 10; 47* Hidehall: 4★).

The land described here as *Wavermede* was a major land clearance scheme evidently dating to the Late Saxon period. In the south-east area of the Clapham Estate, the evidence of later field boundaries suggest that there were probably other areas of assarting either then or earlier (*47*). By 1326 the 222 acres had been broken up into several large pastures:

Over Wavermede	–	85 acres (*47* H)
Netherwavermede	–	20 acres (*47* I)
Goderichfeld	–	60 acres (*47* J)
Shortelond	–	37 acres (*47* K)
Longmeadow	–	10 acres (*47* L)

This 222 acre block of land was farmed from Black (Bleak) Hall (*47* Blackhall: 5★) which survived into the early nineteenth century at the south end of Kingsfield Road. The boundary of the estate was evidently substantial (probably banked and palisaded) and survived as a big semi-circle of land and a major topographical feature on the Clapham tithe map of 1838. The latter still shows evidence of the broad band of headland (*47* Headland: 6★) along the north-western arc in parcels 148 and 149, where plough teams turned for their return trip down the field strips. The old estate name may have been *Wavermede*, which still formed elements of two field names in 1326. In etymological terms, *waver* means pond and *mede* means pastureland which had formerly been arable. The pond (*47* Pond: 7★) is shown in parcel 161 of the 1838 map.

These dispersed farmsteads in the outlands of the Clapham Estate appear to be the result of assart-driven land development of areas too distant or difficult to work for the peasants of the nucleated settlement of Clapham. It is hardly likely, therefore, that the cultivators were drawn from the bondmen of the village community, but may perhaps represent a seigniorial enterprise with tenant farmers. This is all the more likely since the land, when appropriated for grazing after the Conquest, appears to have reverted to the manor. Indeed, the land continued as a discrete manorial holding down to the mid nineteenth century. There is an interesting sidelight to the assarting of this huge block of land from the communal waste. One of the fields of this intake was called Goderichfeld. The personal name Godric was relatively uncommon during the Saxo-Norman period, but may have been used here as a nickname after St Godric, who was notorious for assarting land previously used as peasants' common pasture, as happened here (Bartlett 2000, 311).

The arable land 'lost' at the time of the Conquest amounted to some 371 acres (see above); the total acreage of the assarts described above is 368 acres. It can therefore be postulated with some confidence that this is the missing arable land of 1086. While remaining part of the manor at this time, what exactly was its function?

In 1086 Geoffrey de Mandeville (Goisfrid de Manneville) held the manor, although according to the Hundred Court he did not have legal title to the property. However, this was not something that would have bothered the powerful De Mandeville family overmuch, who claimed that it had formerly been the property, not of Thorbiorn, but of Esger (Ansger) the late Saxon Sheriff of London and Middlesex (Stenton 1947, 717), probably on the grounds that Geoffrey effectively held the same position under William I. However, this legal sleight of hand may explain the otherwise cryptic statement that 'what Geoffrey gave in alms (*eleemosyna*) amounted to 20s', presumably a donation to the Crown to regularise matters.

As Portreeve (*Portirefan*) in the Writ of William I to the City of London, De Mandeville was the most powerful lord in the metropolis and the Surrey area (*Port* here has the O.E. connotation of 'town', and the office of portreeve was later equated with that of the Sheriff of London) (*49*). As a holder of a property (*mansura*) within the city, Geoffrey would have been assured of commercial access to the London market for the produce and animals from his estates (Stenton 1969, 181f.).

In his capacity as Portreeve, Geoffrey must have been acutely conscious of the commercial opportunities that Saxo-Norman London was beginning to present,

49 Late medieval
view of the City of
London catching the
essential character
of 'the most noble
city' (William Fitz
Stephen *c.*1173) whose
commercial needs
always overshadowed
the life of outlying
villages like Clapham.
*Woodcut of 1497 by
Wynkyn Worde*

particularly in the provision of foodstuffs and wool for the flourishing cloth trade (*50*).
The 70 per cent loss of arable land at Clapham might therefore suggest that it was the
new seigniorial policy here to turn over former large areas of arable to pasture to provide
meat and cheese for the markets of the metropolis and, more importantly, wool for the
Flemish staplers (Brooke 1975, 269). Other Surrey properties of De Mandeville show
a similar decline in the amount of farmed arable at this period: Carshalton 13 per cent
and Wanborough as much as 43 per cent. By my estimation therefore some 370 acres of
former arable at Clapham was turned over to pasture immediately after the Conquest,
almost certainly for the benefit of the demesne (*51*).

The use of considerable acreage of demesne land for pasturage is further indicated
by a deed of 1327 in which Robert de Weston, Lord of Clapham, ratified a deed of
Thomas Romayn (formerly Lord) to John Rous which included 'common of pasture
for 600 sheep and 30 beasts, oxen and cows, as the demesne pastures, feeding in all places
where the beasts of the Lord feed ...' (Chart. R 20 Edw. II 1327) (*52*). The cattle and
sheep would have had to be kept in separate hedged enclosures or otherwise managed
separately since sheep crop so closely that cattle and horses can find little to bite. The
procedure that is described in the 1327 Rous deed may represent a version of the *fold*

50 Mule train laden with bales of wool passing through a city. In the foreground a wool stapler's shop with cloth cutting and a merchant checking the quality of wool from a wicker basket. *H.J.M. Green, after vignette in Ambuogio Lorenzetti's fresco 'Good Government' (1337-39), Town Hall, Sienna*

51 Pastoral scene with shepherds and probably a strain of Herdwick sheep, a hill breed kept by Norman abbeys for its coarse, hard-wearing wool. Bones of the four-horned Maux Loughton sheep imported by the Vikings have been found on London sites. *H.J.M. Green after the Cotton Calendar for May (BL MS Julius A VI). Eleventh century*

course by which the valuable dung dropped by the sheep as they roamed over the fallows by day or immediately after the harvest was a manorial monopoly. In other words, Rous obtained pasturage for his animals in exchange for the automatic manuring of the demesne lands by his animals. This must also have included intensive night-folding or *tathing* (53) which was the prerogative of the manorial lord (Williamson, 2003 80).

Given the estimated amount of basic demesne pasturage, say 370 acres, a rough approximation of the number of animals involved can be calculated on the traditional basis of 1, 1½ or 2 sheep to the acre, which were the figures most frequently cited in medieval manorial byelaws. Taking the highest figure of 2 sheep to an acre, this gives us an average of, say, 740 animals in 1086 (Ault 1972, 48).

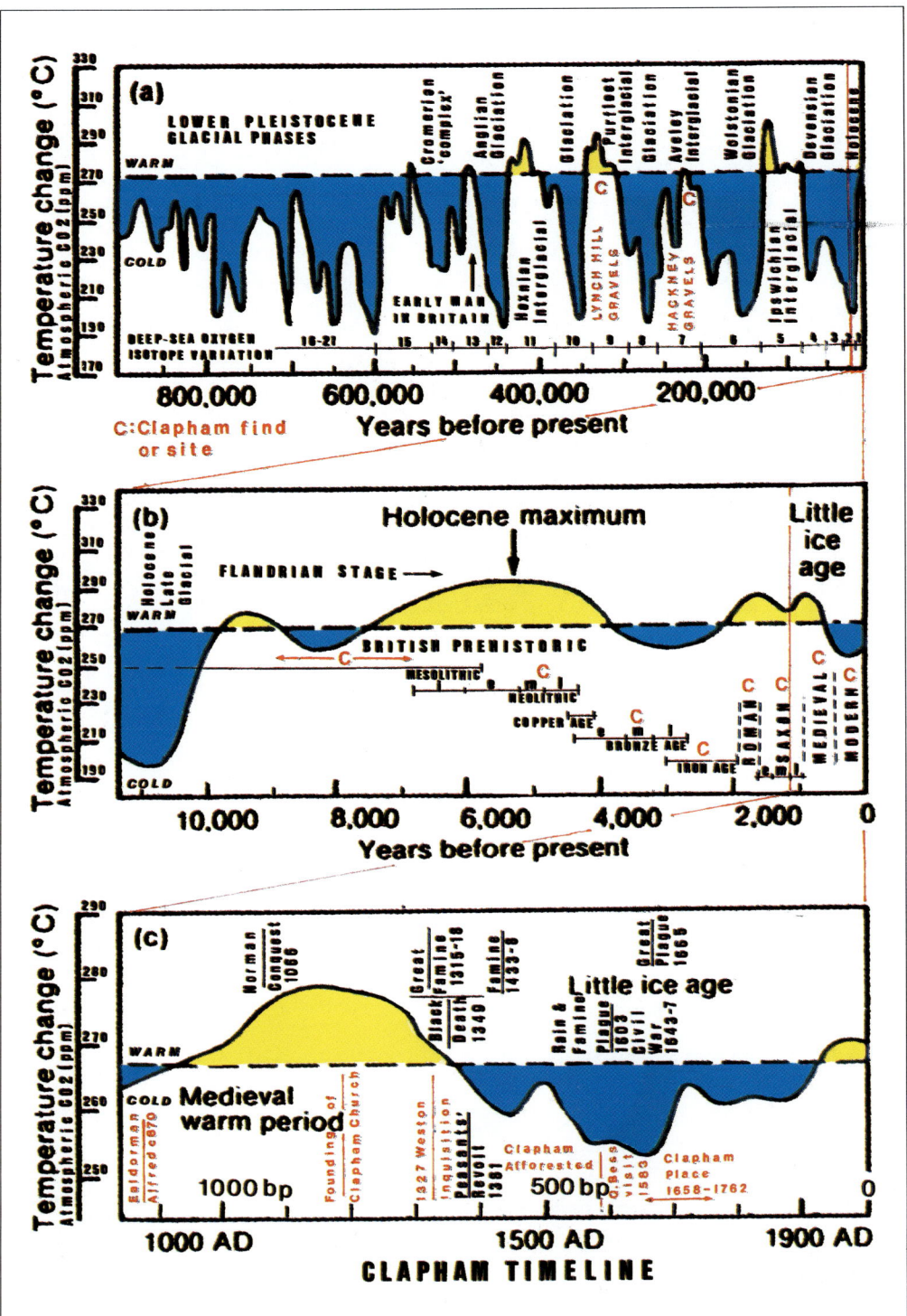

1 Clapham timeline table showing atmospheric CO² with glacial cycles based on the Marine Oxygen Isotope record. The top (yellow) stages are warm periods; the bottom (blue) are cold periods ('ice ages'). The stages are numbered in chronological sequence along the bottom of the top chart (a). Archaeological and historical events at Clapham are indicated in red.

H.J.M. Green, after B. Crackneil

2 Neanderthal encampment reconstruction on the site of Hackney Gravel Terrace (Ilfordian phase) *c*.243,000 years BP. *Model & photograph by H.J.M. Green*

3 Watercolour view looking east from The Avenue towards Holy Trinity Church (completed 1776) showing the heath-like condition of Clapham Common. Unknown artist, late eighteenth- or early nineteenth-century. *Courtesy of the Society of Antiquaries of London*

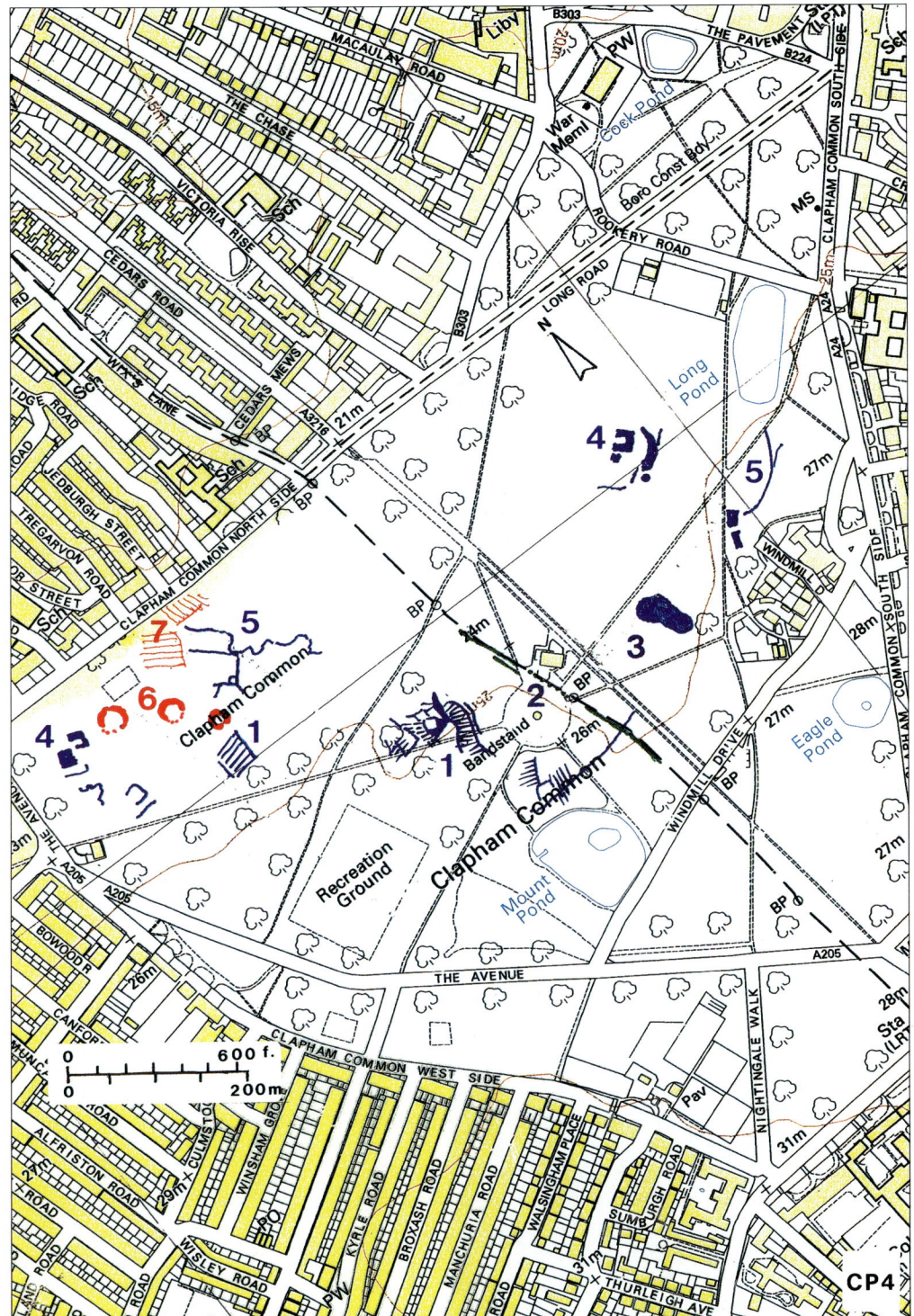

4 O.S. map of Clapham Common with superimposed crop marks (in grass) photographed by English Heritage on 16.09.2003. 1. Spade cultivation marks (medieval lazy-bed agriculture) 2. Parish boundary ditch features of 1716. 3. Pond probably associated with the seventeenth-century Postmill. 4. Medieval house platforms, moats and ditches 5. Stream systems of prehistoric or early historic date 6. Ditches of barrow field of Anglo-Saxon or earlier date 7. Blocks of medieval ridge and furrow. The south-east corner of Wodefield of Wassingham. *H.J.M. Green on Base Plan © Crown Copyright. All rights reserved. Licence number 100047602*

5 Aerial photograph of the bandstand area of Clapham Common taken 16.09.2003. Lazy-bed system shows up dark green against the dried-out grass. The 1716 parish ditch system shows as a dark streak in the lower foreground. *Courtesy of English Heritage. NMR 23180/20 TQ 2875/43. 16 September 2003*

6 Bluebell (*Endymion nonscriptus*) type-fossil of Stockwood, the 70 acre woodland in existence from *c.*1320–1630. Plant from No. 40 Northside. *Photograph by H.J.M. Green*

Right: 7 Hunting scene in 'managed woodland'. *Foreground*: wood pasture with isolated trees (standards) with surrounding undergrowth. *Background*: underwood with Hazel stools producing sucker poles. Flemish sixteenth-century miniature. (*B.L. Add. MS. 18855, f108v.*)

Below: 8 Conjectural reconstruction of Ealdorman Alfred's hall and associated farm buildings at Cloppaham *c.*AD 870. *Model and photograph by H.J.M. Green*

9 Reconstruction of West Stow (Suffolk) settlement (fifth to seventh centuries AD) showing typical wattle and timber framed, thatched huts of the type likely to have occurred at Cloppaham. *Photograph by H.J.M. Green*

10 Hyde Farm in 1906 shortly before its demolition as part of the Hyde Farm Estate Development (site of existing Nos 46–56 Emmanuel Road). The seventeenth-century farmhouse has a Surrey vernacular T-shaped plan with a central hall-kitchen and a parlour in the cross wing. The hall-kitchen premises has a lean-to outshut on the north side. The weather-boarded building at the rear is a barn. *Watercolour by W.F. Palmer dated 1906 looking east. Courtesy of and © of Wandsworth Libraries, Museum and Arts*

11 Hypothetical reconstruction of Clapham manor house with attached chapel *c.*1180. Faramus of Boulogne, Lord of the Manor in the later twelfth century, was probably the founder of this private chapel, later the parish church of Holy Trinity. *Model and photograph by H.J.M. Green*

12 Children of the Manor
Right 12a Francis Clarke as youth from his father's monument of 1589 (see *77*). He held the manor from 1589–1611
Left 12b Rebecca Atkins who died aged 9 in 1661. In part her dedication reads: '*Reader, survey with piteous eye The merciless hand of destinye, Which from a tender parent's breast With fury tore this welcome guest ...*' From the late seventeenth century memorial to the Atkins children (see *colour plate 13*). *Photographs by H.J.M. Green*

Above and opposite: 13 Monumental tomb sculpture by William Stanton of the late seventeenth-century Atkins family when Lords of the Manor. For their original position in the former Lady Chapel see *71b*

13a Heraldic Achievement of the Atkins family: Azure three bars argent, in chief three bezants, quartered with the Arms of Lady Atkins: Azure and chevron argent, in field charged with three bulls heads argent

13b Three Atkins children who predeceased their parents: L. Rebecca d. 1661 aged 9 years (*colour plate 12b*); M. Annabella d. 1670, aged 19 years; R. Henry d. 1677 aged 24 years

13c Recumbent effigies of Sir Richard Atkins (d. 1689) and Rebecca Lady Atkins (d. 1711)

Photographs by H.J.M. Green.

Extant remains of the monument are displayed in the Lady Chapel of St. Paul's Church, Clapham

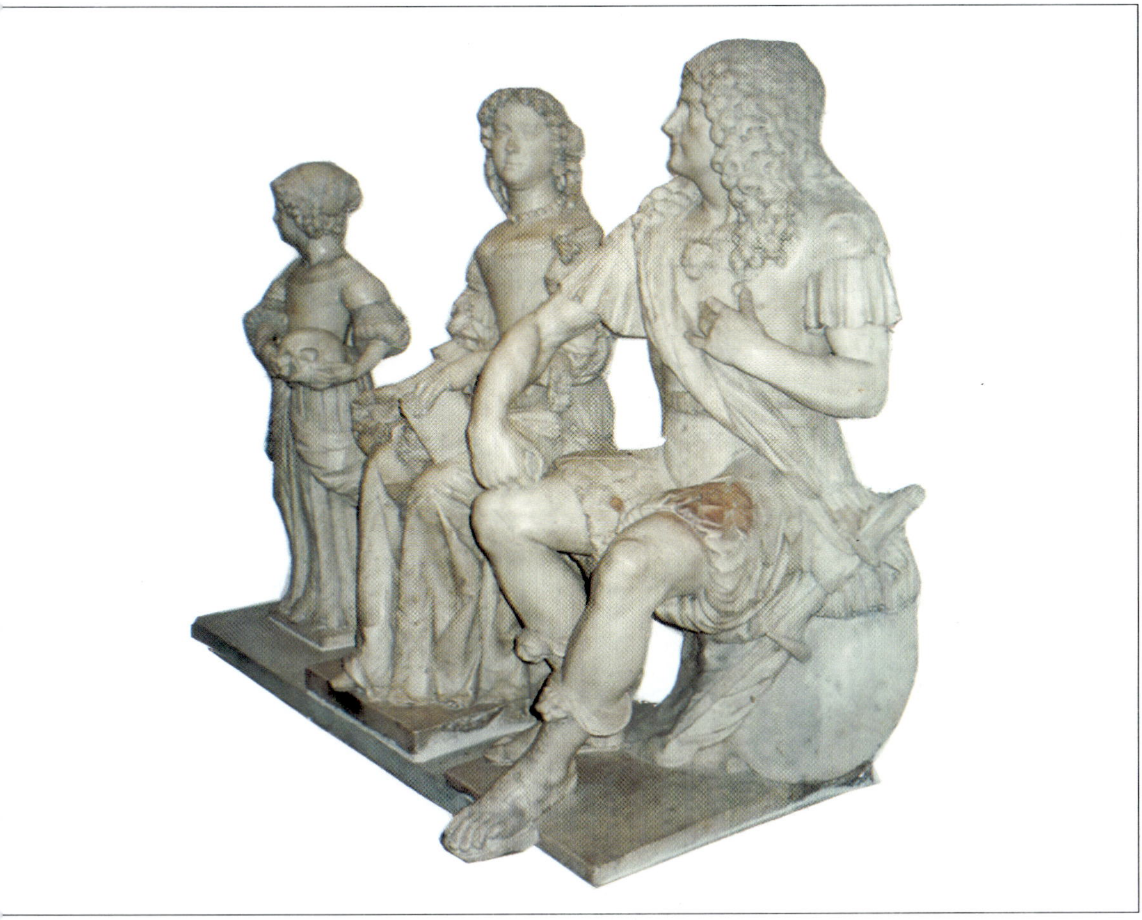

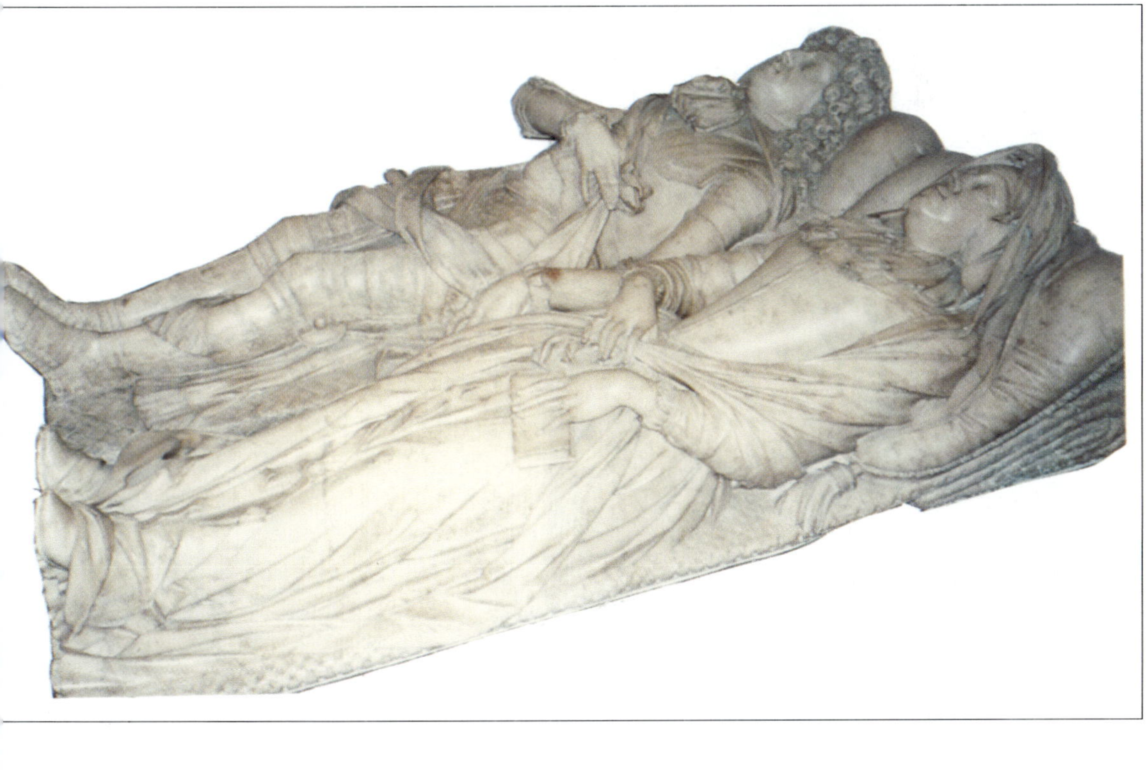

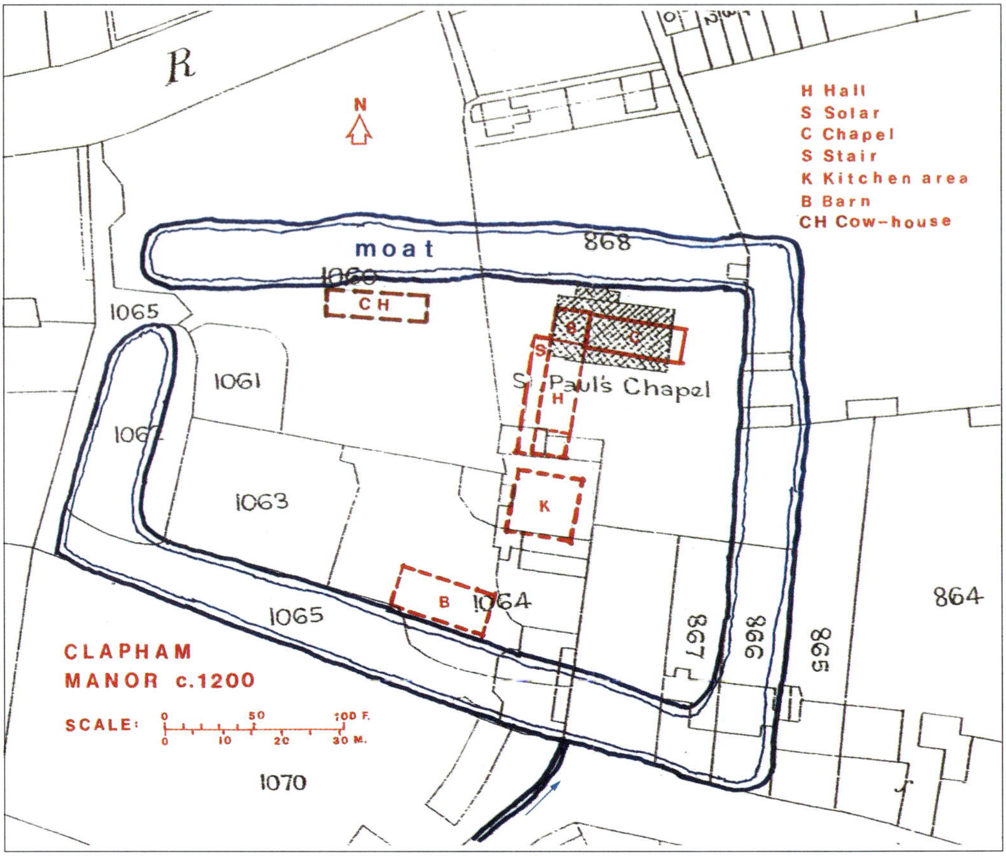

R

N

moat 868
1060
CH
1065
1061
106
St Paul's Chapel
S
H
1063
K
1065
B 1064
CLAPHAM
MANOR c.1200
SCALE: 0 50 100 F.
0 10 20 30 M.
1070

864
897
866
865

H Hall
S Solar
C Chapel
S Stair
K Kitchen area
B Barn
CH Cow-house

Above: 14 Plan of early medieval, moated manor site at Clapham. Hypothetical layout of buildings. *H.J.M. Green. Base map after the Clapham Tithe map of 1838*

Left: 15 Hypothetical view of early medieval Manor House at Clapham looking north-east. *Model and photo by H.J.M. Green*

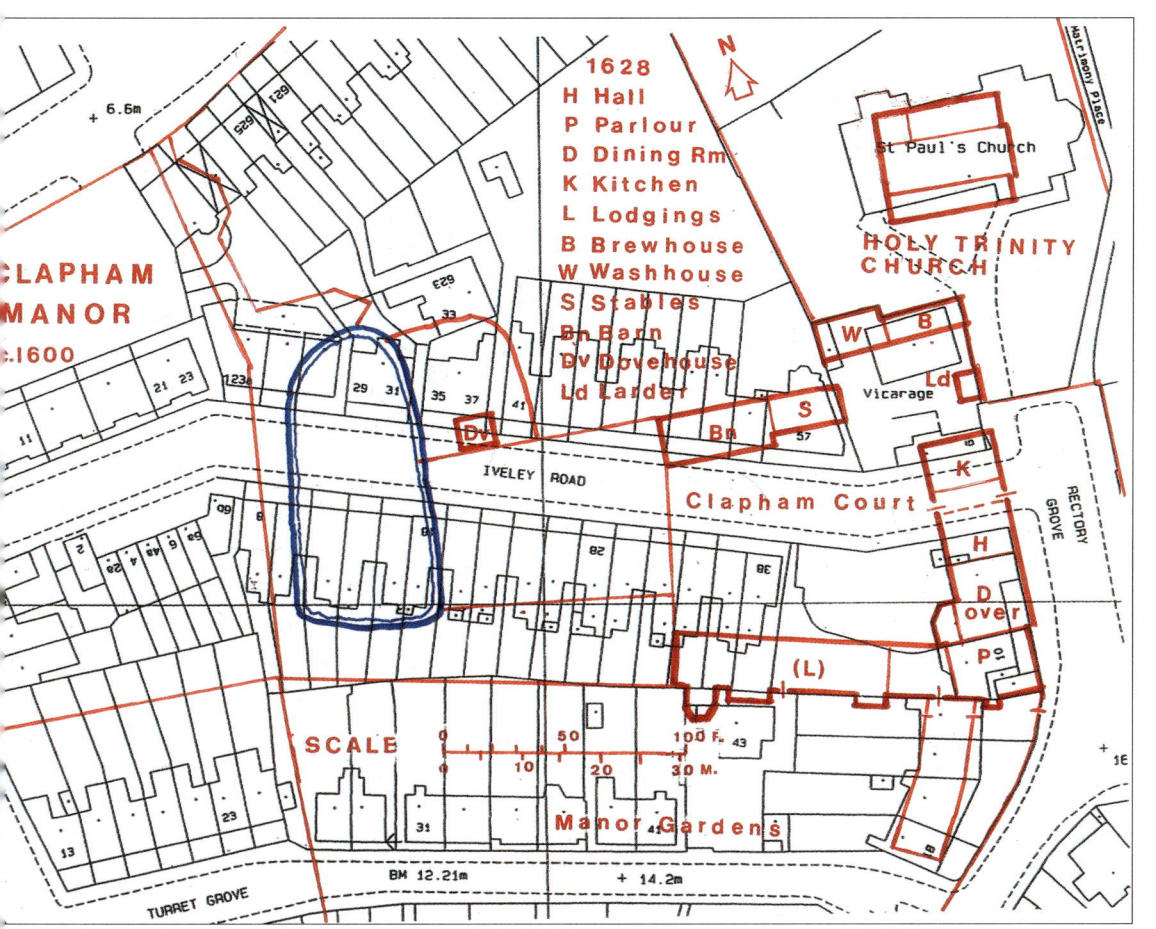

16 Plan of post-medieval manor site at Clapham. Layout of manor complex based on various sources of topographical and historical evidence. *H.J.M. Green. Base map courtesy of the Ordnance Survey © Crown Copyright. All Rights Reserved. Licence Number 100047602*

17 'View of Clopham *c.*1326'. Background detail of *The Peasant and the Birdnester* of 1568 by Pieter Breugel, the Elder (© *Kunsthistorisches Museum Wien*). Flemish village Longhouses of wattle and daub with hipped, thatched roofs with side entrance and main animal entrance in the gable end

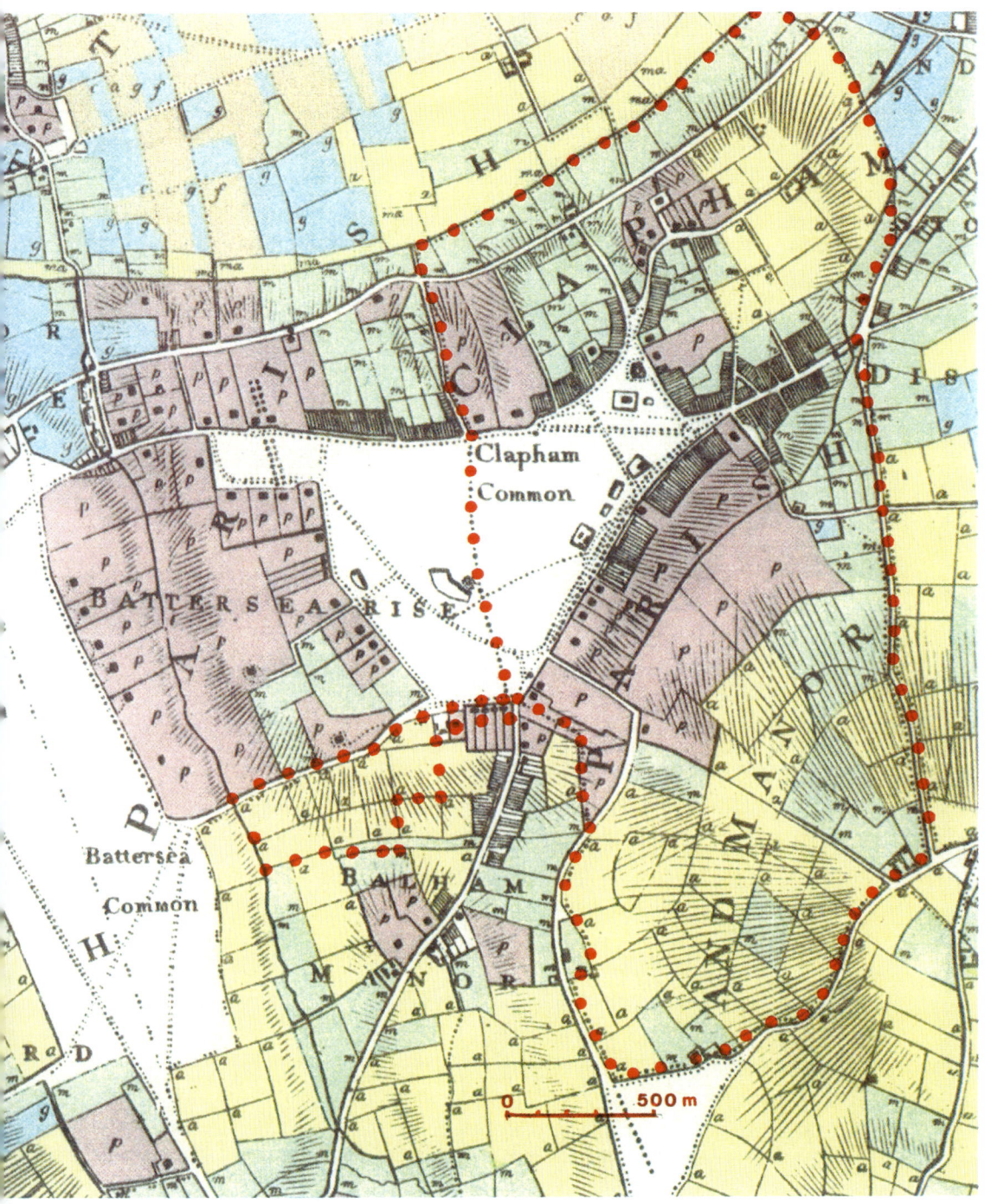

18 Milne's Land Use Map of Wandsworth and District (1801) with the parish of Clapham (and Clapham Detached) outlined in red. Key: a (yellow) = arable, m (green) = meadow, p (pink) = pasture, g (blue) = market garden, f (light brown) = allotments. *Courtesy of Wandsworth Libraries, Museum and Arts*

19a Eatrly terrace development 1714-20 by John Hutt. Nos 13-21 Church Buildings, Northside, Clapham Common. *Photo: H.J.M. Green*

19b End house of former terrace development owned by Clapham Place, *c.1690* by Sir Peter Daniel. No. 45 Clapham Old Town. *Photo by H.J.M. Green*

Sir W. S^t. John's Land
Sr R. Atkin's
Land.
FROM CLAPHAM.
FROM CLAPHAM.
CLAPHAM HEATH.

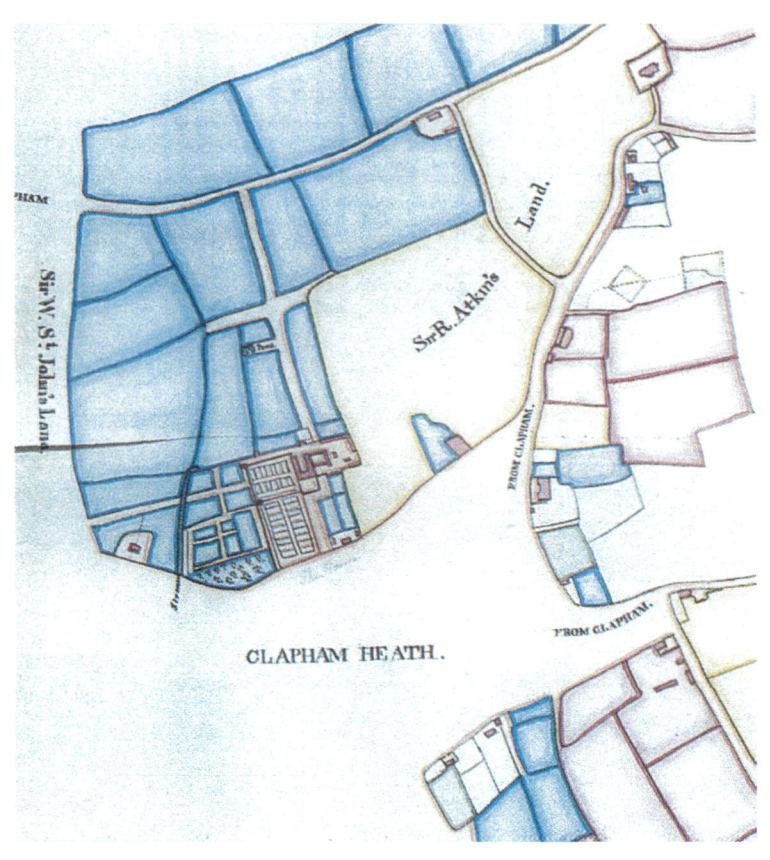

Left: 20a Map of Clapham Place estate *c.*1715. Coloured extra – illustration from Brayley's *History of Surrey* Vol III part 2 (1841). Key: red & blue = extent of Gauden's estate; blue = land sold off by Hewer and Edgeley Hewer owners; yellow = manorial demesne. *Courtesy of the London Metropolitan Archives*

Below: 20b Coloured overlay plan of Clapham Place buildings, gardens and environs based on the Brayley and Rocque maps, and other sources. *Drawings by H.J.M. Green 2004. Base map courtesy of the Ordinance Survey. © Crown Copyright. All rights reserved. Licence number 100047602*

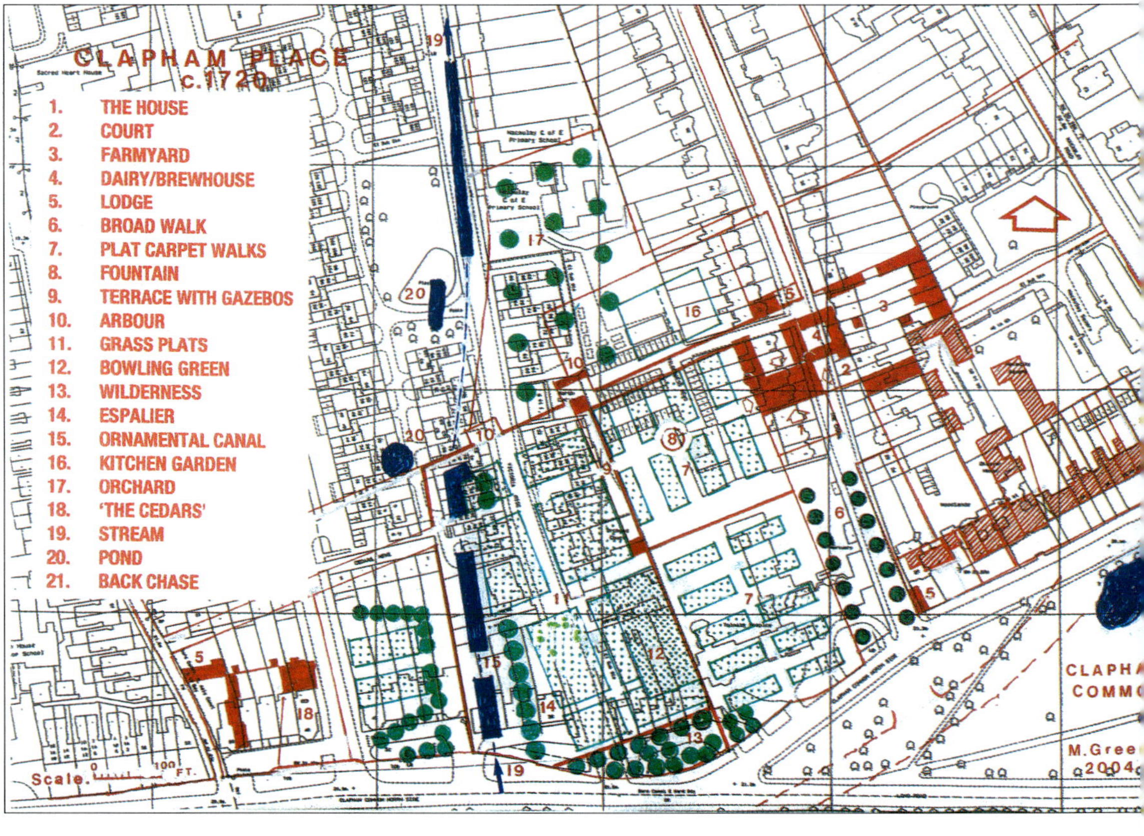

CLAPHAM PLACE
c.1720
1. THE HOUSE
2. COURT
3. FARMYARD
4. DAIRY/BREWHOUSE
5. LODGE
6. BROAD WALK
7. PLAT CARPET WALKS
8. FOUNTAIN
9. TERRACE WITH GAZEBOS
10. ARBOUR
11. GRASS PLATS
12. BOWLING GREEN
13. WILDERNESS
14. ESPALIER
15. ORNAMENTAL CANAL
16. KITCHEN GARDEN
17. ORCHARD
18. 'THE CEDARS'
19. STREAM
20. POND
21. BACK CHASE
Scale.
0
100
FT.
CLAPHA
COMM
M.Gree
2004

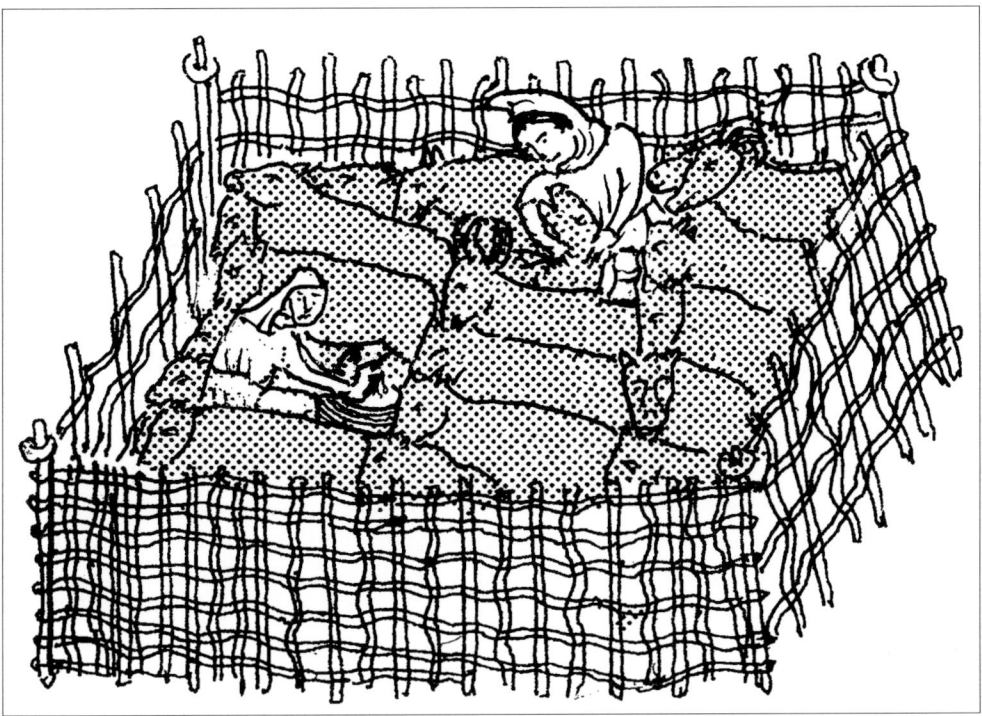

52 Flock of sheep close-penned overnight in a fold of hazel hurdles for the purpose of *tathing* the land. A shepherdess is milking a ewe. *H.J.M. Green after Luttnell Psalter (BL. Add. Ms 42130 folio 163 r)*

53 Communal sheep-shearing supervised by the manorial bailiff. *H.J.M. Green after vignette from calendar of seasonal activities. Fifteenth century (MS Fv. 1872 Bibl. Nat. Paris)*

By the early fourteenth century the likely total of demesne sheep can be calculated on the basis of different criteria. In the 1326 Extent it is stated that 'all customary tenants ought to wash the lord's sheep one day and shear them another day ... and the shearing of each customary tenant is worth beyond reprise [i.e. a deduction, charge or payment due to be made annually out of a manor] by estimation ½d. Total 12d'. In other words, there were 24 shearers at work on the manor's flock (52). Now the number of sheep which could be sheared per day by an individual using traditional methods was about 40 (Jenkins 1976, 52). By estimation, therefore, the number of demesne sheep at Clapham in 1326 was in the order of 960 sheep. This was not all – there was also the Rous flock of 600 sheep to be accommodated (not to mention other animals).

A total of, say, 1560 sheep would require by Ault's figure a minimum of 780 acres. The difference of 410 acres, subtracting the estimated pasture acreage for 1086, must be accounted for elsewhere on the manor. An obvious candidate is the strip of pastureland north of the Wandsworth Road, which must have been brought into use by the late thirteenth century (a total of 49 acres) together with the waste at the Stockwell end of the East Field (some 62 acres). Even this additional pastureland was only a quarter of that required, which suggests that there must have been further intakes, particularly along the east side of Clapham Heath between Stane Street and the Heathwall Brook, to provide the pasture that was evidently necessary if there was not to be serious overgrazing.

The turning of the Clapham outlands or berewicks into what were effectively sheep runs was a stroke of genius by the De Mandevilles. On the self-manured grassland the sheep could be pastured throughout the year in the mild climate of the early medieval period (see *colour plate 1*). At night the flock would have been close-penned in moveable folds of hazel hurdles on the arable strips and closes of the demesne, where the sheep manured (*tathed*) the land by dropping dung and treading it into the soil (53). In return, the sheep provided meat and wool for the burgeoning wool trade of early medieval London. The flock also provided milk for cheese-making, specifically mentioned in the 1326 Extent as a perquisite of the Customary Tenants at shearing. The animals of the manorial tenants clearly did not run with the demesne flocks, but were probably communally pastured, together with other beasts, on Clapham Heath, as is indicated in the 1628 Extent ('a large Common for the tenants').

In 1086, there were 8 villans and 3 bordars at Clapham, with presumably a bailiff or steward to manage the demesne for the absent Geoffrey de Mandeville. Using the Roger's demographic projection of 4.5 heads per family (an approximate which will be followed throughout this study) we have a manorial population estimate of 54 persons living in Clapham vill at this period (Rogers 1972, 16). This is a small population compared, say, with Battersea and Wandsworth, which had between them an estimated 310 souls, not to mention supervisory staff from the 2 or 3 manors which held land in those vills. No church is mentioned in the Domesday Book at Clapham. The vill was evidently a pastoral settlement requiring a relatively small number of shepherds and cowmen to manage the demesne livestock. Geoffrey de Mandeville must have had a quiet smile on his face when he parted from the Domesday Commissioners, who had entirely failed to register the real source of income of the manor!

7

LADY SIBYL'S BEQUEST

The moste partie of this people
That passeth on this eathe,
Have thei worschip in this
Worlde, thei willen no better;
Of other hevene than here,
Holde thei no tale

William Langland, *Piers Plowman* (c.1360), 13.1.6

ECCLIA DE CLOPHAM

The medieval church at Clapham is generally considered to be a relatively late foundation, one of several in north Surrey (Blair 1991, 129). The Domesday account does not mention a church. The first definite reference to a church occurs in 1231-8 (BL 168 Ms. Cotton Cleop. C VILL f. 97) when Henry, Prior of Merton Priory, granted to Stephen, Clerk, the Church of Clopham for life, saving a pension of 20s. per annum. This was given under seal (there is no date on the document, but it falls within the date bracket mentioned above) (Heales 1898, 93).

In the fifteenth century the church was dedicated to the Holy Trinity, as mentioned in a will of Thomas Gower of 1458 (Rudolf, 1904, 6). The supposed medieval dedication to St Mary (Gower 1887, 17 and subsequently copied by other authorities) appears to be incorrect.

At some point in the late twelfth century, Merton Priory became involved with Clapham Manor. It was Lysons who suggested that the *advowson* (the right of presenting a priest to a benefice) was possibly granted to the prior by Faramus of Boulogne, Lord of Clapham Manor (Lysons 1796, xi). The Faramus connection came through Geoffrey de Mandeville (see Chapter 6) who apparently enfeoffed of it his son-in-law Geoffrey, son of Count Eustace of Boulogne (*enfeoffment* – the legal entitlement of a tenant to possession of a land holding).

Faramus was active during the second quarter of the twelfth century. In 1130 he confirmed to the Abbey of Bee a grant of land which had belonged to Clapham Manor: '*Faramus, filius Willelme de Bolonia ... scilicet unam hidam in Belgheham, quae pertinabat*

54 Detail of *Doom* painting on the west wall of Chaldon Church, Surrey *c.*AD 1200. Demons boil sinners in a vat in hell. Similar paintings were to be found in many medieval churches, including probably that of Clapham. *H.J.M. Green after I.M. Kerr*

ad manerium de Clopham' (Round 1895-6, 145). The hide of land concerned was in all likelihood the small discrete holding known as La Hidehall (see Chapter 6) which may have passed out of the ownership of the Manor at this time (*47*).

Such a grant of land had one purpose in mind: the exchange of land for the promise of prayers by the monastic establishment concerned. The medieval mind, whether that of lord or peasant, was traumatised by the Church's relentless emphasis on the prospect of Hell for the sinner (*54*). The concept of Purgatory, i.e. a state in which souls who have departed this life in the grace of God are cleansed by suffering (and thereby prepared for Heaven), was a refinement of this doctrine, indeed it made much better business sense to the clerical mind. Avoiding the fires of Purgatory, by whatever means, became the psychological motor that drove medieval piety. The wealthy had neither the time nor the inclination to perform endless penances, so why not pay for the prayers of a suitably devout religious establishment to do this for you? By the thirteenth century this tried business plan had developed new features which enabled the Church to tap the financial resources of the growing middle class and wealthier peasantry.

> The rewards changed from a remission of penance to a release from God's punishment whether in this life or in Purgatory. In the fourteenth century indulgences were extended even further negating guilt itself or giving the opportunity of acquiring an indulgence for the souls of those already in Purgatory.
>
> Jones & Ereira 2004, 104

It is against this background that the history of the medieval Church in Clapham needs to be appreciated.

Indeed, even the Manor of Clapham was to become involved with the fashionable (and expensive) business of setting up a chantry where a priest would pray for the soul of the deceased (preferably under the eye of the family rather than the uncheckable

55 'Lady Sibyl de Tingria at her toilet, complete with mirror, comb and trinket case.' *H.J.M. Green after Luttrell Psalter c.1330 (B.L. Add. MS 42130 folio 63 r)*

arrangements at Merton). The family of Thomas Romayn established a chantry in the parish church after his death in 1313 (Redstone 1967, 39). It was endowed with 6 marks annual rent 'issuing out of certain houses in London'. Lysons believed that the Archbishops of Canterbury were the patrons. However Redstone states that it was the bishop (presumably of Winchester) who had the advowson (Sharpe, *Cal of Wills* in Ct. of Husting, I, 238) an altogether more likely scenario with Winchester raking in yet another ecclesiastic perk (see *Valor*). The chantry was still in use in 1347, in the time of the Weston family, when a John Clerk of Towester was presented. The small semi-enclosed space of the chantry chapel may have been located on the north side of the high Altar (the south side was usually reserved for an image of the Virgin Mary (*66A, 72A & B, 75*).

ALEXANDER, CHAPLAIN OF CLOPHAM

Faramus of Boulogne 1141–47 was a shrewd operator, as befits someone who was a royal Benefactor (Forsyth Harwood 1895-6, 145) during the troubled reign of King Stephen. In addition to the Bec bequest, he also endowed Merton Priory *c.*1174 with Carshalton Church (BL Cotton Ms. Cleop. C.VII fol. 189) probably because he wished to involve the Priory in a major new project at Clapham in this period.

In the cartulary of Merton Abbey a certain *Alexander, Chaplain of Clopham* is cited as a witness in an advowson case with a dating bracket of *c.*1178-9 (Heales 1898, 39). This is evidently the same Alexander, priest, who was signatory at a slightly earlier date to another document in *c.*1177-86. (Heales 1898, 32). If Alexander's incumbency began *c.*1178, it suggests that a chapel existed at Clapham by this date. For where there is a chaplain there is likely to be a chapel. Indeed, if the endowment of Carshalton is directly linked to this project, it would suggest that building work on the chapel began *c.*1174 under the patronage of Faramus. The nature and location of this putative chapel is discussed below.

56 'Death of Sir Ingram de Fiennes outside the gates of Acre in 1190.' H.J.M. Green after a twelfth-century Egyptian painting, BM (Madden 2004, 73)

In 1187, in faraway Palestine occurred the catastrophic defeat of the Christian army at Hattin by Saladin, who in little more than a year drove the crusaders out of most of the region. In the West, Pope Gregory VIII issued a new call to arms, *Audita tremendi*, and the Third Crusade was launched. Richard of Poitou (from 1189, King Richard I of England) took the Cross and raised an army using the procedures of sub-feudation. The senior nobility, the Plantagenet 'Tenants in Chief' were called on to provide their feudal quota of knights, who in turn called up their enfeoffed 'sub tenants' who held their land as a 'knight's fee', or half a knight's fee as appeared to be the case at Clapham (*Testa de Nevill*) (Brayley 1844, 228). One such was Ingram de Fiennes, who had married Lady Sybil de Tingria (55) daughter and heiress of Faramus of Boulogne, and now the legitimate Lady of Clapham. Did he want to go on this madcap foreign adventure? I doubt it. He was not a young man and was firmly settled in his manor with a wife and young son, William de Fiennes. However, he was honour-bound to respond to his Lord's call-up papers. He probably left in May 1189 with the advance party which, on its eventual arrival in Palestine, was involved in besieging *Acon* (Acre) which, in July 1187, had been captured by Saladin. In July 1190, in the messy campaign which led to its eventual recapture by Richard I, Ingram de Fiennes was killed (*Collins Peerage 1756 ed. IV, 437*) (56). Were his last thoughts on that dusty killing field of Sibyl and William and the mists rising over the lush meadows of Clapham?

> And ye had seen great dust clouds fly
> Our men were greatly harmed thereby.
> > Ambroise, jongleur & eyewitness of the Third Crusade
> > *L'Estoire de la queue Sainte*

57 'Lady Sibyl receives absolution from her confessor'. *H.J.M. Green after Luttrell Psalter c.1330 (BL Add. MS. 42130 folio 74 r)*

The circumstances of that distant tragedy were to have serious consequences for the later history of Clapham. After Sibyl had dried her tears when the news of her bereavement eventually trickled back to the manor, she knew what had to be done and if she was uncertain, there was always Father Alexander of Merton (or a successor) to remind her at confession (*57*). For, although crusading was defined as a penance in itself, who knew what other sins her unfortunate husband might have incurred in foreign parts? A major act of penitential sacrifice was called for.

The widow confirmed her father's charter to Merton Priory as 'Lady of Clapham' (Redstone 1967, 39) a title she held of right following King Richard's charter restoring to her the manor and its privileges as enjoyed by her father and late husband (Brayley 1844, 278). A church at Clapham is not mentioned in these proceedings, but I believe that it was at this point, *c.*1190-91, that Merton Priory acquired the advowson of the Holy Trinity Church. The building ceased to be a private chapel of the De Fiennes family and, in the process of time, became a fully-fledged benefice in the iron grip of the Prior of Merton.

A BENEFICE OF MERTON PRIORY

The Augustinian priory at Merton was founded *c.*1117 and, after a rather uncertain start, was formally chartered in 1121 (*58*). The masonry church was begun in 1130, and recent excavations have revealed that cloistral buildings and an extensive infirmary and kitchen complex were added during the thirteenth century (Saxby 2005, 10).

The Austin or 'Black' canons (named after their black outdoor cloaks) were groups of ordained priests living under a modified Benedictine Rule. This was not one of the stricter orders and it exercised considerable latitude concerning matters such as food. Indeed, analysis of the skeletons from the monks' cemetery at Merton shows that they suffered from a medical condition known as DISH (*diffuse idiopathic skeletal hyperostosis*) brought on by overeating and a rich diet (*59*).

58 Seal of Merton Priory of 1241. Obverse: BMV with Christ Child; inscribed SIGILL ECCLESIE SANCTE MARIE DE MERITONA. Reverse: St. Augustine with background canopy representing the east end of the priory church; inscribed MUNDI LUCERNA NOS AUGUSTINI GUBERNA. *Photograph from Heales 1898, plate facing page 106*

In general terms of education and even political sophistication, ordained canons tended to be a cut above the ordinary choir-monk. They were largely drawn from the ranks of local landholders (in this case London) of middling rank: 'moderate means supported moderate men' (Bartlett). However, this was not strictly the case with Merton, which from an early period had notable Royal patronage and was at the centre of national politics throughout the thirteenth and fourteenth centuries, even to the extent that King Henry III had a suite of private apartments in the Priory in the mid 1240s to accommodate the court during frequent visits. The canons appear to have acted as an informal, administrative think-tank for the Plantagenets as evidenced by their formulating a series of legal codes known as the *Statutes of Merton* in 1236 (Cox 1905, 96). Endowments flooded in (some 202 by 1242) and the Priory's property portfolio was one of the most impressive of the medieval church in England. Although capable of generosity to loyal servants of the House, Merton could be ruthless with anyone who got in the way of their financial interests. Their harsh treatment of the poor tenants of Merton Manor in 1348 was a scandal, even by the rough standards of the time (Cox 1905, 99). It was not that the canons were exactly bad men (and certainly not in their own estimation) but just frightfully good at business (*60*). In the words of Coulton 'a monk was not essentially different from other landlords, in that he was capitalist first and a churchman afterwards' (Coulton 1925, 368).

Above left: 59 Carving of monk carrying bread and ale. Muchelney Abbey. *H.J.M. Green after EH photographs (Wilkinson 2006, 132)*

Above right: 60 Cleric at work in the scriptorium. *H.J.M. Green after Jean de Vignay's translation of Vincent de Beauvais' 'Miroir Historical'. Flemish, late fifteenth century (B.L. C MS. Roy. 14 E1 – Vol. I fol. 3 r)*

The benefice at Clapham would have been very small beer to a 'huge financial machine' like Merton (Jones & Ereira 2004, 103), except in one particular aspect: the pilgrim business. Thomas Becket, a Londoner, was educated at Merton Priory in the late 1120s. As Royal Chancellor and Bishop of London he generously recognised his debt to Merton (including wearing the black cowl). In 1162, he was elected Archbishop of Canterbury and in 1170 martyred at his own altar in Canterbury Cathedral. With his canonisation in 1173 and the establishment of a major pilgrimage shrine at Canterbury, Merton, true to its basic instincts, detected a possible business opportunity. Yet how was it to break into the lucrative pilgrimage trade situated where they were? For, in the words of A. Luchaire 'the true religion of the Middle Ages, to be frank, is the worship of relics' (Finucane 1977, 25). The answer so far as Clapham was concerned was ingenious.

THE PILGRIMAGE BUSINESS

In the normal way, one of the old pilgrim routes from the west round south London (the 'Pilgrim South Circular') and down to Canterbury would have used the ancient Lavender Hill/Wandsworth Road (A3036) route, which bypasses Clapham to the north. It was important to Merton that the pilgrims should be encouraged to visit their recently acquired church at Clapham, one of thousands of so-called pilgrimage churches, where penances could be obtained by offering pious gifts and indulgences would be for sale.

Merton's ingenious scheme was to re-route the pilgrimage trail which now branched off in Wandsworth at East Hill and ran by old existing trackways along Northside, Battersea Rise and Clapham Common Northside (B303). The evidence of aerial photography in 2003 indicates that the new route cut across the south headlands of Wodefield, the eastern common field of Wassingham (*colour plate 4.7*), then proceeded through Clapham Old Town, passing the Holy Trinity parish church, and followed a new route across the furlong headlands of the East Field (now Larkhall Rise) and so back to the main Wandsworth Road (*78 & 85*).

The new pilgrim route was called 'Cannterbury Way' and was mentioned as such in the 1501 Islip lease (see Chapter 4). How did Merton manage to persuade pilgrims to take the new route? Almost certainly by ensuring that the surface was kept in a better state of repair than the rutted, potholed route along the Wandsworth Road. This is not the only road in Clapham in which Merton appears to have had an interest. The church warden's account for 1725 (repeating, no doubt, Clapham folklore) mentions that the road 'now called Nightingale Lane was originally the principal road leading from Tooting to London, then called Tooting Road, and is supposed to have been formed by the convenience of the Abbeys of Merton and Westminster, through Walsingham [Wassingham?] Lane to the Kingston and Lambeth road' (Batten 1827, 133). This route, the so-called 'Tooting Road' would have directed pilgrims from Merton Priory along the old Roman road, Stane Street (now Southside) and so again through Old Town and past the parish church.

For some 350 years, streams of pilgrims chatting and singing (and quarrelling, no doubt) passed along Canterbury Way (*61a*)

> down to Canterbury they wend
> To seek the holy blissful martyr, quick
> To give his help to them when they were sick'.
>
> Chaucer, *Prologue* to *The Canterbury Tales*
(taken from Coghill 1992, 17)

The pilgrims undoubtedly brought custom to the Clapham alehouses and the Church, but were not a wholly unmitigated blessing: 'Charity was a virtue dear to the pilgrims whose ventures would have been impossible without it, for a great many seem to have relied on alms for sustenance' (Finucane 1977, 47). As the nursery rhyme has it 'Hark, hark the dogs do bark, the beggars are coming to town: some in rags, and some in tags, and some in silken gowns' (Opie 1951, 152). A woman at Abingdon (*61b*) importuned by pilgrims is reported to have said 'Not for the sake of Thomas, nor the Lord, nor the Blessed Virgin Mary or any saint whatsoever. Not today: go away you beggars – *abite trutann*' (Finucane 1977, 48).

TITHES, PERVENIENTS AND OBLATIONS

Clapham Church was strictly speaking a *chapel-of-ease* in that it had an absentee rector (Merton) who appointed a vicar who was the residential priest. The harshness of the

Above left: 61a Pilgrims with staves and hats decorated with badge mementos from shrines. *Woodcut from a 'Passional' (Lübeck) 1499*

Above right: 61b 'Woman on her doorstep importuned by beggar with begging bowl'. *H.J.M. Green after illustration for apocryphal tale of Christ's' childhood, the Holkham Bible, B.L. Early fourteenth-century*

Merton regime, both for priest and parishioner, is best exemplified by the whole system of tithes and vicarial dues by which money was wrung out of the community by the church. These fall into various categories which are fairly standard for all livings held by Merton. Although information concerning the particular circumstances at Clapham is minimal, a reasonably full picture can be built up from the historical records of Merton in connection with other holdings (62).

The Obligations of the Rector (Merton)

Repair the chancel of the church , or
Rebuild it if necessary at their own cost.
Provide books.
Provide vestments.
Supply all other ornaments at their own cost;
and provide new ones, and bear all expenses with regard to them in future.
Build a residence for the vicar near the churchyard.

Appointment of tithes and pervenients to Kingston Church
(Heales 1898, 190)

Merton was notorious for neglecting the fabric of its chapels-of-ease (Cox 1905, 100). The parlous condition of the church at Clapham in the post-medieval period was no doubt due to its studied neglect earlier under Merton.

The (Great) Tithes and Pervenients 'That Obtained' received by the Rector (Merton)

An Accustomed Pension (i.e. fee) of 20s. payable by the vicar directly to the Prior of Merton at Easter. The cash-flow of pensions 'played a major role in the recurrent shortage of ready money in the Prior's purse' (Sullivan 2006, 308).

A Praedial Tithe (i.e. a tenth part of the main produce of the land) of all corn and hay of the whole parish. This also included livestock. At a Merton court case in 1316, it was established that the prior could by right claim from each tenant one pig in every 10, and if a tenant had less than 10 pigs, a penny could be claimed for every pig (Cox 1905, 99ff.). These were the core subventions on which the value of the parish was based.

The (Small) Tithes and Pervenients (Alterage) due to the Vicar for his 'Sustenation'

Tithes of corn from crofts and gardens dug with 'foot and spade': herbage of churchyard
   (Tithes due to Effingham Church 1297; Heales 1898, 182)
Obventions from the Tithes of: cows and calves; cheese and milk; honey; pigs (one third
   part of pervenients, see above) pigeons; warrens; mills (two in Clapham).
Oblations (i.e. gifts) at the altar rail (i.e. altarage) on the holy days of: Name-Day of the
   Church (i.e. the first Sunday after Pentecost); All Saints; Nativity of the Blessed Virgin
   Mary (BVM); Purification of the BVM; Assumption of the BVM; Anniversaries of
   the Dead; Bequests and Legacies.
Profit of Oblations on: purifications (i.e. after childbirth etc); espousals (i.e. marriages);
   masses dedicated to the BVM on Saturdays.
   Oblations on confessions in time of: Lent; Holy Week; Easter. (Adjudication of
   Tithes & pervenients of Kingston Church in 1303: Heales 1898, 189-90).
The following routine of services, at which oblations might have been offered, appears
   to have been observed: Matins at 7.00 a.m.; Mass at 8.00 a.m.; Evensong at 3.00 p.m.;
   Midday Mass on Sundays (Rudolf 1927, 18).

The formidable list of occasions on which the vicar might legitimately extract money or goods from members of the community was made worse by the sensitive nature of certain situations (such as bereavements) where this might occur. In a small tight-knit community such as Clapham, the oppressive nature of such dues must have been a great burden in addition to those demanded by the Lord of the Manor. Clapham vicars reduced to a bare living wage by the exactions of Merton (as much as two-thirds of the total tithe) would almost have starved unless they had enforced their customary rights. No poverty excused a parishioner in strict law, however extreme, except where he might die of hunger (*Summa Angelica c.*1480; Coulton 1925, 291). No wonder late medieval sources speak of that 'ancient hatred which has subsisted between peasants and parsons', and that a Dominican friar in 1524 could preach 'woe therefore to such priests and rectors or vicars who are so zealous and clamorous to exact tithes or other altar dues, while they care little or nothing for the souls of their flocks' (Coulton 1925, 536). The parson was hated, but also feared in a way that is difficult to appreciate today in England.

62 Payment of tithes, which includes poultry and animals as well as money. *Woodcut from Rodrigo of Zamora's 'Mirror of Human Life'. German (Augsburg). Bämler 1479*

For not only did the priest exercise the spiritual power of excommunication, but any overt opposition to the exactions of the church might have effects in the temporal sphere also. Opposition could be viewed as heretical, which might result in a legal process leading to imprisonment, even death in extreme cases. However worldly and unspiritual a parishioner might be, it would be these sanctions which made them bite their lip and put up with whatever the priest demanded. There may, indeed, have been medieval vicars like Chaucer's poor parson – 'His business was to show a fair behaviour, and draw men thus to Heaven and their Saviour' – but in reality, ecclesiastical venality was to cast a long shadow over all spiritual teaching and work for hundreds of years in such places as Clapham.

THE INFIRMARY CONNECTION

So what happened to the hard-won tithes from Clapham? Under the Return of the House in the Merton Cartulary for *c*.1242 (Heales 1898, App. LXVI) the entry for Clapham is listed as *Ecclia de Clopham Infirmar*. *Ecclia* (*ecclesia*) indicates that the whole body of the church is referred to as distinct from the chancel, which was the usual responsibility of the rector (Gooder 1961, 113). This no doubt was in the original endowment and probably arose from the fact that the building had a simple unified plan which was incapable of an eastward extension of a chancel due to the proximity of the moat (*colour plate 14*).

The *Infirmar* reference indicates that the profits of the church were assigned to the infirmarer of the priory. This too in all likelihood goes back to the bequest of *c*.1190. There are a handful of such Merton holdings whose profits were designated for particular functions at the House (there is one other for the infirmarer), but most are for the Prior's chamberlain. Monastic and other religious establishments had long-running disagreements (which could become positively internecine) over the allocation of funds between the three main parties involved: the abbot or prior, the obedientaries (the heads of departments of the House) and the vested interests of the body of choir-monks. The prior was formally responsible for the monies of the establishment and thus controlled the 'pot' from which allocations were made to the obedientaries and all other necessary functions. Since the financial interests, indeed capabilities, of priors varied enormously, there were continuous pecuniary battles between the parties concerned, which could erupt into open warfare, as happened at Westminster in 1307 (Sullivan 2006, 322). There was chronic jockeying between the obedientaries of high-spending departments, such as those of the infirmarer and the cellarer, to acquire independent funding from bequests allocated specifically to their needs and which were not subject to the whims of the prior.

The infirmary was a special case in this process. By the twelfth and certainly by the thirteenth century its functions had far exceeded its role as a modest hospital for sick monks. The slippery slope began with the arrangements for bleeding (supposedly to purify the system) which was allowed eight times a year at Austin establishments with a comfortable three-day rest in the infirmary following each blood-letting session. Since the infirmary was one of the few places in a monastery where fires were allowed, senior well-to-do monks began to move in there on a permanent basis, often with the provision of a private suite of study, bedroom and lavatory. Furthermore, the Austin dietary regulations (essentially vegetarian) in the refectory could be avoided by eating in the infirmary instead where meat was on the menu, hence the medical condition of DISH (see above). Rules were equally relaxed about alcohol which appears to have accounted for something like 19 per cent of the monks' energy intake (it provides 5 per cent of ours) (Jones & Ereira 2004, 109) (*63*). By the thirteenth century the enlarged infirmary complex at Merton had taken on the characteristics of a first-class hotel which attracted a number of *corrodians* (paying guests) not to mention frequent royal visitations such as those of Henry III.

Both the infirmarer and the canons would have been extremely anxious that the establishment had independent, bequest-type funding to support its lavish lifestyle. In the normal way, if someone intending to make an endowment to Merton approached the Prior, the money would have been allocated to the central fund or the chamberlain for the Prior's exclusive use. However, the situation at Clapham was different. If the Sibyl bequest hypothesis is correct, Father Alexander from Merton or another chaplain from the House was on hand to steer the Clapham endowment smartly towards the infirmary funds. After all, were not crusades all about supporting sick pilgrims in the Holy Land? Lady Sibyl, who had already suffered so much in that cause, would have been easily persuaded.

63 A 'tasting' session by a monastic cellarer. H.J.M. Green after initial decoration in health manual by Aldebrandius of Sienna: French thirteenth-century (B.L. Sloane 2435, fol. 44V)

'VALOR' (VALUE)

The history of the church at Clapham during the thirteenth and fourteenth centuries is marked by two major financial assessments. The ecclesiastical rate book (*Taxation of Pope Nicholas IX*) was completed *c*.1291. The tithes of all the English ecclesiastical benefices, normally payable to the Pope, had been remitted for six years in 1288 to King Edward I defraying the expense of his abortive crusade between 1270-72 (Heales 1898, 173). The Crown was anxious to assess the precise value of its franchise not only in terms of tithes etc. paid by incumbents to the holders of the advowson, but also the overall value of the property in taxable returns.

In the *Valor* of the 20th of King Edward I (i.e. 20.12.1290-19.12.1291) the financial position at Clapham appeared to be as follows: Church (*Ecclia*) i.e. pension charged to Merton: 20*s*. Value of tithes (*Decima*) payable to Merton: 18*s*. 8*d*. Taxable rate (*Taxatio*) 14 marks, quoted at £9 6*s*. 8*d*. However, Brayley states that in the King's Books the benefice was valued at £8 (Brayley 1844, 283). In 1291 the benefice also paid 7*s*. 7*d*. for *procurations* (fee to diocese in lieu of entertainment of bishop or archdeacon on the visitation round) and 2*s*. 1½*d*. for *synodals* (payment to diocese for attendance at the Episcopal synod). These fees might have been expected to have been borne by Merton as rector of Clapham, but in reality these diocesan 'stealth taxes' may have had to be paid by the wretched parochial incumbent, as occurred elsewhere (Platt 1981, 64), taxed at (*quod taxatus*) 5*s*. payable by Merton to the Crown under the grant of 1291.

These figures, certainly in terms of tithal income to Merton, may not be the complete picture. It does not, for instance, include any income from the pilgrimage business, as postulated earlier. However, it is clear that the Clapham benefice by the late thirteenth century was becoming a financial liability to Merton, a situation that was exacerbated in the following agrarian crisis of the fourteenth century. In the 1291 taxation returns for the Diocese of Winchester in connection with Merton, of 16 entries Clapham has the lowest taxable rate (5s.).

A century later, in 1392, an Episcopal Visitation was carried out by William Wykeham, Bishop of Winchester (the *Ordinary* or ecclesiastical superior of the prior) to sort out various administrative and financial irregularities which had been occurring at Merton. The final session on 2 October 1392 in the chapter house, with the Prior and Brothers arraigned before him (*64*), was in effect a major showdown at which injunctions set out in earlier correspondence were enforced. The Priory objected and the matter was referred to the Crown (King Richard II) for arbitration (Heales 1898, 277-80).

Terry Jones has described Wykeham as someone without any formal religious or academic qualifications whose entire career had been in royal service and who was rewarded with many benefices to become a *mighty pluralist* – that is, he lived off the income from a variety of church appointments for which he did no work (Jones 2003, 153). One of the issues which William Wykeham wished to have rectified by the Crown was of property formerly belonging to Merton which had been sold off and whose advowson (and profits) now belonged to other dioceses. This was a serious matter for the Diocese of Winchester, part of whose income from procurations and synodals came from such benefices. At Clapham for instance, out of a total income of £1 18s. 8d. payable to Merton, a total of 9s. 8½d. was due to the diocese, i.e. 25 per cent. One property sold off was the benefice at Clapham: 'Land comprising 39½ acres, and 30

64 A chapter in session presided over by the prior. H.J.M. Green after a fifteenth-century Flemish illustration

acres and 2 roods of pasture, late of John Queshm in Clapham, held of the Abbot of Westminster by fidelity and 16s worth 3s' was transferred (back) to Merton (Heales 1878, 280). The alienation of a former Merton benefice appears to have occurred as part of a Merton divestment policy of unprofitable benefices and property. Wykeham had this policy reversed by an Order in Council ensuring that sundry items of land and property were returned to Merton 'in perpetuity'.

John Queshm is not mentioned amongst the incumbents of Clapham at this time, nor is a John May in the 1390s when there is a break in the list of appointments in the Diocesan records, presumably during the short period when Westminster Abbey held the advowson. The value of this reference (Heales 1898, 280) is that it established the (not inconsiderable) amount of land held by the Clapham incumbent, the value of the tithes (16s.) and the taxation figure (3s.); to be compared with those of 1291. The fall in titheable value of 13 per cent may have been due to a number of reasons, but the most likely is the loss of 70 acres of arable land in the second quarter of the fourteenth century when Stockwood (6) was afforested (see Chapter 2). In other respects these figures suggest a stable demographic picture, notwithstanding the privations of famine and plague in the earlier fourteenth century. Presumably, the population numbers bounced back fairly quickly, a situation noted elsewhere (Platt 1978, 96).

A POOR CLERK FROM DUBLIN

In R. de M. Rudolf's list of Clapham incumbents (Rudolf 1904, 23-27) there are necessarily some gaps, the major one being the early and mid thirteenth century since the Diocesan Records do not extend further back than 1281. The only exception is Stephen, entered in the Merton Cartulary for 1231-8 mentioned above. Study of the details of these ecclesiastical livings needs to be seen against the background of local politics at Merton, the state of the manor at Clapham and more general social and economic problems in the thirteenth and fourteenth centuries.

The early incumbents, like the chaplain(s) before them, appear to have been drawn from the priests and canons of Merton. Richard de Merton (resigned 1285, but probably holding the living from before 1282) is obviously one such. Nicholas de Lyttlebury (instituted 1285) is from the south-east (Littlebury, Essex). After a 10-year tenure he was replaced by Robert de Broke in 1295, then an acolyte, but formally installed with 'letters of protection' (a significant phrase) in 1296-7. In 1302, William (acolyte) called *Le Botiller* (*botulus* = a sausage) was installed at Clapham.

The late thirteenth century was a troubled time for the manor at Clapham, the descendants of the de Fiennes family having settled in their ancestral estates in Normandy. They eventually parted with the manor to a London merchant, Thomas Romayn *c.*1302, at the same time as the appointment of William Le Botiller (Redstone 1967, 39).

For half a century there is a gap in the record of appointments of incumbents to the Clapham church. This was one of the most critical periods for Clapham with the onset

65 'James Phehw, a poor clerk from Dublin.' *H.J.M. Green after the Macclesfield marginalia (c.AD 1330) MSL 2005 folio 158 r*

of the Little Ice Age *c.*1315 and the arrival of the plague in 1348-9. These dates are thus highly significant at Clapham, as elsewhere in England, and evidently led to a change in Merton's policy for the vicarial staffing of its livings. As Henry Kington, canon of Leicester Abbey, noted in 1349 'there was so great scarcity of priests everywhere that many churches were left destitute … Within a short while, however, a great multitude of men, whose wives had died in the plague, flocked to take orders, many of whom were illiterate, and almost laymen, except that they could read a little but without understanding' (Platt 1981, 67). No wonder, then, that in 1348 the new list of incumbents begins with the appointment of Peter, a poor priest of the diocese of Lincoln, who was the first of a succession of six vicars, each of whom stayed for no more than two or three years. They are clearly no longer drawn from the priesthood of Merton. Indeed, Peter from Lincoln, Nicholas de Limburghe from Weston on Trent and James Phehw [*sic*] a poor clerk from the diocese of Dublin (65) must have been barely able to communicate with their parishioners. Although the Black Death may account for the arrival of a new type of vicar at Clapham, it does not explain why these rather poor quality clergy should have continued to be appointed here for the next 40 years, particularly since the tithe returns were not especially good.

The trouble about appointing local clerics who can communicate easily with their flock is that they may make common cause with the peasants in difficult times, such as the fourteenth century agrarian crisis. Consequently, they might be less likely to be ruthless in exerting their customary rights and the collection of tithes. Indeed, the longer they stayed in a living, the greater the risk that they would 'go native', hence the short-term appointments with poorly educated incumbents whose speech was unintelligible to the parish, and whose sole responsibility was to Merton.

The arrival of the Romayn family, English and bourgeois in 1302, and the succeeding holders of the manor, marked a cultural break with the previous French (largely absentee) minor aristocracy who had held it up to that point. For the new type of residential owners Clapham was an investment, and they probably ran a much tighter ship than the previous holders. They would not have been happy with a string of parish priests sent in by Merton with the sole purpose of extracting the maximum dues from the manor. In any case, the Merton policy clearly failed, tithes reached an all-time low as recorded in 1392 (see above) and the Priory evidently decided to get rid of this unprofitable benefice. The Westminster interregnum ended in 1393, after which a new policy was called for by Merton to handle the Clapham incumbency.

This coincided with the manor lordship of John and Agnes (*née* Weston) Fountain whose family held the manor for the next half century. The next four incumbents from 1399 were all titled (even though the knighthood was probably honorific). They appear to have had links to Cambridgeshire (Cambridge clerks as opposed to the Oxford Merton clerics) and appear to have been an improved calibre of incumbent. Certainly, the value of the tithes improves. In 1394 a memorandum in the Merton cartulary states that Clapham had a value of £2 (Heales 1898, 287). If this figure, as seems likely, includes the value of the pension and tithe, it is evident that the tithe amount has risen by 4s. from 16s. in 1393 to £1 in 1394 (the value of the pension remaining static at £1).

There is a break in the register from 1416 to 1446, but when they resume with Sir John Halton who died in 1447, the same pattern of better class vicars is evident, 11 of whom are knighted. Merton still held the advowson and claimed its 20s. pension until the House was dissolved by Henry VIII in 1538. The fifteenth-century clerics must have been easier men for the manor to collaborate with during the climatic upturn of this period.

After the dissolution of Merton Priory, the benefice was appropriated by the Crown and the advowson was sold in September 1544 to Sir Thomas Arundel. Subsequently, it was vested in the Lord of the Manor starting with the late sixteenth-century Clarke family (Redstone 1967, 410).

FABRIC AND FITTINGS

The old parish Church of Holy Trinity, after many vicissitudes and a steady deterioration of its physical condition due to generations of neglect, was eventually pulled down in stages between 1791 (Edwards 1801, 21.22) and the end of the eighteenth century (70). So bad was the state of the church in 1769 that Mr Couse the surveyor had to be brought in to superintend its propping up 'to quiet the minds of the inhabitants' (Batten 1827, 143). Mr Couse later went on to design the existing Church of Holy Trinity. However, the north aisle of the old church was retained for funerals, until it too was demolished *c*.1813/4. The new replacement Church of Holy Trinity was built between 1774 and 1776 on common land donated by the manor. On the site of the former medieval church a new chapel-of-ease, St Paul's, was constructed in 1814.

Of the medieval church nothing of the structural fabric survives above ground level and probably not very much below it either, thanks to the construction of extensive burial vaults. Even the precise location of the old Holy Trinity in relation to the present day St Paul's is uncertain. The site of the high altar is said to be marked by the tomb slab of Sir Lawrence Bromfeilde (d. 1668; Batten 1827, 74), but since this memorial has long been covered by floor coverings (if, indeed, it still exists at all) even this location is uncertain. The old church was probably on the same alignment as the present St Paul's, if only to line up with the existing burial vaults when the new building was erected. However, even this is not certain.

The evidence for the physical structure of the old church as it survived in the later eighteenth and early nineteenth centuries comes from a number of sources: a plan of *c*.1776 and another of *c*.1780 (*66* and *67*); a bird's eye view of 1675 (*68*); a sketch view of 1754 (*69*A and B); and a series of existing views of the north aisle *c*.1800 (*70* and *71*a) including an interior of the same date (*71*b) (for an early nineteenth-century romanticised view of the old church, see Jefferson Smith and Wilson 2007, 15).

On the basis of these various sources, a possible structural history of the old church can now be postulated (*72*A-E). Brayley describes the building as consisting originally of a nave and chancel only (Brayley 1844, 285). It is possible to detect this arrangement below the palimpsest of later alterations. The building appears to have been a long simple rectangle, 60ft 6in x 18ft internally. Its function as a chapel, mentioned earlier, is suggested by two factors. Firstly it lies centrally within the moated area identified as being that of the manor bailiwick. Secondly its walls, which vary in width between 2ft and 2ft 6in, widen to 3ft 6in at the west end (*66*). This is highly significant since it suggests that it was attached to a substantial masonry structure, the rest of which no longer exists, but is postulated here as being the east wall of the Norman Manor House. Indeed, the chapel plan form has close parallels with those of the Crusader military orders where these were attached to commanderies or granges of thirteenth- or fourteenth-century date in this country. A case in point is the former Hospitaller chapel at Chibburn, Northumberland (*73*). There is no suggestion here that the Clapham building was a commandery, but the parallel is close enough to suggest the influence of this type of Crusader architecture and the links that Faramus of Boulogne may have had with the military orders of the mid thirteenth century. The Chibburn chapel was a simple two-storey structure with a gallery at the west end, adjoining the *solar* end of the Manor House (*colour plate 11*). If a separate chancel was not required to be built at Clapham (see note on the use of the expression *Ecclia* above) Merton would have been keen to partition the building close to the east end of the building, dividing the nave from the chancel to ensure that they only had the responsibility for the upkeep of the latter portion as rector (*74*).

There appear to have been no substantial alterations for over 250 years. Brayley suggests that the next substantial addition to the church was that of a Lady Chapel to the north-west corner in 1500 (Brayley 1844, 285). This date is based no doubt on the 'Tudor' character of the fenestration. However, there is circumstantial evidence which indicates an earlier date for this addition. The will of Thomas Gower Esq. of 11 July 1458, mentioned above in connection with the dedicatory name of the Holy Trinity (Rudolf

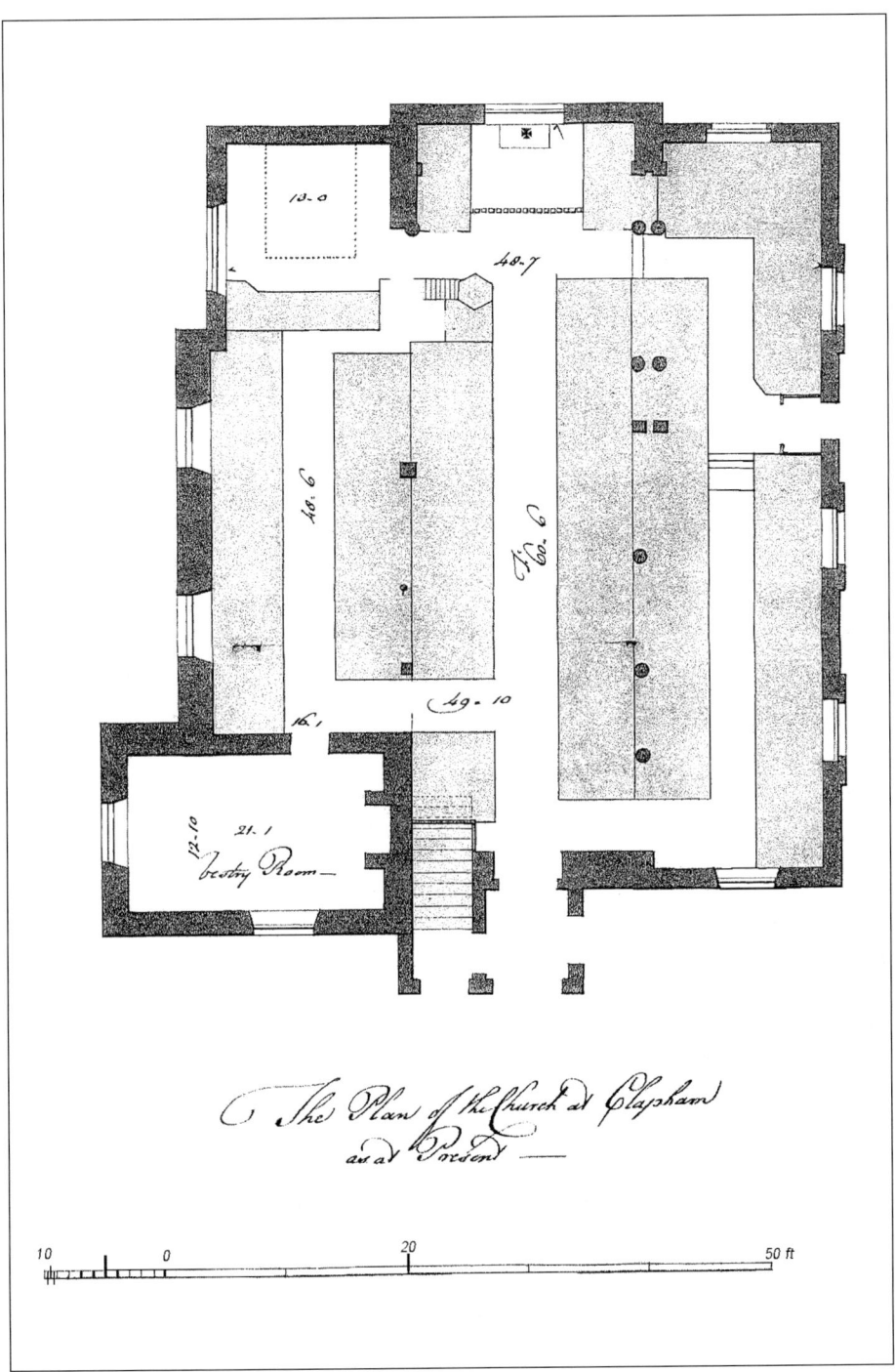

66 Scale plan of *c.*1776 of the old parish church of Holy Trinity shortly before its demolition on the completion of the new building on the Common. One of a set of three surveys in the same hand, including the present church, possibly by its architect Kenton Couse, or an assistant in his office. The plan of the present church has a monogram 'M' in one corner. *London Metropolitan Archives*

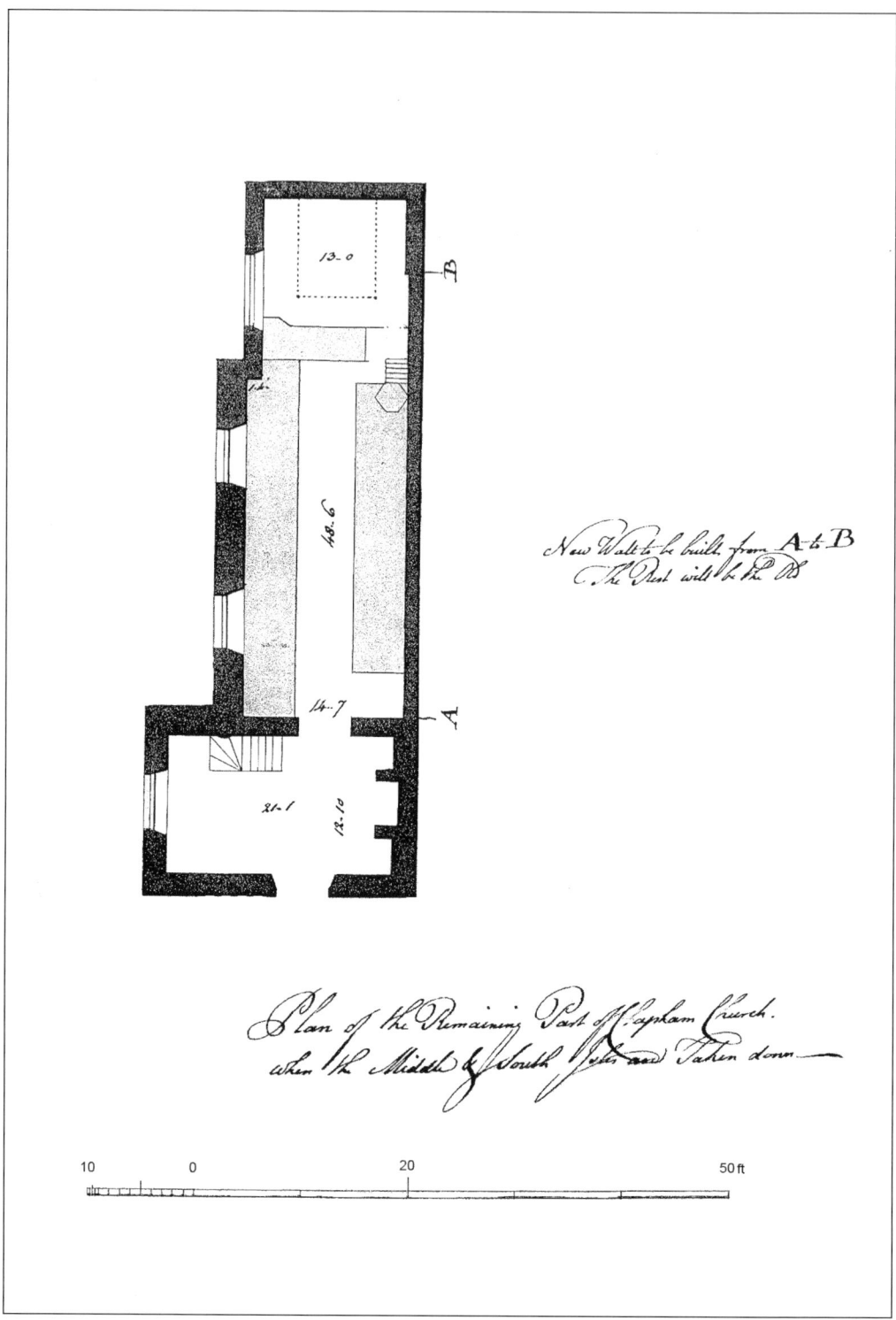

67 A scale plan *c.*1780? (the second of the 'Couse' series) surveyed after the demolition of the old Holy Trinity Church leaving only the north aisle and vestry. *London Metropolitan Archives*

68 Diagrammatic birds-eye-view of the old parish church *c.*1675, looking south-west. *From John Ogilby's* Britannica. *'Road from London to Portsmouth' 60, pl. 30. Courtesy of the Society of Antiquaries of London*

1904, 6) specifically instructs that he should be buried 'before the image of the blessed Mary of the same church', as well as appointing a chantry priest to pray for his soul and those of his parents and benefactors. All of this suggests that we are looking at a new chapel as opposed to just an image somewhere else in the church.

Amongst the devout of late medieval England, the cult of the Blessed Virgin Mary (*75*) was second only to that of Christ himself, and towered above that of all other saints. 'Englishmen were encouraged to think of their country as being in a special way "Mary's Dowry"' (Duffy 1992, 256). The patriotic Thomas Gower, who may have fought at Agincourt (1415), was a rich city gentleman with property in South Lambeth and elsewhere. He was a pious product of his time with the wealth and power at Clapham as Lord of the Manor to indulge it (Rudolf 1904, 6). He had bought the manor from William Wetenhale, citizen and grocer of London who had, in turn, acquired it from the Weston family *c.*1437-8 (Redstone 1967, 39). The early eighteenth-century north aisle was a rebuild of an earlier structure, and it seems likely that Gower was not only responsible for the Lady Chapel in the north-east corner but the contiguous north aisle and tower with vestry below at the north-west corner (*72B*) all apparently constructed in brick. The Ogilby map of 1675 shows a two-stage tower, and the mid sixteenth century inventories of church goods specifically mention two small bells *in the steeple*, the latter apparently having disappeared by the late seventeenth century. The only structural features of late medieval date surviving externally to be recorded *c.*1800 were the three light windows with pointed, arched heads and a hood mould in the north wall of the Lady Chapel. A similar hood mould at the east end of the Lady Chapel indicates another window there too, but it was blocked when the Atkins' memorials were installed in the late seventeenth century. Windows of this type were beginning to appear in the mid fifteenth century, to which date these suggested additions by Gower probably belong.

Above and below 69a & b: Sketch drawings looking north-east (a) and south-west (b) of the old parish church. 1754. *Philipps MS 15719 Minet Library, Lambeth. Reproduced by permission of London Borough of Lambeth, Archives Department*

70 Wash drawing by W.F. Zincke, 1796, showing the north aisle of the reduced church looking south-west. The most accurate of the surviving views, it shows the poor state of the fabric and the ruins of the old church behind. *Reproduced by permission of London Borough of Lambeth, Archives Department*

Above and below 71a & b: Wash drawings by Bartholomew Howlett *c.*1800 showing the north aisle of the reduced church looking north-east (a). The ruins of the old church had been cleared away by this date. Interior of the north aisle (b) looking east. *From Smith (1976) pl. 4 reproduced by permission of and © Surrey History Centre*

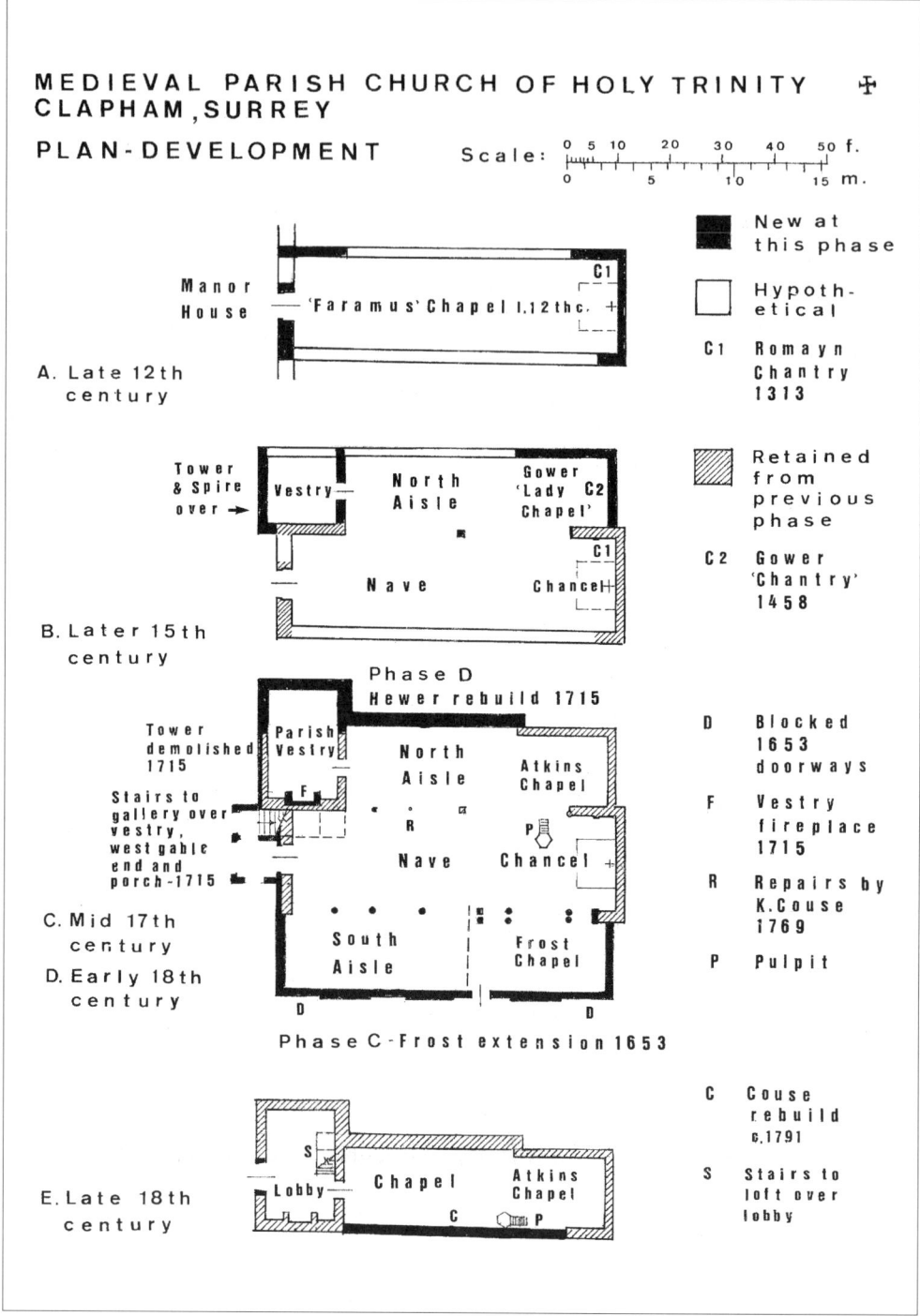

MEDIEVAL PARISH CHURCH OF HOLY TRINITY ✠
CLAPHAM, SURREY

PLAN-DEVELOPMENT   Scale:

A. Late 12th century

Manor House

'Faramus' Chapel l.12thc.

C1

B. Later 15th century

Tower & Spire over →

Vestry

North Aisle

Gower 'Lady Chapel' C2

C1

Nave

Chancel

Phase D — Hewer rebuild 1715

Tower demolished 1715

Parish Vestry

North Aisle

Atkins Chapel

Stairs to gallery over vestry, west gable end and porch-1715

F

R

Nave

Chancel

C. Mid 17th century

D. Early 18th century

South Aisle

Frost Chapel

D   D

Phase C - Frost extension 1653

E. Late 18th century

S

Lobby

Chapel

Atkins Chapel

C

P

Legend:
- ■ New at this phase
- □ Hypothetical
- C1 Romayn Chantry 1313
- ▨ Retained from previous phase
- C2 Gower 'Chantry' 1458
- D Blocked 1653 doorways
- F Vestry fireplace 1715
- R Repairs by K. Couse 1769
- P Pulpit
- C Couse rebuild c.1791
- S Stairs to loft over lobby

72 Phase plans of the medieval Church of the Holy Trinity, Clapham. A: Faramus chapel, late twelfth-century. B: 'Gower' Lady chapel, north aisle and tower, late fifteenth-century. C: Frost chapel and south aisle, mid seventeenth-century. D: Hewer, north aisle and vestry 1715 E: Demolition of church retaining Hewer additions, early nineteenth-century. *H.J.M. Green*

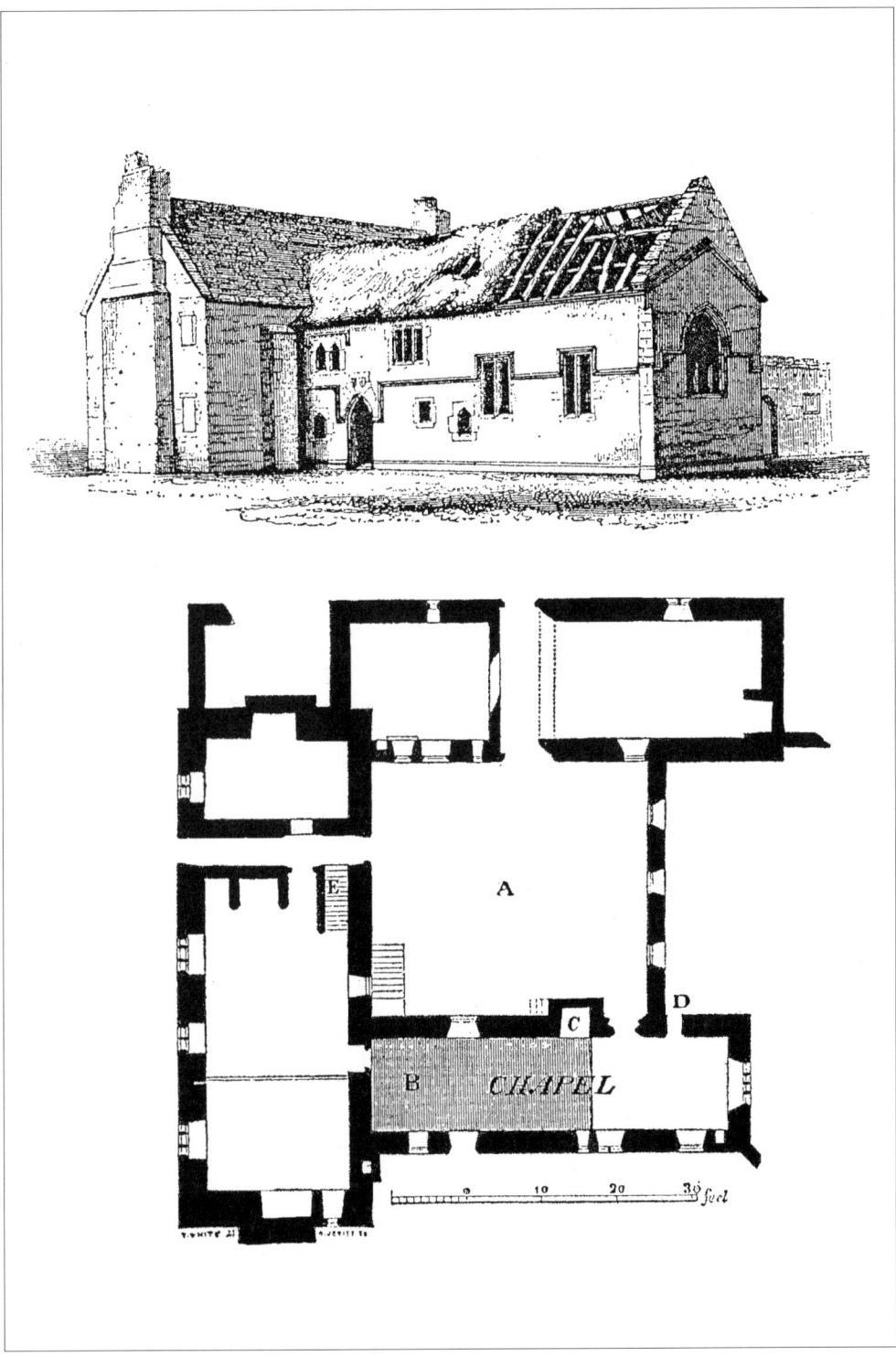

73 Commandery chapel at Chibburn, Northumberland. Late fourteenth-century. View and ground plan. *Drawing by T. White del. C. Jewitt, 1856*

74 View of medieval chancel sanctuary. Stone altar on a step (*predella*). The altar frontal with
embroidered *patée cross* and superfrontal band. The *retable* (shelf behind altar) carries a hanging cross
with integral crucifix backed by a *dossal* (curtain) acting as a *reredos*. From *Tractato di Oratione mentale*
by Savonarola, Florence. Late fifteenth-century. At Holy Trinity, Clapham in the early sixteenth
century the altar frontal was of green *chamlett* (camlet or worsted cloth) with a fringe, also a canopy of
red *sarcenett* (sarsenet or silk material) and small silk *grysshions* (cushions) for the altar (Rudolf 1927, 20)

A brass from a former tomb slab originally positioned in front of the altar rails survives
from this period. It carries an inscription to William Tableer who died on 13 October
1401 (*76*). Tableer, evidently a city merchant, was an early incomer to Clapham and a
relative, Roger Tableer, is recorded in a document of 1411 (Smith 1976, 7).

The 'Gower' aisle of *c.*1450 has an internal area of 544 square feet (excluding the
Lady Chapel and vestry). The main body of the nave has an area of 953 square feet. The
additional floor space for the congregation was therefore 36 per cent. This was in part a
reflection of the growth of the village population from the time of the agrarian crisis in
the mid fourteenth century to the more buoyant economic situation a century later.

Political events of national importance tended to pass over the heads of the small Clapham
community. This could not be said, however, of the religious and social movement which
resulted in the destruction of traditional Catholic religion in the sixteenth century and its
replacement by forms of Protestantism. This more than anything else marked the end of the
Middle Ages for most communities in England, rather than the historian's benchmark of
the Battle of Bosworth in 1485. The destruction of the monasteries in the 1530s by Henry

Right: 75 Virgin and Christ Child, holding a sceptral lily and orb respectively. Alabaster, painted and gilded. English, late fifteenth-century. Height: 98cm. The type of devotional statue which might have been displayed in the Lady Chapel at Clapham. *H.J.M. Green after BM MME 1956, 7-1, 1*

Below: 76 Funerary brass inscribed in Black Letter Gothic HIC JACET WILLMS TABLEER QUI ORBIIT XIII°. DIE MENS(IS) • OCTOBRIS • ANNO DŇI M • CCCC •PMO • CUJUS AĪE•PPICIETUR DEUS • AMEN • 'Here lies William Tableer who died 13 October AD 1401 on whose soul may God have mercy. Amen'. *Photograph by H.J.M. Green*

VIII was a political act undertaken for largely economic reasons. Although devastating at a cultural level in national terms, there would have been few tears shed at Clapham over the demise of Merton in 1538. The Protestant reforms by the government of Edward VI was something else, and starting with the *Injunction for Religious Reform* in 1547 a process known as the 'stripping of the altars' began which was eventually to change wholly the nature of religious expression in England and destroy the medieval character of its churches.

The trauma was marked at Clapham by the survival of inventories of church goods in 1552 and 1553 prepared by the church wardens (Rudolf 1927, 19-22). This was the closing stages of a process which had progressively removed lights, images, altars – indeed, all adjuncts of worship. The pathetic list of remaining furnishings and vestments – one cross of latten (base metal) gilt, four candlesticks of latten, diverse stained and painted clothes for the 'doing of ceremonies lately used in the church' – are the last remnants of 400 years of village piety. In 1553, what was saleable was sold, including the chalice and the 'two bells in the steeple' for 25s. 8d.

A century later in 1645 during the Commonwealth, when Major Richard Salway, a noted Roundhead, was at the Manor, the parish accounts recorded the taking down of 'ye Cross' (presumably in the churchyard) and removal of the (medieval) font, in both cases no doubt because they had superstitious 'Romanish' carvings. Even the altar *rayles* (rails) had to be taken away. They were valued at 10s. and were bought by a Joshue Foote of Whitechapel (Rudolf 1927, 356).

The stripping of the church's interior left room for another type of monument, this time an expression of the power and piety of the Lords of the Manor. The interior view of the north aisle (*71b*) shows how the former Lady Chapel was appropriated for this purpose. The south wall had an elaborate tomb of Bartholomew Clerke accompanied by wife and son, who was Lord of the Manor in 1583-9 (*77 & colour plate 12a*). However the central area is filled with the splendid Atkins' monuments of 1689 (*colour plate 13a-c*) – the three Atkins children against the east wall (*colour plate 13b*) – and in 1691 a chest tomb with the recumbent figures of Sir Richard Atkins and his wife, Dame Rebecca (*colour plate 13c*). After the demolition of the north aisle in 1814, the parishioners, who had never cared much for the Atkins family, shovelled the monuments into the burial vaults of the family, whence they were rescued in 1886 by the local antiquary, J.H. Grover. Apart from one figure (*colour plate 12a*) which was recovered, the rest of the Clerke memorial is probably still buried somewhere in one of the vaults.

PARISHIONERS

The population of Clapham *c.*1330, based on the figures in the 1326 Extent (see Chapter 8) and the Surrey Taxation Return of 1332, was approximately 184 souls (using the Rogers Demographic Projection). This census was taken after the 'Great Hunger' of 1315 and subsequent years but before the arrival of the Black Death in 1348-9. The Hearth Tax Return for 1664 (Meeking 1940, with additional information from Susan Rose, Roehampton University of Surrey) with 91 households, gives us a population figure using the same demographic projection, of 409 persons and this notwithstanding plague, economic recession and civil war. In 1326, the floor area of the congregational part of the church is 953 square feet or nominally 4 square feet per person. The additional floor space of the 'Gower' extension with 544 square feet would have provided space for an extra 136 persons, a reasonable growth for the mid fifteenth century giving an approximate total of 285 persons in Clapham vill. A population jump of one-third over the next 200 years would have necessitated another extension of the church to accommodate the additional villagers, and, indeed, this is what happened. Now there is no suggestion here that the vicar and churchwardens worked out the additional extra space needed using the type of calculations and projections set out above. It was based

77 Monument to Bartholomew Clarke, Dean of the Arches and Lord of the Manor 1583-89 (d. 12 March 1589) with his widow Elenora and boy Francis. The memorial was on the south wall of the former Lady Chapel (*71b*). Francis survives (*colour plate 12a*) but the remainder of the monument apart from the dedicating inscription is missing. *Drawn by Bartholomew Howlett, 1811*

on an *ad hoc* approximation taking into account other factors such as the need for private pew provision and non-conformist absenteeism. There appear to have been no galleries at any point. Nevertheless, as has already been seen, the extra provision for worshippers does seem to be directly related to successive levels of population growth.

The parish accounts for 1653 relate that 'Leave given to Walter Frost to erect a chapel over the sepulchre [monument or, more likely, burial vault] of his father, on the south side of the church 29 feet by 14 feet 6 inches' (Batten 1827, 113). The chapel can be precisely located on the south-east corner of the church and is marked in the interior by paired columnettes and responds on to the chancel (*66*). It appears at this stage to have been a private chapel for use by the Frost family and had a separate external entry from the churchyard at the east end (*72c*). The eastern window had a panel of stained glass bearing the arms of the Frost family from York (Smith 1976, 7).

The Frost family were evidently people of some consequence and wealth, but do not appear on the parochial rental assessment of 1638 and were evidently incomers of the

Commonwealth period. A possibility is that they were lessees of Brick Place, the lodge in the former West Wood (see Chapter 2) owned by the Lord of the Manor. If so, they were the last tenants before the Gaudens purchased the estate from the Atkins *c*.1655, and it became Clapham Place. The Gaudens had had a small house in the village since 1648. The erection of the chapel would have been a last gesture of piety by the Frosts before they left Clapham.

Three years earlier, on 16 June 1650, the parish accounts state '... Ordered, that the church be enlarged, and that churchwardens make an assessment of £50 to be laid out upon the premises'. By the time the church had got round to carrying out the work, Frost came along with his chapel proposal. As a consequence, the work was co-ordinated as a single project which included the erection of the south aisle. The evidence for this is the uniform fenestration which the 1776 plan (*66*) shows as having provided a raised band surround to the windows. At this stage, the chapel was separated off from the south aisle, which also had a separate entrance from the churchyard at the south-west corner. Unlike the north aisle of *c*.1450 which had square bases for (timber?) posts carrying the wall plates of the roof valley, the south aisle had small round columns with the same function, which, if not of timber, might be of later cast iron. A similar column in the north aisle, irregularly positioned, may well be part of the remedial work carried out by Mr Couse in 1769.

In 1678, the church accounts specify that the 'Frosts' vault and chapel [be] allowed to the parish for the benefit of the poor. The vault is now the parish vault ...' It is clear from this entry that the Frost connection having ended, the chapel and south aisle were now thrown together as a combined space for accommodating the poor of the parish at worship. The two outer entrances as shown on the 1754 drawing (*69a*) were blocked off and a new single entrance was provided to the south aisle at the west end of the former Frost chapel. This separate entrance 'for the poor of the parish' was no doubt organised to ensure that they did not mix with the 'carriage folk' arriving at the main west entrance. Parochial regulations of 1764 stipulated that 'Beadles do wait on the ladies and gentlemen keeping coaches and inform them that ... they should order their coachmen when they have set down to draw off their carriages ... and return to take up their masters and mistresses as they come out of church.' A porch was provided at the west end in case of wet weather (*66* and *69a*). The combined area of the Frost Chapel and the south aisle is 883 square feet, thus providing theoretical space for an additional 220 worshippers. Using the previous projections of church floor space, this amounts to about 500 persons overall who could be accommodated in the church. However, this has to be set against the introduction of pews (normally people stood for services) which would reduce the amount of space available. The seventeenth century developments are designated as phase C (*72c*).

The last major addition to the medieval church occurred in the early eighteenth century – phase D (*72d*). The church accounts are again the source of information (Batten 1827, 128). An excerpt from 1711 reads: 'Vestry room ordered to be built. Voluntary subscriptions for enlarging the church produce £155-09-03. Church rate for ditto £102-11-00'. Nothing much seems to have happened until 1715 when 'Hewer Edgeley Hewer Esq [of Clapham Place] offered to enlarge and rebuild the north aisle of the church, and also to build a vestry room for use of the parish, at the west end [at his own expense]'. There must have been a collective sigh of relief in the vestry at this last clause since it is recorded that the final cost of the work amounted to £600 6s. (Dale 1927, 256). The new works commissioned by Hewer are clearly visible on the plan (*66*) and various views (*69, 70 & 71a*). The north wall of the fifteenth-century north aisle was demolished and a new wall with segmental leaded windows (cf. *71b*) was built further out to provide extra room in the aisle. To the east, the wall was taken as far as the limits of the old Lady Chapel, now housing the Atkins Memorial and regarded (by the Atkins) as *their* chapel. In 1716, the will of the late Rebecca Atkins (d. 1711) left £30 to the parish 'upon condition that the parish keep in repair the chapel and monuments therein belonging to the Atkins family'. The parish refused the legacy! (Batten 1827, 130)

The old fifteenth-century tower which had formerly carried a steeple and had housed the two bells (removed in 1553 – the steeple disappeared subsequently) was evidently demolished, and the north wall of the old vestry below the tower was rebuilt further out to enlarge the space. The elevations of the new works in rendered brick were provided with a scheme of Doric pilasters between the bays which was carried round the west end with lunettes in the gables. The classicising style was, of course, extremely fashionable in London at this period with the work of Wren on the City churches.

The Clapham population growth by the mid eighteenth century (from about 400 persons in 1664 to 1625 people in 1774) meant that no amount of tinkering with the decrepit fabric of the old church could provide space for the additional parishioners. In 1773, moves were made to build a new parish church on a different site, which was finally opened in 1776.

The last phase E (*72E*) of the old Holy Trinity's life began c.1791 with the demolition of all of the building except for the Atkins chapel, the north aisle and the vestry, which was now converted into an entrance lobby (*67* and *71a*). The internal colonnade between the former north aisle and nave was blocked off and provided with lunette windows. The building continued in use as a funerary chapel. As recounted above, the remnant of the old church was pulled down c.1813 and replaced by the present St Paul's. Some of the old burial vaults of the lords of the manor and other notable families survive below and immediately adjacent to the existing building, blocked off but probably still containing in some cases the remnants of their tomb sculptures.

The existing churches of Holy Trinity and St Paul's are not considered here. Both have been the subject of a number of historical and architectural studies over the years. There are individual guide books to each church: Bryant (1986) and Lush (1993) respectively, the latter revised by Peggy Aylen (2007). Apart from these, the more important publications include Brayley (1844), Redstone (1967), Smith (1976), Pevsner (1983) and Clegg (1998). The Clapham Society has produced a series of publications since 1968 of which the *Buildings of Clapham* (Alyson Wilson ed., 2000) is the most important.

Holy Trinity Church under its charismatic vicar, the Rev. Henry Venn, was the spiritual centre of the 'Clapham Sect', through whose exertions, focused by William Wilberforce, the slave trade in the British Dominions was formally abolished in 1807.

This, arguably one of the greatest humanitarian achievements of any age, was fostered in the numinous atmosphere of Clapham – a product, perhaps, of the Seven Winds (the Seven Spirits of God) which are traditionally said to meet on Clapham Common.

8

VILLATA DE CLOPHAM

Nymphs and Shepherds
Dance no more
> J. Milton, *Arcades*

The dancers are all gone under the hill
> T.S. Eliot, *East Coker*

MEMBRANE I D

The most important document concerning the history of Clapham surviving from the medieval period is that laconically described as Membrane 1d from the Calendar of Close Rolls of 19 Edward II (1326). It concerns the

> Partition of lands that belonged to Juliana Romayn, deceased etc., in the king's hands by reason of her death, made by William de Weston, escheator in COS. Surrey, Sussex, Kent, Middlesex, and in the City of London, by the assent of Roesia de Boreford, one of the daughters and heiresses of Juliana, and of William de Weston and Margery his wife, the other daughter and heiress of Juliana, according to the tenor of the king's writ sent to the escheator.
>
> *Cal Close*, 1323-27 (PRO 1898, 582)

Evidently Juliana Romayn had died without a direct male heir and Clapham Manor had therefore reverted to Crown by the process known as Escheat. Membrane 1d sought to regularise matters and divide the property equitably between the two daughters and heiresses of Juliana, Roesia and Margery, as conveyed by King Edward II's ruling and administered by the royal official (Escheator) responsible, who in this instance appears to have been by a happy coincidence William de Weston of Albury, husband of Margery! (Redstone 1967, 39)

Although the immediate circumstances of the issue of the writ are clear enough and relate directly to the death of Juliana Romayn, Lady of the Manor, the production of a detailed custumal at this time may have been regarded as providential by the manorial authorities. (A customal was a written statement of the customs of the manor, the services owed by free and unfree tenants, and the rights and obligations of their lord. This was periodically read out at manor courts). As mentioned above the arrival of the Little Ice Age and the onset of the Agrarian Crisis of *c.*1310-20, had precipitated demographic and social change which the monolithic feudal system found difficult to handle. There had undoubtedly been starvation and a fall in population numbers at Clapham within the previous decade, as evidenced by the loss to arable of the great West Field by its recent afforestation. It was critical for the manor to reassert their traditional rights, privileges and responsibilities as they had previously been exercised in the thirteenth century. In the process, a vivid window is briefly opened revealing peasant life in Clapham, which was not to be repeated again on the same scale until the mid seventeenth century, hence the chapter heading *Villata de Clopham* 'the village of Clapham', taken from the Surrey Lay Subsidy Return for 1332. In this return, incidentally, Clapham was assessed for tax purposes at 21*s* 10*d* (Johnson 1932, 125).

THE MANOR

The Manor premises of *Clopton* belonging to William and Margery de Weston were described succinctly in the opening clauses of the customal as being a messuage with garden worth yearly in the fruit and herbage of the garden 5*d.* and a dovecot worth nothing (a messuage comprised a house, its outbuildings, yard and, when applicable, a garden). The property share of the other sister, Roesia, and her husband John de Burford was the manor of Stockwell, as previously mentioned (see Chapter 2). The customal of 1326 is also described in this study as an Extent, i.e. it includes a statement of the extent and valuation of the manor lands and tenancies.

Phase 1

The site of the Clapham 'messuage' was initially on a salient of higher ground (16m OD) projecting northwards in the vicinity of the present St Paul's church, and to the east of the stream running down from the Common (*78*). Archaeological evidence suggests that the Saxon Hall may have lain slightly further south (see Chapter 4). If the suggested site of the Norman manor house in Chapter 7 is correct the building lay immediately west of the old parish Church of Holy Trinity. The width of the possible east wall of the manor house as recorded in the late eighteenth century was 3ft 3in which suggests that the fabric was of masonry, possibly two storeys in height, of a range that had a north-south alignment (*colour plate 15*) . Short of proper archaeological investigation this is as much as can be hypothesised at this stage. An important locational discovery which has emerged from recent topographical research is that the early medieval manor site was moated. The sister manor house site held by Roesia and John de Burford at Stockwell is clearly shown as moated on all four sides on the Rocque map of 1746. This early manor site lay on the north-east corner of the former Stockwell Green in the vicinity of what is now Sidney Road SW9.

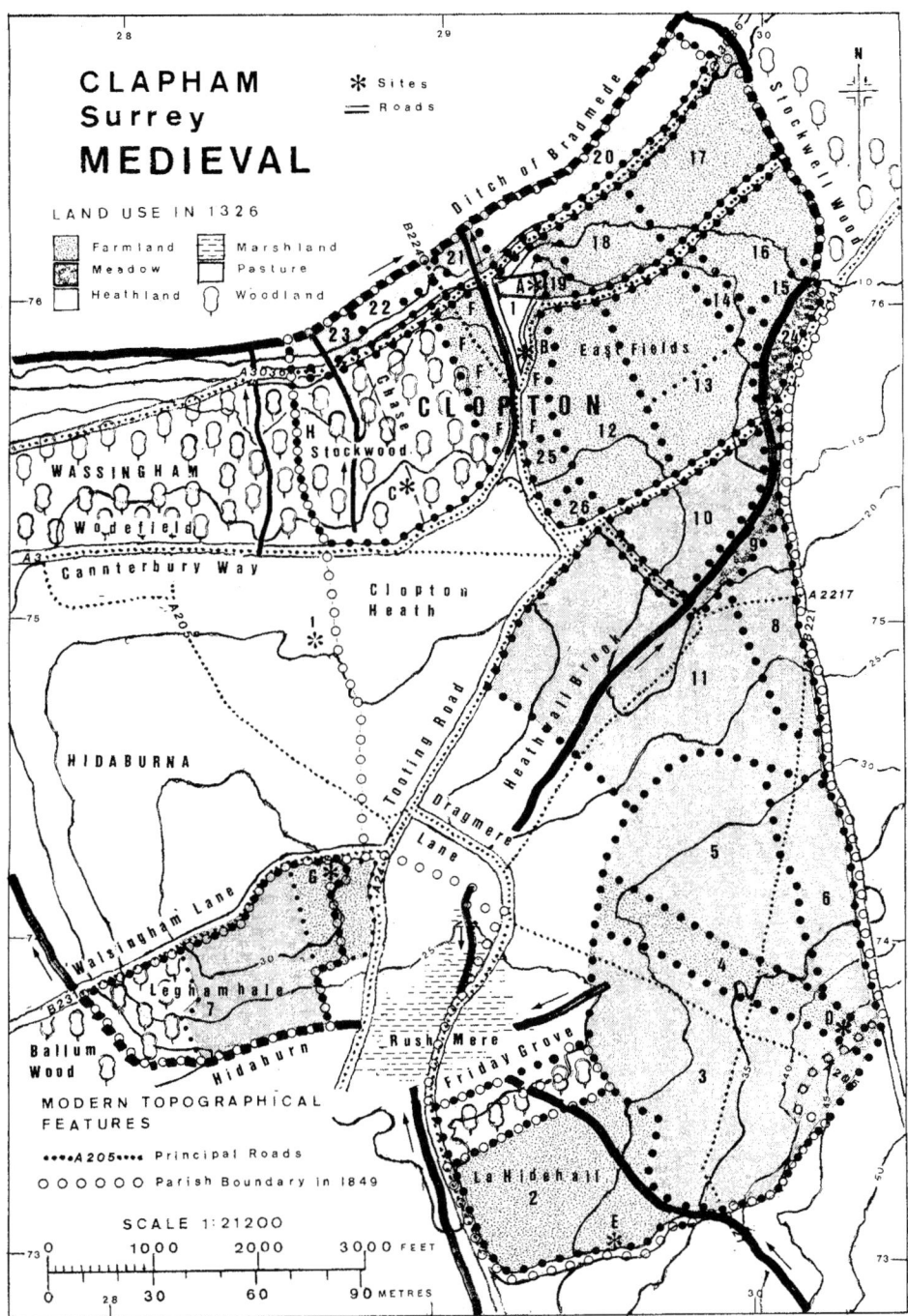

78 Map of Medieval Clapham showing land use and field systems based on various sources of topographical and historical evidence. A: Moated manor house and church B: Rectory C: Lodge, later Brick Place *c*.1500 D: Black Hall E: Hide Hall F: Clopton tenements and tofts G: 'Legham Hall' farm H: manorial warren I: lazy-bed fields. *H.J.M. Green, Base Map based on the British Geological Survey published 1990. By permission of the B.G.S.*

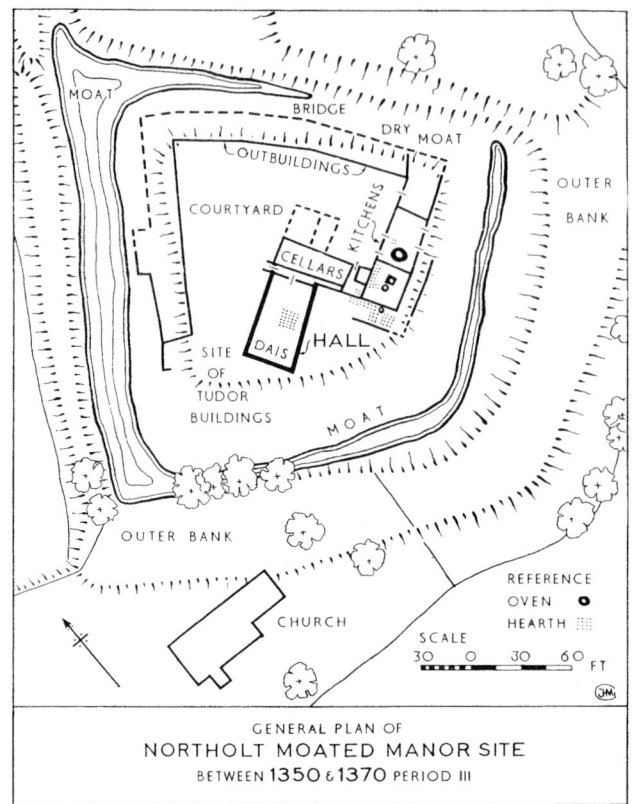

79 Plan of Northholt Manor site *c.*1350-70, excavated 1953-58 (Hurst 1961, fig. 56) *Drawing by H. J.M. Green*

It is a reasonable assumption that the Clapham manor site was similarly moated, and so it proved on investigation. The moat at Clapham is nowhere mentioned in the historical record as such, but early maps, topographical research and fieldwork indicate its former position. Indeed the filled-up and levelled remains of the moat are still clearly visible on the north and east sides of the site (*colour plate 14*) and are still marked by a residual pond to the west on the Tithe map of 1838. As regards the general character of the manor site during the early medieval period, comparison should be made with Northolt, another of the De Mandevilles' manors in Middlesex comprehensively excavated by the late J.G. Hurst (Hurst 1961, 211). By the mid fourteenth century the kitchen and farmyard building complex was grouped around a rectangular winged hall at Northolt (*79*). The arrangements at Clapham were probably very similar in character (*colour plates 14 and 15*). Although at Northolt the first moat was dug *c.*1300, at Clapham the moat appears to be much earlier, possibly by Faramus of Boulogne in the later twelfth century. It has a trapezoid plan with external dimensions, 400ft long by 320ft at its widest point to the east. The ditch was on average 40ft wide and had an entrance at the north-west corner leading out to the Wandsworth Road, an arrangement which survived into the nineteenth century (on the approximate site of No. 623 Wandsworth Road). The moat extended down to the old village stream and road through from Old Town to the Wandsworth Road. The western edge of the moated area coincided with the old road

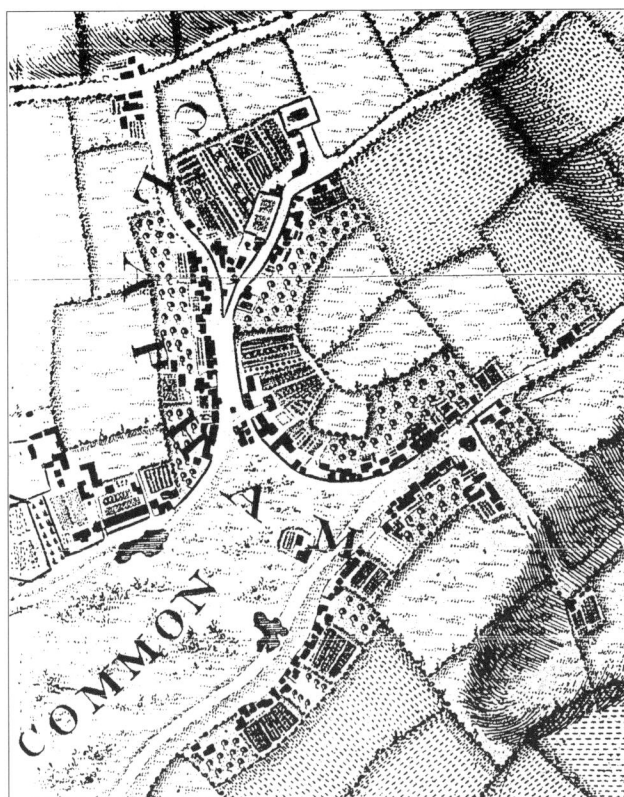

80 Earliest comprehensive plan of Clapham by John Rocque, surveyed 1741-5 and published in 1746. The village is still essentially agricultural with the old nucleus centred along Rectory Grove and Old Town, but with eighteenth-century suburban development alongside the Common. *Map courtesy of the City of London Metropolitan Archives*

which is why the manorial entrance was traditionally located here (*85*). At a later stage the demesne boundary was extended further westwards towards Stockwood, necessitating a diversionary route from the village (*80*). There must have been some displacement of villagers as a result of these encroachments by the manorial demesne.

The construction of the moat necessitated some system by which it could be kept filled (or at least wet) with water. As mentioned in Chapter 1, the early village was served by a stream (*6A*) whose spring was near the site of the present Holy Trinity Church. The stream appears to have run alongside the old (now abandoned) village street as it descended down to the Wandsworth Road, with sections of the route still surviving into the mid nineteenth century (Bland map of 1849). At some point in the later twelfth century the source of the stream was tapped to provide a leat following the winding course of Rectory Grove and feeding into the upper level of the moat. It is possible that the whole stream was diverted for this purpose (*85*). The 1326 Customal states that it was one of the duties of manorial tenants to keep the banks of this water course repaired. The construction of homestead moats round manor sites and substantial farmsteads was a feature of the twelfth and thirteenth centuries in south-east England. Smaller homestead moats have been noted from aerial photographs on the Common, whose wet conditions required such measures for drainage (*colour photo 4.4*) The late Christopher Taylor argued that this was not primarily a defensive measure, but a foible of feudal fashion at the time in some measure copying castle defensive systems (Taylor 1973, 127). Certainly moats were no defence against a determined assault, as occurred at Stockwell manor in 1450 over an ownership dispute (Hawtrey 1967, 57). Homestead moats were clearly a social statement of seignorial power and a measure to distance the Lord of the Manor both literally and figuratively from the rest of the village population.

Phase 2

In the later medieval period the manorial premises were moved further south away from the church and were positioned on what is now the west side of Rectory Grove and the east end of Iveley Road. Extra land for the manor demesne grounds was taken in and eventually included most of the property north of No. 52 Rectory Grove (the old vicarage site) stretching over to North Street, as mentioned above (Rocque map of 1746, 80). In this second phase the former manorial range of buildings is clearly indicated on the Batten map of 1827. The main block at this stage included the sites of what is now Nos 6-8 Rectory Grove with outbuildings to the north in what is now the vicarage premises. A yard, gardens and a large pond (the residual remains of the former moat) lay to the west, in the area of what is now Iveley Road (*colour plate 16*). The late sixteenth-century range to the south-west (phase 3) is described below.

In the 1628 Extent the manorial property is described as follows:

> A faire mansion house of bricke with a faire hall, parler, dining chamber well wainscotted, a good kitchen, brewhouse, washhouse served with water in leaden pipes, a larder, a good seleridge (cellarage) and other convenient houses of Office [i.e. Lavatories]: [also] a barn, stable, dovehouse, a good orchard and gardens well-walled and set with all manner of good fruit, and water coming into them in pipes of leade.
>
> *State Papers Domestic*, Charles I 154/93: 1628, a particular of the town of Clapham

When did this major move of the medieval premises take place? By the fifteenth century with a steady growth of population the churchyard was full to bursting, including mass grave pits of victims of the 'Great Hunger' of *c*.1320 and the bubonic plague pandemics, notably that of 1348-9. There was also the sheer nuisance and security risk of having the parish traipsing through the manorial premises to reach the church. However, it would have taken a lord of considerable wealth and determination, not to mention piety, to put in hand this major development exercise, which will have included a substantial gift of manorial estate to the church. There is no indication of who this Lord of the Manor might have been in the historical record, but there are some slight archaeological pointers.

Of the phase 2 manor buildings, there is only one view of significance and this is a pencil sketch of probably early nineteenth-century date looking south down Rectory Grove showing the east frontage of the building (Smith 1976, 28: *81*). It is of two storeys with 3 large gabled dormers. Of brick construction and rendered, the range has a broken platt band at first floor level suggesting different periods of refacing. The fenestration is a mixture of seventeenth-century casement windows and eighteenth-century sashes, but

81 Pencil sketch of view looking south down Rectory Grove showing the east frontage of the old Manor House, *c.*1800. Artist unknown (*B.M. library Smith 1976, pl. 26*)

the bay at the southern end (*colour plate 16D*), the former solar end of the hall, appears to have paired arched lights under a hood mould. The doorway has a quasi 'Gibbs Surround' of mid eighteenth-century date. The building, while probably retaining a core medieval structure, had evidently by this date been extensively refurbished with openings of post-medieval date inserted.

The key diagnostic feature is the hood-moulded first floor window and this, taken together with the fact that the building was of brick, suggests an early sixteenth-century, or more likely, a later fifteenth-century date. Similar windows occur in the mid fifteenth-century brick Lady Chapel of the old church, which I have postulated as being the work of Thomas Gower, who was Lord of the Manor and active in Clapham in the middle years of the century (see Chapter 7, *Fabric and fittings*). Indeed it would have been difficult to build the north aisle and bell tower, as postulated above, if the Manor House had been retained on its old site. The circumstantial evidence thus suggests that phase 2 of the Manor House is the work of Gower *c.*1450.

Phase 3

The building that has always been associated with the Manor House was that built by Bartholomew Clerke, Dean of the Arches and Member of Parliament for Bramber (Sussex) who took up residence in Clapham as Lord of the Manor *c.*1580 (Smith 1976, 22; Redstone 1967, 39). This range (phase 3 of the Manor House sequence) was at right angles to the street and (originally) was not connected with the older manorial buildings of phase 2. Lysons writing about the building as it existed at the end of the eighteenth century describes it as follows:

... some coats of arms in one of the rooms having been destroyed some years ago ... Both from the external structure and the panels and chimney pieces in the rooms, it appears to be of as old a date as Queen Elizabeth.

Lysons 1796 XIII

One of these coats of arms was preserved in a building in Old Town, Clapham, said to be that of the eighteenth century Bowyer family with a motto '*Contentment passe Richesse*' (Contentment surpasses riches); not wholly appropriate for most Lords of Clapham Manor (Battley 1938, 29)!

Clerke must have started building soon after he took possession in 1580 because in 1583 he entertained Queen Elizabeth I at Clapham, according to the accounts of the Churchwardens of Lambeth − 'item, for ringing for ye Queenes majestie when she dined at Clappam and went to Grenwitche 3*s* 4*d*' (Smith 1976, 22). The occasion must have been an expensive success, because in 1594 the Queen sent a member of her Guard to Clapham indicating that she wished to make another visit. By that stage Dr Clerke had died (1589-90) and the manor was under offer to a Henry Maynard. Greatly alarmed on hearing of the Queen's intentions he wrote to Robert Cecil, head of the Privy Council, threatening to cancel the sale if the visit went ahead. In fact he never became Lord of the Manor, evidently frightened off by the prospect of a Royal 'Visitation' (Dale 1927, 40). It was something of which to be seriously frightened, since the Queen with her large retinue of courtiers and retainers had a nasty habit of bankrupting loyal subjects who were obliged to lay on lavish entertainment for the court (*82*).

No detailed plan survives of Clerke's building work, but the general arrangements can be worked out from a series of views of the façade from the south and west made in the late eighteenth and early nineteenth century. It was approximately 120ft long east to west and 25ft wide. There are two large external chimney stacks on the south side, with another on the gable end of the extension marked parlour (*colour plate 16*). The arrangement is typical of sixteenth-century lodging ranges (Thurley 1993, 132) with eight sets of rooms on two floors with attics above. The building was of brick, as was

82 Queen Elizabeth I on a 'royal progress' accompanied by courtiers, outriders, guards, servants and dogs. *H.J.M. Green after sketch by Joris Hoefnagel's view of Nonsuch Palace, 1568*

83 South front of the phase 3 Clapham Manor House by Bartholomew Clerke *c.*1580 with the 'Viewing Tower' on the south-west angle. *Print by J.P. Malcolm 1798. Reproduced by permission of and ©London Borough of Lambeth, Archives Department*

the outstanding architectural feature of the structure, the 6-storey Viewing Tower on the south-west corner. Each stage of the octagonal tower was fenestrated and carried an elaborate cove-moulded cornice. It was surmounted by an ogee leaded dome with a weathervane (*83*). Such Viewing Towers were designed for hunters to register the movement of game in the adjacent 15-acre hunting park, to which part of the great West Wood at Clapham had been turned over to at this stage (*78*).

The building as left by Clerke has an unsymmetrical, unfinished look about it. A view of the contemporary Vaux Hall Manor House shows a winged, half-timbered building with octagonal viewing towers on the inner corners of the wings (*84*). Indeed so similar is one of these towers in terms of its roof and cornice arrangements that they could well be by the same mastercraftsman as that at Clapham. This symmetrical arrangement suggests that Clerke's original intention may have been to have a similar building in terms of plan, but only the northern wing was actually built, no doubt due to the shortage of funds after the Queen's financially ruinous visit in 1583.

There is a curious feature surviving in old plans and views of the building which suggest that this was indeed the case. There is an odd small enclosure set within the walled garden and abutting the 1580 range. It is about 20ft wide and 65ft long, forming

84 Vaux Hall Manor House, or possibly Sir Thomas Parry's house known as Copt Hall, which is described as being made of wood. Engraving seventeenth century? (*Renier 2006, fig. 27*)

an approximate right-angle to the Clerke building (*colour plate 16*). Views of this enclosure indicate that it was of old brown brick (Jefferson Smith and Wilson 2007, 17). The gateway is of eighteenth-century Gothick (*83*). However, the plan strongly suggests that this might be all that remains of the north-south range of the projected Clerke building, which here got no further than the foundations before work ceased on the project. Later owners used the footings as foundations for a garden wall.

An even better example of viewing towers built as a feature of a symmetrical façade in a local house is the earlier phase of Clapham Place. Brick Place of *c.*1500, probably constructed on the site of a park lodge in Stockwood and built by Thomas Marrowe, evidently had two such flanking towers on the north façade. These were retained by Sir Dennis Gauden in his new house of Clapham Place *c.*1660 (see Chapter 9) and are shown in the Ogilby map vignette of 1675 (*96b*) and, more importantly, in the Streater view of *c.*1662-4 (*99b*). They may well have been the inspiration for Clarke's projected design.

The later history of the Manor House (Clapham Court) is complicated by its evident use as two separate establishments by the Lords of the Manor and their tenants. The Clerke interest passed on to one or two other, short-term, city investors until it was acquired by Dr. Henry Atkins *c.*1616-17. Dr. Atkins was president of the College of Physicians and as doctor to James I is traditionally said to have purchased Clapham Manor with the £6000 received in presents from the king after attending the infant Prince Charles in a dangerous illness in 1604 (Redstone 1967, 39). The Atkins connection with Clapham has continued through affiliated lines of the family down to the present day.

The Atkins family's main estate was in Hertfordshire and early members of the family were buried at Cheshunt Church. Dr. Henry Atkins died in 1635 and was succeeded by Sir Henry Atkins who is recorded as living at Clapham and died in 1638. However, the late Eric Smith stated that the Manor was leased to Sir Robert Heath in 1624 (Smith 1976, 22) and argued that the Atkins family appeared to have 'seldom lived there for any great length of time'. What actually happened, however, was that the old (phase 2) manor buildings were separated from the Clerke extension (phase 3) which continued to be lived in by branches of the Atkins family.

The old, phase 2, manor buildings described earlier continued to be leased out to various owners including Sir Robert Needham in the 1640s. By the late eighteenth century this block was in private, multiple occupation and by the early nineteenth century the various housing units were being replaced piecemeal by the existing buildings.

The Clerke range (*83*) continued in use by the Atkins family, who were very much in evidence during the late seventeenth century (*colour plate 13a*). The tombs of Sir Richard Atkins and his wife Dame Rebecca, together with 3 of his 8 children are in St Paul's church and are described in Chapter 7. The Atkins family finally sold up their part of the Clapham Manor buildings in 1749 when it became the Old Turret House School until it was finally demolished in 1837 (Smith 1976, 23).

The loss of the manorial premises in 1624 as a Court Leet for the business of the manor and parish was a serious matter for the Clapham community (Smith 1976, 22). Evidently proceedings were moved to the cramped, unheated vestry at the bottom of the church tower built by Thomas Gower *c*.1458 (amongst other places). It explains why Hewer generously offered to enlarge (with provision for heating and a gallery) the parish vestry in 1715.

THE VILLAGERS

The composition of the inhabitants of Clopton (or Clopham) at the time of the 1326 Extent falls under a number of heads: the manorial residents, the 'free' tenants, the 'customary' tenants or bondsmen, (*nativi* who were divided into two categories according to the amount of land held) and 'cottars'.

The manor

In demesne (i.e. held directly by the manor) there were:

254 acres and 1 rood of land, worth £4 4s. 9d. annually and priced at 4d. an acre;

20 acres of meadow, worth £3 6s. 8d. annually and priced at 3s. 4d. an acre;

6 acres of pasture worth 2s. annually priced at 4d. an acre.

Woodland (Stockwood) 'as divided by bounds' (i.e. parcelled up) containing by estimation 70 acres worth £3 6s. 8d., price 11½d. an acre and 5d. more on the whole. As will be seen the manor held parcels of land in practically all the fields, closes, pasture and meadowland of the vill, a practice known as 'demesne farming', which was evidently well established at Clapham at this date (Platt 1978, 46).

Free tenants

Tenants are not named in the 1326 Extent, but do appear a few years later in the Surrey Subsidy Rolls for 1332 which probably represents the situation in 1326 in all essentials (Johnson 1932, 83). These Subsidy Rolls recorded the medieval national tax on movable (i.e. personal) property which was instituted basically to pay for the Crown's foreign wars and lasted until 1623, the date of the last grant to be levied. The key 'County Roll' or 'Particulars of Account' for Surrey was that of 1332 which is the only one which provides an assessment of individuals. All other Returns are merely in the form of an agreed total. The internal evidence from Clapham indicates that a flat tax rate of 1*d.* per acre was being levied on holders of land in the vill. Nineteen separate individuals are named in the 1332 Tax Return, of whom the wealthiest top five are likely to be 'free tenants' whose services to the demesne had been commuted by the payment of money rents. Since the tax return for these individuals is supplied in the roll, it is possible to assess the amount of land they held and consequently which of the smallholdings they are likely to have farmed in the vill.

Willelmo Cristemasse (William Christmas)

Assessed at 3*s.* tax. He should probably be considered with Simone Cristemasse (Simon Christmas) a son (?) who was assessed at 20*d.* Their combined holding would have been 56 acres. Hide Hall is the most likely estate farmed by the Christmas family, which had 63 acres (*78E*). It may be the same land which was the subject of a grant to the Abbey of Bec by Faramus of Boulogne in 1130. Two hundred years later it was evidently back as part of the Clapham manorial demesne and was described as La Hidehalle in the 1326 Extent. Its return to Clapham may be seen as part of a movement at this time to reverse the growing trend of long-term leases turning into hereditary tenures, thereby constituting losses to the demesne and titheable income to the Church. Canterbury See instituted a policy of 'recall of land into demesne' in the late twelfth century (Platt 1978, 46). Although remaining within the later parish of Clapham, the Hyde Farm Estate was finally alienated from the manor in 1392 (see Chapter 6, *Assarting and Pastoralism*)

Johanne le Harpere (John the Harper)

Assessed at 2*s.* 2*d.* tax giving a land holding of 26 acres. Probably the estate known as Black Hall (*78D*) with the land listed in the 1326 Extent as the 29 acres of Netherwavermede (*78.4*).

Willelmo le Almier (William the Almoner)

Assessed at 2*s.* tax, giving a land holding of 24 acres. Probably a smallholding at the north-east corner of Leghamhale (*78G*) of some 28 acres. This small estate was subsequently broken up and passed into the Manor of Balham, although remaining part of Clapham Parish Detached (Gower 1996, 12).

Jul' atte Welle (Jules or Julien at the Well)

Assessed at 2*s.* 2*d.* tax, giving an estate of some 26 acres. The holding may have been on land near the old village spring at the southern end of the vill (*85*) where there was

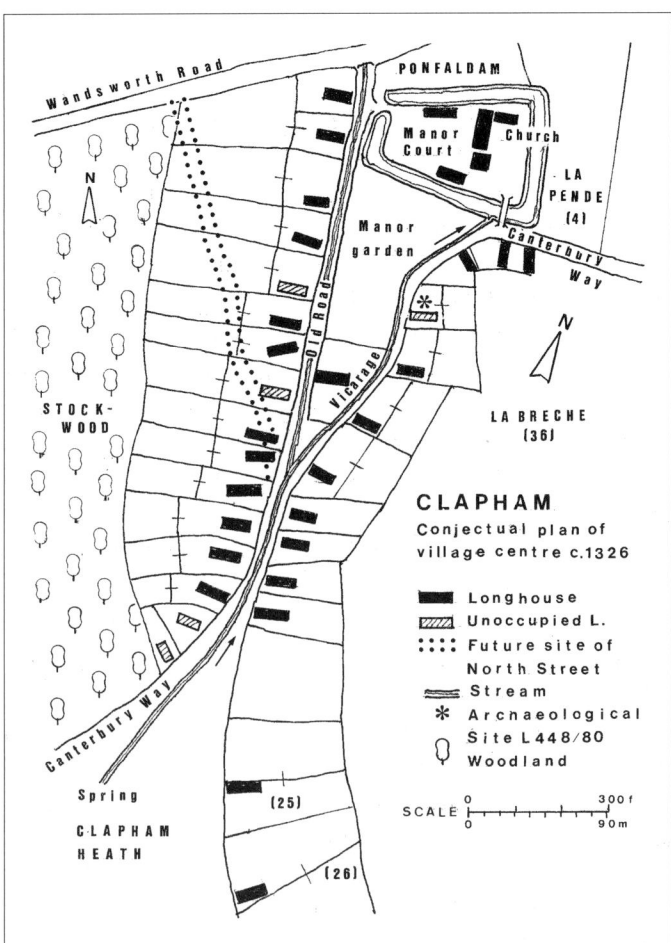

85 Conjectural plan of the medieval village of Clapham c.1326 showing the moated manor site and church, the vicarage, road system, streams and messuages with longhouses and attached crofts. H.J.M. Green based in part on the Clapham Tithe map of 1838 and other sources

a discrete group of five closes (including *78.25* and *26*). No. *78.25* is described in the 1326 Extent as 'formerly belonging to William de Kent' so was evidently a vacant 'free' tenancy at that time. The total area is about 27 acres. It may be significant that all these tax returns show a shortfall compared with the known acreage of these holdings. They do not appear to take into account the holdings of the demesne on this land.

Bondmen

At Clapham there were 31 Bondmen divided into two categories according to the amount of land they held (for a discussion of the acreage of land holdings at Clapham see Chapter 4, *The Alfred Estate*). The Bondman was an unfree tenant (villan in Domesday) who was tied to the land and subject to a range of agricultural services (customal) and payments. Neither he nor his family could marry without the Lord's permission. Upon his death a fine (*heriot*) was paid by the heirs. In return he had a landholding and the right to graze a fixed number of animals on the Common, gather fuel there and take hay from the meadows of the vill.

According to the 1326 Extent, five bondmen (virgater) held virgates (16 acres or ¼ of a hide) and 26 (virgat) held half-virgates (nominally 8 acres or ⅛ of a hide) which at Clapham amounted to 17 virgates of land or 272 acres. There is an immediate problem when these figures are compared with those of the 1332 Tax Return which mentions only two 16-acre bondmen (Edmundo Le Harpere and Hugone Mapel) instead of the five in the 1326 Extent, and eleven 8-acre-bondmen (Willelmo Le Brewer, Roberto ate Welle, Willelmo Baud, Johanne in the hale, Thoma Longe, Alamo Iacob, Roberto Longe, Simone Colin, Willelmo Mornill, Johanne Warin, Ricardo Rykedon). In addition there was Waltero Col(e)n who was paying 6*d.* tax instead of 8*d.* This leaves 14 bondmen unaccounted for, with only approximately a third of the tax owed being paid to the Exchequer! It is difficult not to regard this as a *prima facie* case of fraud perpetrated by the Lord of the Manor, William de Weston, and/or his bailiff (the business manager and, along with the reeve, the agricultural organiser of the manor). We can be quite sure that the last penny of tax was extracted from the wretched bondmen including the 5*d.* owed by the four cottars. So how did the manor pull off this piece of skulduggery?

When the Surrey Collector rode into Clapham vill in 1332 with his clerk and escort, they will already have carried out a rough count of the messuages. In the Manor Hall they will have been presented with a list of those contributing tax and the money itself, which according to the return amounted to 21*s.* 10*d.* (you can be quite sure that the 1326 Extent and Customal would have been carefully kept out of sight). It would have been explained that some of the houses were empty and that others belonged to the landless cottars. The remaining messuages each contained one named bondman contributing his allocated tax. However in reality, of course, the longhouses contained large families of whom one or more sons or relatives will also have held land in the vill. The Collector was evidently satisfied with the explanation he was given because beside the total (*summa*) drawn up by his clerk is written *probatur* (approved) in a different hand.

The 1332 Tax Return was important. It was the last time that named individuals are assessed. In future the Particulars for each year were broadly based on the totals of previous years, i.e. 22*s.* 2*d.* for 1336 and a standard rate of 18*s.* 1*d.* for most other years. However, in 1348 the assessment was reduced by 3*s.* with a note in the Rolls that the figures for this share was on the good word (*pro bonis dicti*) of Walteri de Chiryton, who was presumably the bailiff or reeve at that time. This, however, was an exceptional year when the Black Death reached southern England. The 16 per cent fall in the tax rate for Clapham suggests that the vill had been seriously affected by bubonic plague, evidence for which comes from other sources also (see below). In 1350 there was taxation relief of 2*s.* also due to the after-effects of the pestilence. There were some other bad years, with deductions of 2*s.* in 1436 and 3*s.* on another occasion in Henry VI's reign (1422-61) when there was a downturn in the climate and an agrarian crisis in the 1430s (Fagan 2002, 83).

Cottars

At Clapham there were 'also four cottars who hold amongst them 4 cottages and 5 acres of land'. The cottar was the lowest social level at Clapham. He held no communal land, only his messuage and approximately an acre of attached ground which would have been worked by hand agriculture to provide basic subsistence. The cottar was obliged to labour on the Lord's land either free or for a fixed sum. The social restrictions of the bondmen also applied of course to the cottar, and there were also many other menial duties required of him. The 1326 Extent states that the 'rents of assize' (i.e. those agreed at the Court Leet between the manor and the tenants) of the free tenants and bondmen was £7 11s. 9¾d. The rents were payable in instalments throughout the year on the medieval Quarter or Rent Days which usually coincided with a church Feast Day.

Cartselver
(cart = charter; selver = silver – payment or toll)
Effectively an authorised payment by bondmen holding land in the manor to the lord at the Court Leet (i.e. Manor court) on *Le Hokeday* (usually the second Tuesday after Easter Sunday, but sometimes Easter week itself). The total of cartselver quoted by the customal is 6s. 8d. This has evidently been based on each customal bondman paying ¼d. per acre, and with the quoted 272 acre total this amounts to 6s. 8d. Clearly free tenants and cottars were not included in this particular payment.

Medselver
(med = mid i.e. midsummer or 6 July at this period)
The total medselver quoted by the customal is 8s. 3d. This again is based on a flat rate of ¼d. per acre, but in this instance includes the free tenants as well who farmed between them 108 acres. Cartselver and medselver are effectively local or manorial taxes, in part to offset the cost of meals and ale due to the free and customary tenants for certain *boon work* during the year (see below).

Romscot
22d. (presumably again the total amount from the vill) at the feast of St Peter ad Vincula or Lammas Day, 1 August. A tax imposed by the Papacy of a penny on each house (cot or cottage). This is an early form of hearth tax and important evidence for the size of the vill at this period. If the manor and the five free-tenant farms are excluded, it suggests that there were some 17 houses in occupation in the village centre. These will not have included empty properties and possibly not those of the cottars (*85*).

Michaelmas
(St Michael's mass or feast day: 29 September at this period). This is the third quarter day (the fourth being *Cherset* at Christmas) and the second of the two statutory Court Leet meetings. The free tenants will have paid their annual rent to the manor on this occasion based on a flat rate of 1d. per acre, providing a total of 9s. to the manor. This is effectively a form of *tallage*, a tax on tenants by the Lord of the Manor payable at Michaelmas.

However that was not all. At the Court-Leets (Cartselver and Michaelmas) 'each person being in the tithing (*decenna*) shall give the Lord 1d. Total by estimation: 2s. 8d.

and no more, because the king shall have 3*s*. from the leets.' Tithing was a system by which young men when they reached the age of 12 swore before the manor Leet to become law-abiding members of a tithing or *frankpledge* group. This ancient system of primary law-enforcement at the lowest levels of society, had its origins in the Anglo-Saxon period but was gradually being phased out during the later medieval period. This particular tithing does not relate to the ecclesiastical tithes, but functions here as a form of 'national income tax.' The figures here suggest that there were 32 persons 'in the tithing' at Clapham who were paying 1*d*. a year. Perhaps only the cottars were again excluded, probably the free tenants made up the balance of 4*d*.

The reorganisation of the central government taxation system 'The Assessment and Collection of the Fifteenths and Tenths' as it was formally termed, came into force *c*.1334 and enormously increased the rate of tax for such places as Clapham — much to their dismay no doubt! No wonder the manor felt no compunction in defrauding the system (see above).

Herset

A tax ostensibly in kind at Christmas. At Clapham there is a rent of assize for bondmen of three cocks and six hens worth 16½*d*. Since the individual price of each bird is supplied (a cock 1½*d*., a hen 2*d*.) this rent was probably intended where possible to be commuted to a money payment.

Whilst considering demographic issues there is the matter of the total population figure of the vill in 1326. Following the Roger's demographic projection of 4.5 heads per family (used throughout this study) we have a manorial population estimate of about 184 persons living in Clapham at this period, including the Weston family at the manor (Rogers 1972, 16). It should be compared with the Domesday figure of 54 persons at Clapham in 1086, an approximate growth of 70 per cent in the population. The feudal social categories described here were already in a state of flux by the early fourteenth century, partly due to an earlier rise in population and intense competition for land. Holdings were tending to become smaller and more numerous, and more land was being brought into cultivation. The demographic disasters of the fourteenth century gradually terminated the older feudal practices.

CLAPHAM VILLAGE

In studying the possible layout of the medieval village of *c*.1326 (*85*) certain features have already been established. The plan form was essentially linear following the course of the Holocene stream (*7A*) whose spring was somewhere in the area of the present Holy Trinity Church (see Chapter 1). The course of the old village street is still preserved at its southern end in Old Town but from the Rectory Grove Centre northwards to the Wandsworth Road the route is now lost under urban development. As late as the mid nineteenth century, however, the old road could still be traced by pathways and property boundaries (Clapham Tithe Map of 1838 and the Bland Map of 1849).

At its southern end, the Common 'funnels in' to meet Old Town, a feature noted by Oliver Rackham on 'wood pasture' commons where animals have to be herded into the village centre and the byres in the longhouses (Rackham 1986, 141). This layout, probably dating back to the Saxon period, is still a feature of the existing layout.

The first major change to the topography of the vill was the digging of a moat round the manorial site. As postulated above this may have been the work of Faramus of Boulogne in the later twelfth century, as part of his scheme to upgrade the status of the manor, which included the erection of a private chapel. The moat is on a slope running westwards down to the village street and stream in the valley bottom. There would have been no difficulty keeping the western end of the moat wet with a feeder from the stream, but the eastern, higher end was more of a problem. The solution was to direct the stream (or provide a branch) in the area of the village green (now the bus station) so that it wound its way along what is now Rectory Grove and fed the upper, eastern end of the moat. Whether both watercourses ran concurrently or there was some sort of sluice gate to the moat leat is uncertain. As mentioned earlier it was one of the duties of the customary tenants to 'repair the wall of the watercourse as far as the churchyard' (Redstone 1967, 414) in 1326. Alongside the stream there was a path or trackway which was later developed by Merton Priory as a route passing the church and known as Canterbury Way in the late twelfth century. The adjacent manorial demesne included not only the moated site but a block of land to the south, the garden of the manor mentioned above.

At the southern end of the manor gardens was the messuage of the Vicarage, about ½ acre of land. One of the 'pervenients' (gifts) that Merton expected when they obtained the advowson of a parish church was a 'sufficient and convenient area nigh to the Church' on which Merton could build a residence for the priest (Heales 1898, 182). This parcel of land (*85*) formerly a part of the manorial demesne, was presumably a gift of Lady Sibyl in the late twelfth century. The vicarage, later rectory, was to stay on this site, rebuilt many times, until 1886 when it was pulled down and the site redeveloped (Smith 1976, 20).

The last major medieval development occurred, as has been argued above, *c.*1450 when the Lord of the Manor, Thomas Gower, effectively vacated the manorial, moated site, part of which was turned over to the church for use as a burial ground. The new manorial premises were located further south in the northern area of the manor garden (*colour plate 16*). New land needed to be appropriated for the gardens and grounds. It was at this point, I believe, that the old village street was abandoned and a new road, North Street, was built across the sites of former messuages and crofts (*85*). The triangular area of land vacated now became the manor gardens (*80*). The social upheaval with the demolition of several village houses and acquisition of their land might not have been possible had the vill not been going through another agrarian crisis at this period, as evidenced by the Surrey Taxation Returns (see above). As in the second quarter of the fourteenth century, crops failed and there was starvation. There may well have been vacant property in the village into which displaced customary tenants could be moved.

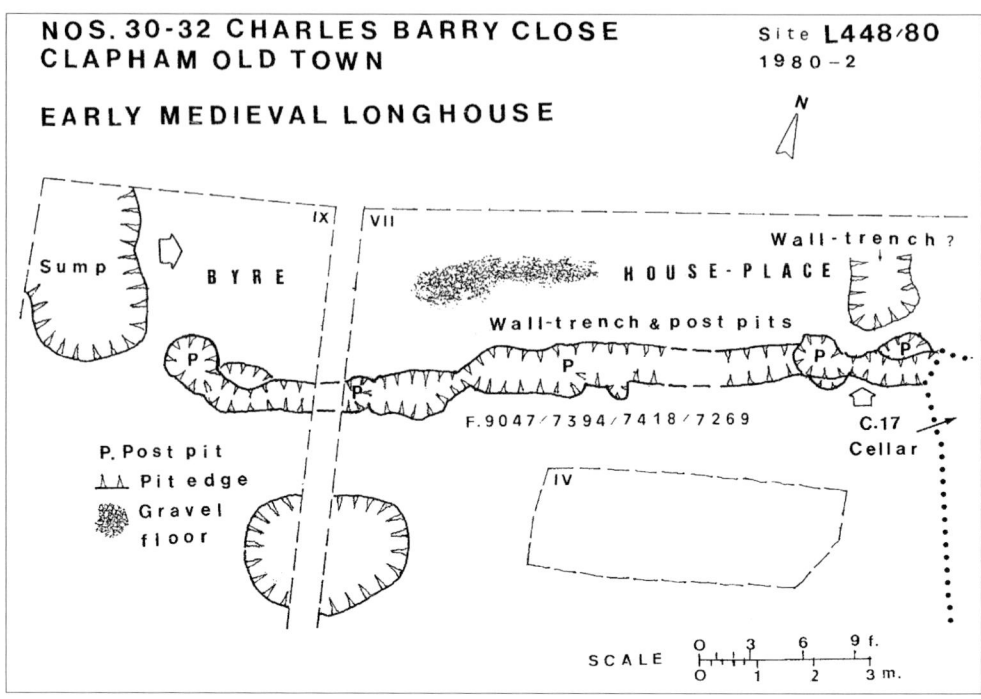

**NOS. 30-32 CHARLES BARRY CLOSE
CLAPHAM OLD TOWN**

Site **L448/80**
1980−2

EARLY MEDIEVAL LONGHOUSE

N

Sump

BYRE

IX VII

HOUSE-PLACE

Wall-trench ?

Wall-trench & post pits

F. 9047/7394/7418/7269

C.17
Cellar

P. Post pit
Pit edge
Gravel floor

IV

SCALE

0 3 6 9 f.
0 1 2 3 m.

86 Plan of part of an early medieval longhouse excavated below the existing Nos 30-32 Barry Close (east of Rectory Grove). For site location plan see *28. H.J.M. Green, reinterpreted plan of site L448/80 excavated by R. Densem and D. Seeley in 1980-2. Courtesy London Museum*

87 View looking west of medieval longhouse wall-trench with post-pits and post-holes in site (marked by scale rods). Site L448/80 (*86*) excavated by R. Densem and D. Seeley in 1980-2. *Photo courtesy of London Museum*

Buildings

The history and structure of the medieval Manor House and church of Holy Trinity has already been discussed in some detail (see Chapters 7 & 8). In turning to the longhouses, cottages and byres, which can only now be elucidated by archaeology, there is the problem of finding sites where sufficiently large-scale excavations have taken place to identify their transient remains. One such site (L448/80) was that excavated in 1980-82 by Densem and Seeley at the top of Rectory Grove under what is now Nos 30-32 Barry Close (*28*). This site produced an early medieval horizon (*85, 86, 87*) of some importance to this study.

The draft archive report of this and other sites in the immediate vicinity prepared *c.*1988 by the Museum of London summarised the results as follows: 'No medieval buildings were found, though the discovery of a well suggests that one stood nearby'. However, an irregular linear feature (9047/7394/7418/7269) identified tentatively as a drainage trench is in fact a wall trench, probably of two periods, recut and with irregularly spaced post-pits. The feature was 11.5m. (37ft 9in) long and varied in width between 0.9m (3ft) and 0.4m (1ft 6in). The filling consisted of lenses of 'silt and sand', i.e. redeposited, backfill make-up. There are indications of what might be interpreted as post-pits on the draft plan (LM fig.3; redrawn here in *86*) and are visible on site photos (*87*) as indeed is a gravel floor overlying the natural to the north of the feature.

This linear feature would therefore appear to be the south wall of a longhouse with a gravel floor which extended northwards beyond the limits of the excavation. The post-pits suggest a structure of three, possibly four bays, irregularly spaced and probably with cruck frames (see *41* for general type). The wall was probably of lightly-framed wattle and daub construction set in a foundation trench. This is a type of building construction known as 'earthfast'. The lack of clear structural features and postholes probably indicates that the building was deliberately demolished and the materials removed. At the east end what appears to be a wall-trench may indicate a return wall here. There is a possible entrance flanked by door posts at the east end of the main east-west wall leading into the house-place. The west end of the building was clearly open onto the trackway and the wall trench terminated with what is described as a butt-end, presumably a post-pit. The roof was undoubtedly thatched, a craft mentioned in the 1326 Extent. The material used was probably the straw left over after the corn had been threshed. Another possible source were reeds from Rushmere (*78*).

The building that has emerged from the 1980 excavation is a very ancient type of longhouse where the main entry to the house is through the byre as described in *Breuddwyd Rhonabwy*, one of the fourteenth century *Mabinogion* tales. In the *Dream of Rhonabwy*, three members of a Welsh war-band seek shelter in a peasant longhouse. The owners were obliged to give them hospitality as was expected under the Welsh traditional laws of the time. There is no contemporary description of this period which conveys so graphically the conditions in which such communities lived.

> And as they came towards the house, they could see a black old hall with a straight gable
> end, and smoke billowing from it. And when they came inside, they could see a floor full

of holes and uneven. Where there was a bump upon it, it was with difficulty that a man might stand thereon, so slippery was it with the mire of cattle. Where there was a hole, a man might go up to his ankles in water and the urine of cattle. And there were boughs a plenty of holly spread over the floor whereof the cattle had browsed the tips. And when they came to the main floor of the house (the houseplace) they could see bare dusty dais boards, and a crone feeding a fire on the dais, and when there was a cold draught she would throw a lapful of husks onto the fire, so that it was not easy for any man alive to endure that smoke entering into his nostrils.

And after they had sat down they asked the crone where were the people of the house. But the crone was rude to them. And thereupon the people came in: a bald and wizened man with a bundle of sticks upon his back, and a little skinny, livid woman also carrying a bundle under her arm. And a cold welcome they had for the men. And the woman lit a fire of sticks for them and went to cook, and brought them their food, barley-bread and cheese and watered milk. And when their resting place was examined there was nothing on it save dusty flea-ridden straw-ends ... A greyish red, threadbare, flea-infested blanket was spread thereon, and over the blanket a coarse broken sheet in tatters, and a half-empty pillow and filthy pillow-case thereon, on top of the sheet.

The Mabinogion
(after Jones and Jones 1949, 137-8)

It is significant in connection with the Clapham building that the excavators noted that the wall trench (and presumably the floor) sloped down to the west so that manure and urine from animals drained off into the watercourse in the trackway (*86*). At the west end there was also a wide shallow scoop in the ground where cattle may have trampled the surface, but which also acted as a sump for the effluvia.

The external appearance of such a building, and indeed of Clapham village at this period, is well caught in a background detail by Pieter Breugel, the Elder, of *the Peasant and the Birdnester* of 1568 (*colour plate 17*). Peasant buildings in north-west Europe were very similar in character on both sides of the Channel at this time. The longhouse at Strata Florida, Cardiganshire, illustrates the internal character of such a building (*88*).

The Black Death

Pottery in deposits and features associated with the wall trench included a small amount of (residual) Late Saxon material and a more substantial group dating to *c*.1150-1350. Some of this material came from a circular, timber-lined well in trench XX lying slightly to the north of the longhouse, it also had clearly been abandoned *c*.1350.

The dating brackets of the pottery from the house and the well are highly significant. It confirms the postulated date of the construction of the watercourse, accompanying road and house plot development as occurring in the later twelfth century under Faramus of Boulogne. The closing date of *c*.1350 must be directly associated with the appearance of the Black Death in 1348-49. As has already been noted above in connection with the Surrey Tax Concession for Clapham in 1348 and 1350, there was clearly some sort of socio-economic crisis in the vill at this time. It is not merely the closing date of the

Above and below 88 Internal views in 1888 of a traditional Welsh longhouse at Strata Florida,
Cardiganshire. Apart from being constructed in wattle and daub throughout, the Clapham
fourteenth-century longhouses would have been very similar in scale and character
88a View through byre towards the house-place. Cruck truss with collar propped up by tree trunks
88b View of hearth. Chimney canopy and shelf for roosting chickens. Side entrance by hearth as at
Clapham *(Peate 1946, figs 35 and 36)*

pottery sequence that is of significance in this context, but what happened to the site subsequently. The longhouse was evidently pulled down and the site was uniformly covered by what is described as 'ploughsoil' 0.3m (1ft) to 0.45m (1ft 7in) thick containing material dating up to the mid seventeenth century when post-medieval structures begin to appear again on the site. The ploughsoil horizon was found on all five archaeological sites around Rectory Grove reported in the Museum of London archive report. Strictly speaking it should perhaps be regarded as the product of 'allotment' activity, i.e. spade agriculture in crofts which had formerly been messuages or house sites. This is not land on the margins of the settlement, but in the very centre of the village where the built-up area might be considered to have been at its densest. It is the clearest possible evidence for considerable depopulation in the mid fourteenth century.

Apart from this indirect (but telling) evidence, no record has come down of the horrors of the Black Death in Clapham at this time. Unlike the effects of the agrarian crisis and starvation in the earlier fourteenth century, which, although devastating, was a slow process and took several years to take full effect, the bubonic plague was horrible and immediate, with death occurring within days or even hours of a person developing the disease. An inscription scratched on the wall of St Mary's church Ashwell (Herts.) by probably a distraught incumbent speaks of a 'wretched, terrible, destructive year ... the remnants of the people alone survive' (Ziegler 2003, 138). At Clapham there is only a much later account of another visitation of the plague in the early seventeenth century which demonstrates how comprehensively an entire family could be wiped out within a few days (*89*). The Parish Register of Burials in 1603 records how Edward Coochman, Parson of Clapham, Judith his wife, Edward his son, his two daughters Elizabeth and

89 Bedroom in seventeenth-century London house afflicted by the plague, with dead and dying members of the family attended by a doctor and officials (with staffs). *Broadside 1665-6 by John Dunstall*

Judith, together with Susan his maid servant, all died of the plague between the 3rd and 24th of September. Perhaps it was old Joane (John?) his keeper, who witnessed his will on the 2 of September, who was found dead in the parsonage barn on the 11 October (Rudolf 1904, 28).

The squalid conditions in which most of the Clapham peasantry evidently lived in the mid fourteenth century would have made the effects of this highly infectious disease even more lethal in the community. The progress of the Black Death across Southern England after its arrival in the West Country ports has been charted. It reached Surrey at the end of 1348, with the most virulent outbreaks occurring in the early summer of 1349. At Farnham it has been calculated that 20 per cent of the inhabitants died of the plague (Ziegler 2003, 121). London was devastated with a casualty rate of 20,000-30,000 out of a total population of 60,000-70,000. Many Londoners went out into the adjoining countryside to places such as Clapham to escape, or to search for food, thus providing an additional source of infection. There were further outbreaks of bubonic plague over the next 300 years and its reappearance in Clapham in 1603 has already been noted.

At a manorial level, one of the immediate effects was to speed up the commutation of manorial services for cash payments, a process evidently already well under way at Clapham judging by the 1326 Customal. However, the psychological, indeed spiritual, effects of this evil visitation were longer lasting and became the catalyst for dramatic social change in the later medieval period.

THE FIELDS

At the beginning of this study it was emphasised that it was of major importance to understand the nature of the land at Clapham and, by implication, the use of it at different periods. In particular, an appreciation of the exact amount of property that was held in the past, who owned it and its name at the time has been critical in establishing the history of Clapham.

As is standard practice with such a problem it has been necessary to work backwards from the known to the unknown. Nothing of the old field systems, woodland and heathland of early Clapham survives today, but 150 years ago there were still traces of the ancient countryside. Fortunately, the map-makers of the early and mid nineteenth century were highly proficient surveyors. In particular there are two important parish surveys. The 1838 Clapham Tithe Map held by the Lambeth Minet Library consists of a meticulous large-scale survey (scale 1:1250 approx.) accompanied by an inventory in which every parcel of land, however small, is listed and measured, and its ownership and name (where appropriate) is provided. From this survey the Bland cartographical map was prepared and published in 1849 amongst others (*91*).

Working backwards there is the Batten survey of 1827 and the Ordnance Survey carried out between 1780 and 1801, on which the Milne 1801 Land Use Map was prepared (*colour plate 18*). Earlier in the eighteenth century there is the famous Rocque Map of 1746 of 'country near ten miles round [London] begun in 1741 and ended in

1745'. Unfortunately, Rocque did not accurately survey the field systems away from the main roads, but this information is supplied in part by what survives of one or two estate maps. Of these the most important for our purposes is a coloured plan of the Clapham Place lands in the parish of *c.*1715 published in Brayley's Surrey Vol. III part 2 held in the London Metropolitan archives (*colour plate 20a*).

The cartographical information is supplemented by local historical records and in particular Batten's 1827 account of boundaries and 'parochial occurrences' which takes the history of the parish lands back to 1600 and beyond. From these and a wide range of lesser sources it has been possible to reconstruct the landscape of post-medieval Clapham with some accuracy, and, by projection, earlier periods still.

The Extent of 1326 is exceptional in Clapham studies in providing a detailed list of all the lands, described by name, in which the manor had holdings, together with totals of the amount of land involved. Many of the field names are familiar from later evidence, but one great asset has been the realisation that the survey was methodically carried out (with one or two exceptions) anticlockwise round the parish starting with Hide farm in the south-west corner and ending at the north-west end of the parish by the Wandsworth Road. It has thus been possible to reconstruct this landscape, given our knowledge of later boundaries, although some details must necessarily be conjectural (*78*). What is much more difficult to establish is the precise land use of any given parcel of land (unless specifically stated) since much was in a state of flux at this time due to the agrarian and demographic crisis affecting the vill at this period. (The history of some of these fields, closes, pastures, meadows and woodlands has already been touched on in earlier chapters, in particular Chapter 2, *The Woods of Clapham*, Chapter 4, *The Alfred Estate* and Chapter 6; for land parcel numbers, see *78*, listed as they occur in the Extent.)

1. Demesne grounds (see above, *the manor*)

2. *La Hidehalle* (between Hydethorpe Road and Emmanuel Road SW 12). 63 acres: manor, 20 acres. *Hide* = a unit of Saxon land measurement. Farmed by Hide Hall.

3. *Overwavermede* (between Poynders Road and Thornton Road SW 12). 85 acres: manor, 20 acres. *Over* = beyond; *waver* = pond; *mede* = meadow, i.e. '*Further pond meadow*'.

4. *Netherwavermede* (Monish Road — Sulina Road SW2). 29 acres: manor, 12 acres. *Nether* = lower, i.e. '*Lower pond meadow*'. Farmed by Black Hall.

5. *Goderichfeld* (between Clarence Avenue SW4 and Lyham Road SW2). 60 acres: manor, 14 acres. Goderich is a personal name, probably after St Godric (see Chapter 6, *Assarting and Pastoralism*) *feld* = open (arable) field, i.e. *Godric's field*.

6. *Shortl(and)* or *Shorteland* (between Lyham Road and Kingswood Road SW12). Possibly divided plots in what had originally been one parcel of land. 37 acres: manor 3 and 4 acres respectively. *Land* = strip in open field, i.e. '*Shortstrip*'.

7. *Leghamnhale* (?) (between Nightingale Lane and Temperley Road SW12). 44 acres (may have included part of Ballum Wood,) 18 acres: manor 5 acres. *Leghamn* = Leigham Manor; *Hale* = small corner of land, i.e. '*Legham Corner*'. Farmed by Leghamhale farm.

8. Longelond (between Kings Avenue and Park Hill SW4). 27 acres; manor, 9 acres. '*Longstrip*'.

9. *La Groveshote* (between Bowland Road and Haselrigge Road SW4). 9 acres; manor 6 acres. *Grove* (*O.E Graf*) = thicket. *Shote* = strip (referring to its former waterside condition before becoming meadowland).

10. La Battesland (between Clapham High Street and Clapham Park Road SW4). 30 acres: manor 12 acres, 1 rood. *Battes* = *Baetti* is a personal name and a side-form of *Betti* (Ekwall 19437, 29) i.e. *Baetti's strip*.

11. *La Fridaysfeld* (between Clapham Common Southside and Rodenhurst Road SW4). 109 acres: manor, 24 acres. *Friday* = *Frigedaeg*, a personal name (Ekwall 1947, 179) which also occurs in Friday Grove (*78*). It probably refers to the same 'assarter' who brought both areas back into cultivation, possibly during the twelfth or thirteenth centuries, a time of population growth and pressure on arable land in Clapham.

12. *La Breche* (between Old Town and Manor Street SW4) 24 acres: manor 16 acres. *Breche, breach* or *breech* = land newly cultivated (Richardson 2003, 12). The field name evidence suggests that the East Field at Clapham was brought under cultivation at a later period than that of the West Field (Stockwood by 1326) possibly during the late Saxon period (see Chapter 6, *Arable and Meadowland*).

13. *Richemmens lond* or *Firsfeld* (between Clapham Road and Larkhall Lane SW4). Possibly two separate fields, originally each of 20 acres, which had been amalgamated by 1326: manor 14 acres. *Richemont* is a personal name (Ekwall 1947, 368) *Lond* = strip in the open field; *firse* or *furze* = heathland; *feld* = open field.

14. *La Longelond* (Gauden Road SW4). 7 acres. *Lond* = land or strip in the open field.

15. *Shortelond* (between Clapham Road and Chelsham Road SW4) 3 acres. *Lond*, see 14 above.

16. *Maltecroft* (Bromfelde Road SW4). 22 acres. *Malt* or *Barley Croft* = enclosure or small holding distant from the village (as here on the edge of the parish). In the 1326 Extent, parcels 14, 15 and 16, perhaps originally separate closes, had evidently been lumped together to form a large, arable open-field of which the manor had 16 acres.

17. *Hemereshull* (Union Grove SW8) 30 acres: manor 5 acres. *Hemere* (O.E. *Hemm*) = border. *Hull* = hill. This open field on rising ground borders the boundary between Clapham and Stockwell.

18. *Cherchehull* (between Albion Avenue SW8 and Brayburne Avenue SW4). 10 acres: manor 9½ acres. *Cherch* = church; *hull* = hill. There is no tradition of a church in this area, so perhaps originally a gift of manor land to the church in the early thirteenth century to support the priest, but by 1326 was evidently back in demesne ownership.

19. *La Pende* (near the church, between Brayburne Avenue and Netherford Road SW4). 4 acres: manor 2½ acres. *Pende* = pound or pinfold for stray animals. This close is too large to have been the pound itself, but may have been adjacent to it, lying in the small parcel of land north of the moated manor (*85*). This ground abuts the old village street and Wandsworth Road where straying animals were most likely to be found. It is also under the eye of the manor, and may therefore be identified with the Lord's pinfold (*ponfaldam*) of the 1326 Extent. The customary tenants were obliged to maintain the earthen (cob) walls of this enclosure, a labour worth annually 3*d*. Stray animals impounded had to be redeemed by their owners for a money payment to the manor.

20. *Le Medshote* (strip of hillside north of Wandsworth Road running down to the former ditch of Bradmede, stretched between Thessaly Road and St Rule Street SW8). 27 acres (as measured in 1838): manor 28 acres. *Med* = meadow; *shote* = selion, land or strip. This is probably the meadowland owned by the manor in 1326 and is described as comprising 20 acres in the Extent, where it is valued at 66*s*. 8*d*. yearly (price 3*s*. 4*d*. an acre) making it some of the most valuable land in the demesne.

21. *La Waterslade* (Rule Street School SW8). 7 acres: manor 5 acres. *Slade* = valley with a stream. The '*Water*' is the continuation of the stream which flowed through the village down to the Ditch of Bradmede (*6A*, *78* and *85*). Perhaps the 6 acres of pasture worth 2*s*. annually, priced at 4*d*. an acre in the Extent belonging to the demesne.

22. *Chekeneye* (Heath Road SW8). 8 acres: manor 5 acres. *Chekeneye* is a fourteenth-century corruption of the Late Saxon, *Ceokan Ege* (see Chapter 5 *Westminster Charter item 4B*) = Ceaccas' island or promontory, i.e. where the land juts out in the area of Silverthorne Road SW8.

23. *Bradenham* (between Daley Thompson Way SW8 and Ashley Crescent SW11) 7.5 acres: manor 3½ acres. *Braden* (O.E. *Braegd*) possibly a personal name (Ekwall 1947, 55). *Ham* = pasture enclosure. The three parcels of land 21-23 which lay north of the Wandsworth Road or the steep slope which ran down to the Ditch of Bradmede (approximate line of Heath Road SW8) were all probably pastureland at this period. The remaining enclosures 24-26 were closes elsewhere in the vill which either belonged to the parson or free tenants.

24. *La Clerkesland* ('in divers parcels'). This appears to be a discrete unit of land divided into many small parcels rather than a reference to various holdings of the vicarage in the open fields. This land, described as *glebe* property, survived into the nineteenth century (see Chapter 2 *The Agricultural Lands of Clapham 5*). It formed a long strip on the north side of the Clapham Road between Union Road and Gauden Road SW4, and constituted the water meadows of the Heath Wall Brook, 9 acres as surveyed in 1838, but recorded as demesne land of 11 acres in the Extent. *Clerke* (O.F. *Clerc*) = a cleric of the church, but not in Holy Orders. *Lond* = a field strip. As hay meadows it would (theoretically) have been of great value as a source of income to the vicarage, but appears to have been held by the manor in 1326. The appropriation by the manor of glebe land at the time of the 1326 Extent (see also 18 above) suggests that the living had been subject to a long vacancy at this time, probably not filled until 1348 (Dale 1927, 24).

25. *Land formerly belonging to William de Kent* (between Grafton Square and Bromells Road). 13 acres: manor 8 acres (see under *The Villagers* for a discussion of this property).

26. *Land that was Le Maples at Withiebed* (between The Pavement and Venn Street SW4). 7 acres: manor 1½ acres (messuage?). *Le Maple* is a personal name of a former free tenant owning marginal land close to the spring line, *withiebed = withy bed* (O.E. *Wipig*) or osier willows growing on waterlogged ground (see under *The Villagers* for a discussion of this property).

Also a moiety [half share] of the Wood there [i.e. Clapham] on the west side as divided by bounds, to wit the moiety containing by estimation 70 acres, worth yearly 66s. 8d., price 11½d. per acre and 5d. more on the whole

(Between Wix's Lane and North Street west-east and Wandsworth Road and Northside north-south SW4) (PRO 1898, 583). This woodland, formerly the West Field(s) of Clapham during the Saxo-Norman period, is discussed in Chapter 2 under *Stockwood* and elsewhere. It was evidently planted in the 1320s following the climate downturn of the Little Ice Age and the ensuing agrarian crisis when much of the arable land of the vill was abandoned (see *6* and *78*). It was not finally felled until the early seventeenth century.

THE FARMING YEAR

The medieval mindset
One of the difficulties in studying the lives and lifestyles of fourteenth-century people in Clapham is understanding, let alone empathising with, the psychological motors that drove their world. In a nutshell, the motivating force was sheer physical survival, but

90 A view of neighbouring Wandsworth in 1750 showing the different types of fields and closes which would have been in use at Clapham at this period and earlier. *Foreground*: Common open field under corn with headlands (between the furlong blocks of land) used as access paths. *Middleground*: Communal pasture with herdsmen tending groups of cattle. *Background*: Village houses with adjoining crofts under intensive cultivation. The stout fencing round the closes is in place to prevent livestock from straying into crofts and the corn fields. *Courtesy of and © Wandsworth Libraries, Museums and Arts*

for its achievement certain structures of communal discipline needed to be in place. The community, effectively, had no support services whether educational, medical or custodial, with only the most casual and uncertain help from the manor and church in times of dire need. The community was utterly reliant on the mutual support of its members. In an economic situation where so much of the farm equipment and agricultural services had to be shared, it was imperative that you got along with the other members of the village community, whether you liked them or not. A high premium was therefore set on mutual cooperation, compliance and conformity.

There was absolutely no privacy, either at a domestic level or socially: everyone knew everyone's business and habits. For the ordinary simple villager there was in all this a certain measure of security and acceptance: everyone knew you and your place in the community. In a world of limited social mobility, however, such constraints for the independently-minded and maverick were sheer hell, with only escape to the relatively anonymous slums of nearby London as a possible release.

In such rural communities bottled-up emotional tensions could run high, breaking out in sudden acts of domestic or social violence, with concurrent high levels of incest and illegitimacy. Eliza Clapham (named after the village) was one such hired by Lady

Gauden in 1679 (see Chapter 10). Strangers and incomers were viewed with deep suspicion as being only too likely to upset the carefully balanced social structure of the community. Such attitudes are neatly caught by the 150-year-old Punch cartoon in which two locals are watching a visitor to the village: *'First: "Oos Eee?" Second: "A furriner" First: "Then eave 'arf a brick at im"'*.

It was imperative that such communities learned at a rudimentary level to run their own affairs, thereby maintaining their own social order and discipline. This was achieved by using certain well-tried administrative structures to enforce the corporate will of the community on all its inhabitants. It is against this psychological background that the fourteenth century socio-political structures described below should be seen.

It started at the very bottom of society with the system of tithing (*decenna*) briefly mentioned earlier under Court Leet payments. Associations of 10 or 12 village households were held corporately responsible for the good behaviour of their members. In practice the *decenna* was probably run on a clan basis, being comprised of large extended families or those closely related by marriage. Each association was presided over by a *tithingman* who was answerable to the Court Leet for the working of the tithing through regulations known as the *Frankpledge*. On reaching the age of

91 Plan of the Parish of Clapham in the County of Surrey, 1849, with section across the Common. Messrs A. and R. Bland surveyors, engraved by H Martin. *Reproduced from the G.L.C. Map Collection by kind permission of the Greater London Council. Published by the Clapham Society 1873*

12 every boy of a village *decenna* was obliged to swear in public before the Court Leet that he would be an obedient member of his tithing. It was in effect a form of institutionalised 'binding over' as a guarantee of good behaviour, enforced on all male members of the community. By the late fourteenth century with the emergence of national and county legal systems, the ancient *Frankpledge* arrangements were beginning to be phased out, but still lingered on in some places into the sixteenth century.

THE MANOR LEET

As already noted above the Leet (*leta*, perhaps derived from the A.S. *Laestan* = to make good a vow) was central to the workings of the village and manor. It is only mentioned briefly in the 1326 Customal, where it is stipulated that it should meet twice a year at Le Hokeday and Michaelmas and that 1*d*. should be collected from all individuals in the tithings on those occasions (see above under *The Villagers*). The Customal also mentions 'the pleas and perquisites of the court there, which are worth yearly by estimation 6*s*. 8*d*.' In a sense these brief references represent only the tip of an iceberg of social and legal management of the *villata de Clopham*. The Court Leet proceedings has not survived at Clapham, but has done so elsewhere, notably at Ramsey, Cambridgeshire, the subject of a magisterial study by Anne and Edwin de Windt (De Windt 2006, 86ff).

The process appears to have worked at two levels of the village community, the lower level perhaps being focused on the *Tithingmen*. A relatively large group of householders at Clapham would have met on a fairly frequent basis in the village centre, probably in the open air, to decide what issues should be aired at the manorial leet and in particular to appoint the Twelve Presenters or Sworn Men (*Jurati*). At the manorial Leet, or upper level, in the Lord's hall, presided over by the bailiff, the *Jurati* were obliged to swear an oath put to them along the following lines:

> Ye shall loyally enquire among yourselves and loyally present all the articlers of which ye shall be charged on behalf of the King and the Lord of this court to the best of your knowledge. So help you God in the day of judgement.
>
> De Windt 2006, 92

Such oaths, made before the lord and the village community, were considered to have great binding force, which was only possible in these circumstances through trust in one another's word. The bailiff would then put to the sworn men a series of questions on a number of different issues, legal, fiscal and management, which they were expected to answer honestly, even though on occasions it meant 'shopping' their neighbours. The *Jurati* thus exercised great responsibility which extended to recommending the level of fines and remedial action for various offences, and a whole range of financial arrangements covered by the expression in the Customal 'of assize'. A top priority was the management of the lands and animals of the vill, and, in particular, the financial value of all the various agricultural tasks. This cut both ways of course. It decided the level of fine if a task was commuted for payment, but it also ensured that an agreed price was paid if labour was hired for a particular task.

From all this it is evident that the management of the vill was very much a shared responsibility between the Lord of the Manor and the villagers. An ancient Breton saying has it that the difference between the sexes in these communities was that 'men exercised power and woman exercised control' in the family unit. To extend this to a wider village context, the same might be said of the relationship between the manor and village, the lord having the ultimate sanction in any line of action, but that it was the community that determined the real control over its way of life.

MANAGEMENT OF THE LAND

As already noted in Chapter 2, the ploughlands were apparently situated in a large number of smallish open fields (of which some might be run together for ease of working, as in the case of fields 14-15). Each field was divided into plough ridges or lands which were raised strips of variable length with a furrow on both sides for drainage purposes, hence the ridge and furrow system. The 'land' would be ploughed up and down, and round and round with the plough team turning at the top of the ridge on the headland. Each block of strips or furlong was treated as an arable unit, which were in turn grouped into larger units or fields.

All the customary tenants together with the Lord of the Manor and the parson would have had their various lands scattered throughout the fields and closes, intermingled with those of his neighbours, to ensure that as far as possible everyone had a share of good and poor land. As mentioned in Chapter 2, traces of the ancient ridge and furrow system were noted on aerial photos of Clapham Common (*colour plate 5*).

Free tenants, who rented their land would tend to have it in one unit, usually termed a close (i.e. an enclosure) from the common fields. In field 4 (Netherwavermede farmed by Black Hall) it is clear that the close had been formed out of a furlong comprising several strips. In theory the vill at this time was farmed on a crop rotation system with approximately a third of the land being left fallow in any one year. Another third would be given over to the winter cereal (wheat and rye) which had a long growing cycle. The last third would be the spring crop (barley, oats and legumes) with a shorter growing cycle and harvested within the calendar year.

DUNGING

Apart from fallowing, the manuring of arable land was the principal way of maintaining its fertility. The animal and human manure from the longhouses would have been shovelled out of the byres in the longhouses (see *Buildings* above) and heaped in front of the building along the old village street, whence it would have been carted off by the villagers to their crofts and strips. A similar process took place with the manure of the Lord's demesne piled in the stock-yard of the manor court, but in this case it was the 26 bondmen who had to gather, carry and spread the lord's dung whenever and as often as necessary throughout the year, the work of each bondman being worth 6*d.*, total 8*s.* 6*d.*

Each bondman would evidently have been expected to pay a flat annual rate of 6*d.* for commuting this service based, apparently, according to the amount of land he held. The nominal holdings of the bondmen should have been 288 acres of arable, but, in fact, the actual total stated by the Customal is 272 acres, a shortfall of 16 acres, which implies that not all the virgaters held the full amount of land. It has already been noted that Walter Colen apparently held only 6 acres in 1332.

Manuring was one of the most onerous and time-consuming of manorial duties, and would need to have been carried out, probably weekly, throughout the year, although clearly the manor was prepared to be flexible on this point.

PLOUGHING

> Also each of the aforesaid bondmen [i.e. all the 31 customary bondmen] having a plough or plough-beasts [i.e. Oxen] shall come twice a year to the boon ploughing [benerth], and shall plough for one day for winter seed and for one day at Lenten seed at the Lord's meat, and each ploughing is worth 1½*d* beyond the meat.
>
> PRO 1898, 583

Boonwork was a day's work performed by tenants for their lord on special occasions, and was rarely commuted for money payment. The lord fed the workers ('the Lord's meat') on the day they carried out this work. William de Weston could thus be assured of the joint services of his bondmen to till his 254 acres of arable at the time of the winter ploughing (between Michaelmas and Christmas) for sowing wheat and rye, and again at the Lenten ploughing between Ash Wednesday and Easter) for sowing barley, oats and legumes – in all two months' work.

The term 'ploughing' (or 'seed' as in the 1326 Customal) covers several staggered activities or 'works' which include breaking up the ground with a wooden swing plough (*92a*) manuring the land (see dunging above) and harrowing. 'Also they ought to harrow the land thus ploughed by them, and each harrowing is worth ½*d.*' The tine harrow had a box frame with projecting spikes (*92b*). It would be used to break down the ploughed land into tilth suitable for seed sowing.

The critical stage of seeding was next brought into operation using the skilled technique known as *broadcast*.

> You sowed only about 2 pounds, or half a peck at the outside, of seed per acre; and this had to be sown in step with two hands alternately. The sower took only a pinch of seed between his thumbs and finger at a time, and it was broadcast as he walked in step

92a Medieval seasonal activities: ploughing and sowing. *H.J.M. Green after fourteenth-century MS. (B.L. Add. Ms. 47682f.6 BL)*

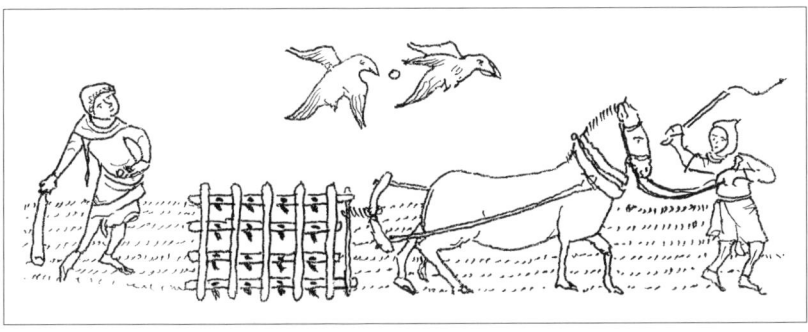

92b Harrowing the ploughed field, with slinger to deter crows from eating the seed. *H.J.M. Green after the Luttrell Psalter. B.L. f.172v c.1330-1345*

92c Harvesting supervised by the manorial bailiff. *H.J.M. Green after the Queen Mary Psalter. English early fourteenth century (B.L. Add. 19720f 11 7v; BP, MS Parrs. 1870f 36v)*

(synchronizing foot with hand). He used a seed-container, which was called a hod, hung on his chest with a strap over his neck; and he dipped his hands into this alternately and just took a pinch out and it was sown. (Suffolk farmer, R.M. Sherwood 1885-1963 in Ewart Evans 1969, 33) (See *92a*).

The bondmen when sowing their crofts or small-holdings would have used a simpler method of sowing known as dibbling. 'A man with a dibbler [basically a pointed stick] walked backwards and made holes in the seed bed. A woman or child followed with a hod of seed corn dropping a few seeds into each hole' (Ewart Evans, *ibid*). As a method of growing corn it was reckoned to be very labour intensive but was claimed to be four times more productive than broadcast sowing.

With broadcast sowing the seed had next to be covered over by further harrowing: 'Also each virgat[er] of land ought to harrow at Lenten seed daily with one harrow until the lord's plough be reached, and the harrowing of each virgate is worth 6*d*. Total 8*s*. 6*d*.' (PRO 1898, 584). This harrowing during the spring growing season would have been intended to pull out weeds, bring them to the surface and drag them to the edge of the field. The amount of work required each day was evidently carefully regulated by the placing of the lord's plough as a marker at a defined spot along the lord's strip or land (presumably by the bailiff or reeve).

As the corn shoots appeared a further process was required, that of weeding.

> Also each virgater [i.e. 16 acre tenant] ought to hoe with two men, and each half-virgater [i.e. 8 acre tenant] with one man, and they shall hoe until the hour of noon, at the lord's meat once a day without ale, and after dinner they shall go and hoe in winter no more, and the hoeing of each man is worth 1/2*d*. daily. Total by estimation 3*s*.
>
> PRO 1898, 584

The cottars were also included in the weeding operation. 'And each of them shall hoe with one man, as half virgaters do at the lord's meat, as above'.

REAPING

> Also each of the said customary tenants and cottars shall come to the lord's great boon-work in autumn with all his family, except his wife and shepherd, and shall work at the lord's meat twice a day [i.e. The lord will provide two meals daily], without ale at noon [*ad nonam*], and with ale at supper, and the work of each is worth beyond reprises [*reprisa* = deduction] 2*d*. Total by estimation: 21*s* 10*d*. (*92c*)
>
> PRO 1898, 584

Summoned by the blowing of a horn the women and children would bring out the food provided by the manor in baskets called *frails* and the beer in special small barrels to the workers in the field, at *elevenses* and *fourses*. Apart from bread and cheese there would have been an allowance of mutton for each of the harvesters. Harvesting was generally reckoned to have been completed by Michaelmas (September). The corn was cut using an iron sickle with a serrated, saw-edge blade. The reaper used the sickle's point to divide the corn and then grasped the stalks below the bunch of ears in his left hand, inserting the sickle round them and drawing it back with a sawing motion (*92c*). The reaping action itself was simple and the sickle easy to use, but the constant bending was very tiring.

With the reaper worked a gaveller (Medieval English and Old French *Gavel* = a quantity of corn cut and ready to be made into a sheaf) who raked the mown corn into gavels or rows for bundling and tying into sheaves ready for stacking, carting or carrying. Barley was gavelled in this way and carted on wagons loose, but wheat, oats and rye were bound into sheaves, and possibly set up in *stooks*. The corn was cut about halfway down the stalk leaving the remaining straw to be removed from the field as a separate operation. The 1326 Customal makes no mention of stooks but there may have been a mixture of cartage and physical carrying of the harvest corn to the lord's barns, as indicated below.

POST–HARVEST ACTIVITIES

Also the customary-tenants ought to bind all the aforesaid corn, carry it into the barns [in the manor court], and stack it, without meat, and the work of each [virgater] of them is worth 12*d* and of each half-virgater 6*d*. Total by estimation: 19*s*.

Also each virgater shall come with two men after harvest, and each half-virgater and cottar with one man to gather straw for one day until the hour of noon, and shall carry the straw to the lord's court without meat, and the work of each of them is worth 1*d*. Total: 3*s* 4*d*.

PRO 1898, 584

One important activity which must have formed part of the straw gathering or occurred shortly afterwards (but is not mentioned in the 1326 Customal) was gleaning. Traditionally it was the women and children who were the gleaners, and went to the fields on an agreed signal, usually the church bell. The ears of corn were picked up and put in apron pockets and thence into sacks. An industrious family group might glean enough to make all its bread through the winter or feed the poultry at the messuage.

HAYMAKING

Also each of the customary-tenants shall mow the lord's meadow, at the lord's meat twice a day, and shall have of the lord's grass as much as he can lift with his scythe without aid, and the mowing of each of them is worth 3*d* a day. [The total is noted above with the rent under the tithe of 'medselver' i.e. 8*s* 3*d* at Midsummer of medselver – also see above, *Villagers*]. But the lord shall find a man to spread the grass, and the customary tenants ought to gather, carry and make into stacks [*tassare*] the said hay within or without the barn at the lord's will, without meat, except that the lord shall find a master-stacker, and the work of each customary tenant is worth 2*d*. Total: 5*s* 2*d*.

PRO 1898, 584

Hay was of critical importance for feeding the draught animals of the vill, not only over the winter period but also during the spring lean months up to April when grass was not growing. In the East Midlands only after Stocking Day (1 April) would animals be regularly put out to pasture on the Commons. Gathering hay from the valuable but somewhat limited meadowland (see *The Fields* above) took place in June or July before the corn harvest and depending on the state of the weather – 'making hay while the sun shines'. This was another intensive operation requiring the labour of the entire community. As indicated in the Customal, the hay was harvested using scythes (*14*) which were in general use by the fourteenth century. It was imperative that during the gathering and storage process the crop was allowed to dry out properly, hence the lord's provision of a man to spread the mown grass and a master stacker.

MICHAELMAS ACCOUNTS (29 SEPTEMBER)

At the end of the harvest season at Michaelmas there was a general settling-up of accounts in connection with the agricultural year. 'Also five virgat[ers] shall give the Lord at Michaelmas 2*s* 6*d* for a part of the work of mowing and lifting sheaves to the carts in harvest time released to them' (PRO 1898, 584-5). This probably refers to the corn harvest when it appears that the five virgaters (16 acres) had commuted their share of the back-breaking work of harvesting for a payment of 6*d* each.

Also each virgater of land shall give to the lord at Michaelmas 2 bushels [16 gallons or 7.274 dekalitres] of rye for the work of one holder of a plough released to them by custom. Total: 6 quarters, 2 bushels, worth in common years 27*s*, price of quarter 4*s*.

PRO 1898, 585

There are features about this penalty that are now obscure, not least how it had become 'a custom of the manor.' The careful tabulating of the value of the crop and its theoretical price 'in common years' suggests that the manor as elsewhere in the country was still suffering from the after-effects of the early century agrarian crisis, mentioned previously in this study. There had been a serious crop failure as recently as 1321, and evidently cereals were still subject to inflationary prices.

Rye (*Secale Cereale*) has been described as 'the poor relation of wheat grown usually on lighter soils' (Dudley Stamp 1955, 112) than those at Clapham. A clue may be that this producer of dark nutritious bread was the preferred bread grain in continental Europe, and thus perhaps the choice of the French lords of the manor who probably encouraged its cultivation and may indeed have introduced the crop in the first place. Certainly it did not appear amongst the carbonised grains of the sixth and seventh century Anglo–Saxon settlement at Clapham (see Chapter 4).

Another interesting feature of this penalty was that it was imposed on all those who were 'holders of a plough'. By deduction therefore it is possible to work out how many customary bondmen had ploughs in the vill at this period, the answer being 25 out of 31 virgaters.

> Also all the customary tenants who have not plough-beasts to do the boon-ploughing
> twice a year, shall come and do other work at the lord's will at his meat, and the work of
> each of them is worth ½d a day. Total by estimation 2s 1d.
>
> PRO 1898, 585

This is another penalty, this time working against those people without plough beasts (oxen in this instance). Again by calculation it would suggest that 24 bondmen lacked draught oxen, so that all the ploughing work had to be done by the remaining 7 virgaters (who may not of course have had complete teams of four oxen, see *13*). This is an extraordinarily low figure, especially bearing in mind the large number of ploughs in the vill at the time. It suggests that no less than 18 bondmen with ploughs had lost their stock of draught animals.

Between 1319 and 1321 England suffered from a devastating pandemic of cattle murrain (Platt 1978, 96) and it is clear from the Clapham figures that by 1326 the vill had not yet built up its stock of draught beasts. This lack of animals to work the ploughs is yet another reason for the abandonment of the West Field(s) at this period and their putting down to woodland.

SHEEP

> Also all customary tenants ought to wash the lord's sheep one day and shear them
> another day, and on that day they shall have all the cheese [*cas*] made from the said
> sheep, and if there be no cheese [*caseus*], they shall have bread and ale once a day, and
> the shearing of each customary tenant is worth beyond reprise by estimation ½d.
> Total: 12 *53d*.
>
> PRO 1898, 584

Pastoral activity in Clapham during the Norman period has already been mentioned (see Chapter 6 *Assarting and Pastoralism*). It is evident from the costings that 24 bondmen were involved in shearing, probably most of the half-virgater bondmen (*53*). As calculated earlier it can be estimated on the basis of the number of sheep that could be sheared in a day (40), that the number of sheep in demesne might amount to as many as 960 animals. In addition there were the flocks and herds of John Rous which in a deed of

1327, mentioned earlier, gave him rights to 'common of pasture for 600 sheeps and 30 beasts, oxen and cows, on the demesne pastures, feeding in the places where the beasts of the lord fed and rendering 8s 2d.'

There must have been many more sheep to the acre than the medieval maximum of two quoted by W.O. Ault (1972, 48), probably kept in the many small holdings of the various closes and enclosures occupied by the manor. However, most of the sheep were probably kept in the southern areas of the demesne where the old Norman sheep runs were located (on some of the worst arable land of the vill) and also north of the Wandsworth Road (see *The Fields*, nos 21-23). The still fairly extensive area of the Common (*78*) provided rough grazing for the customary tenants of the vill. Sheep were kept, of course as earlier, for their wool and use was made of ewe's milk for cheese, as indicated in the Customal. Lambing took place in late April or May and shearing in July.

Of other animals, horses for instance or pigs, there are no references in the 1326 Customal. Most peasant families kept a pig or two, which would have been killed in the autumn and smoked or salted down to provide meat over the winter. 'Pannage' or woodland pasturage for pigs, who fed on acorns from oaks and 'mast' of the beeches, could have been provided by the Clapham Woods, but there is no mention of it (*18*). There is mention, however, of rabbits at this period, which were valued as fresh meat. In February 1309-10 Thomas Romayn, Lord of the Manor, and Juliana his wife, had a royal grant of free warren (Redstone 1967, 39) although it is not established where it was located. It is possible that the warrens were in the field or woodland park embankment on land held by the manor (*78.1*).

One permitted use of the demesne woodland was the collection of firewood.

> Also each virgater of land ought to carry a cartload of brushwood for the lord's fire from his wood [i.e. Stockwood *78*], as often as he will, and shall have a faggot for each cartload, and the carriage of each cartload is worth 1d. Total of the value by estimation: 2s 10d, to wit [that is to say] each virgater twice in the year.
>
> PRO 1898, 583-4

These totals suggest that 17 virgaters were involved, perhaps only those who had carts (or were able to borrow them) and some sort of draught animal. The Cotton Calendar would suggest that the carts in question were open-sided pole-carts (*48*) pulled by a pair of oxen.

> Also each virgater or half virgater ought to carry [*averare* = by farmhorse or ox] to London or elsewhere where the lord wills within the county of Surrey all sorts of victuals for the lord and his household, and each carriage [journey?] is worth ½d. Total of the same by estimation: 5s 2d, to wit each of them four times a year.
>
> PRO 1898, 584

This amounts to something in the order of 10 trips a month from the manor carrying food by packhorse/mule/ox to perhaps supply the London market. Thomas Romayn,

Lord of the Manor *c.*1300-1313, was a merchant and senior official in the City. He, undoubtedly, had a residence there, which his daughter Margery and her husband William de Weston probably inherited. The amount of traffic from Clapham, however, might suggest a business arrangement rather than the cartage of merely domestic supplies.

The remaining sections of the 1326 Customal are concerned with what might be termed odd-jobs about the manor premises. 'Also all customary [*tenants*] ought to find a boy [*garcionem*] to serve the thatcher covering [*cooperienti*] the barn and the cowhouse when need be, and this work is worth yearly by estimation 12*d*'. The barn and the cowhouse, already mentioned earlier in the Customal, would have been outbuildings in the manor court sited inside the moated area.

> Also all customary [tenants] ought to repair suitably the walls about the said manor, to wit from a certain bank of the water on the south of the court to the churchyard, and the lord shall find what is necessary for repairing the said walls and the master-workman, and this work is worth yearly by estimation 12*d*. And in the same way they ought to enclose the lord's pinfold [*parfaldam*].
>
> PRO 1898, 584

It is unlikely that these boundary walls in the vicinity of the Manor House were of masonry: compacted earth or cob is much more likely. The reference to the water has been translated elsewhere as 'and repair the wall of the watercourse' (Redstone 1967, 414) (see Chapter 1 *A spring of soft water*).

The 1326 Customal and Extent of William de Weston has thus proved to be a mine of information about the life and economic structure of the manor and people of Clapham at a moment in time. It should be emphasised again, however, that this is not a complete picture of the vill. It only deals with the tenurial duties and rights of the village inasmuch as they affected the economic and administrative position of the manor and its lord. The document is a tribute to the careful work of the clerk who drew it up, and the bailiff who supervised its compilation. The day-to-day management of the peasant labour force and scheduling of its activities was the responsibility of the reeve (literally 'deputy'). If the bailiff represented the lord's interests, the reeve fronted for the villagers by whom he was elected. We do not know who the reeve was at this time. He is likely to have been a member of the community and possibly a free tenant. The work of organising the feudal management of even a relatively simple village organisation must have required considerable intelligence and organisational skills.

In reviewing the detailed picture of the lands of the manor and village that has emerged from this study one is reminded of the findings of A.R.M. Baker studying the field patterns and farming practices of medieval Surrey, Sussex and Kent. He detected a changing kaleidoscope of 'flexible rotations, subdivisions of larger fields by temporary fences for folding and sowing purposes, the early cultivation of legumes, the almost continuous cropping of some fields and the intermittent cropping of others' (Baker 1973, 429) but all at this date still under the firm control of the manor.

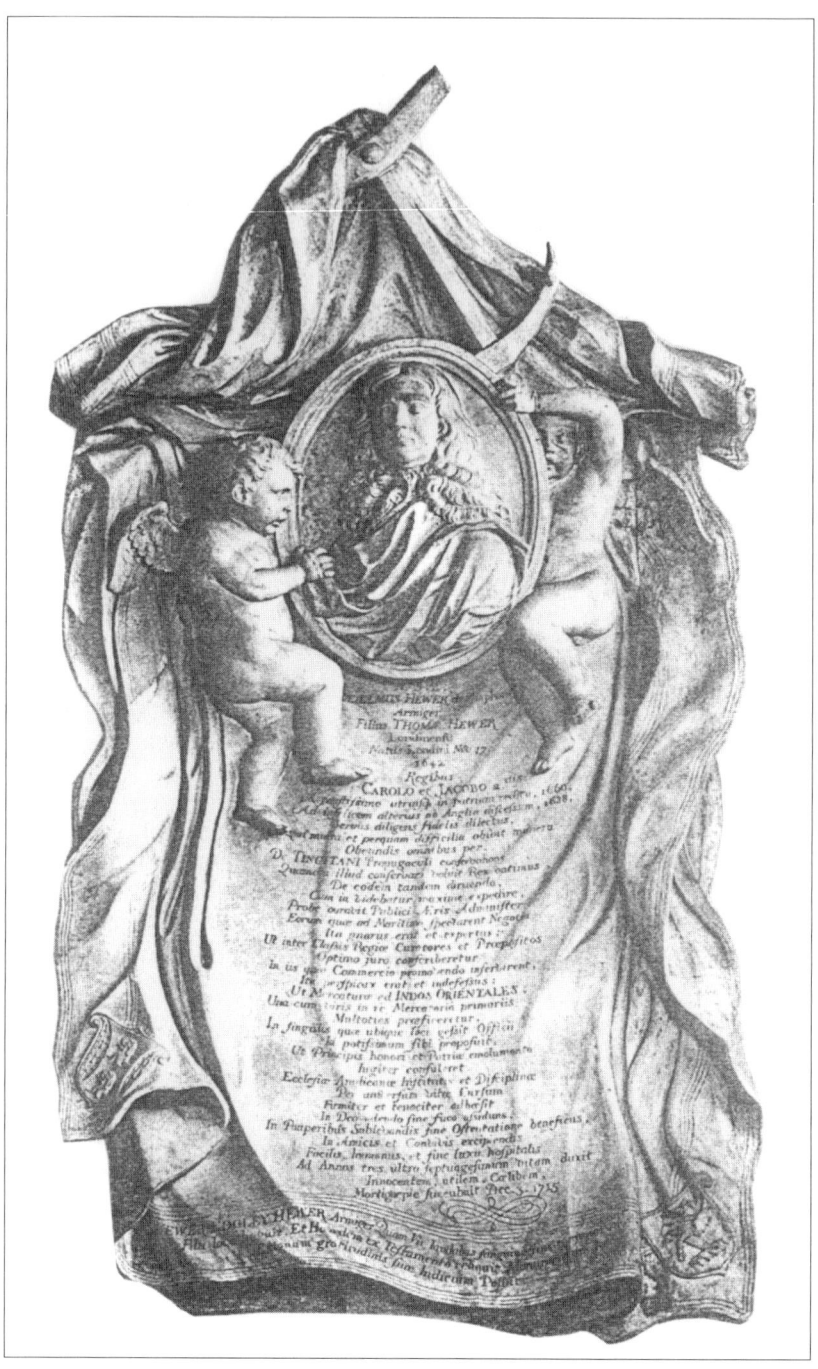

93 Monument to William Hewer in St Paul's Church, Clapham. Hewer died at the age of 74 in 1715 at his house, Clapham Place. A decent and kindly man, he took in his former employer Samuel Pepys from 1700-1703. Sculptor Francis Bird.
Photo: Gerald Harvey

9

PARADISIAN CLAPHAM

The House was built upon the Place
Only as for a Mark of Grace:
And for an Inn to entertain
Its Lord a while, but not remain.

　　　　　Andrew Marvell 1653, *Upon Appleton House*

THE LOST HOUSE

This evocative quatrain by Marvell with its veiled allusion to the transitory nature of human existence could equally well apply to the seventeenth century house erected by Dennis Gauden at Clapham. It was certainly a place of lavish meals and entertainment as well-nigh every contemporary literary reference testifies. Its life was also extremely short, exactly 100 years – a brief enough time for an ordinary house, let alone for the splendid mansion that Gauden built.

The expression of admiration, 'Paradisian Clapham' used by John Evelyn about Samuel Pepys' lifestyle as a guest in the House, is a memorial to one of the great lost residences of London. At the time of Pepys' stay, the House was owned by his former clerk, Will Hewer, and became the diarist's home on a permanent basis from 1700 until his death in 1703, and thus has earned a footnote in English social and literary history.

The circumstances of Samuel Pepys' life and interests at Clapham are referred to in a number of biographies, a notable recent study being that of Claire Tomalin (Tomalin 2002). It is not my purpose here to review again such well covered material, but to investigate the topographical and architectural evidence, such as it is, for identifying Clapham Place, the setting for Pepys' last years. Such a study presents something of a problem since the literary references are brief and the cartographical and architectural evidence is sparse and scattered. Hitherto, there has been no recognised pictorial representation of the building; indeed no agreement even on its exact location, notwithstanding the interest of historians in it over the last 200 years. However, the case is not hopeless, as will become evident as the investigation proceeds.

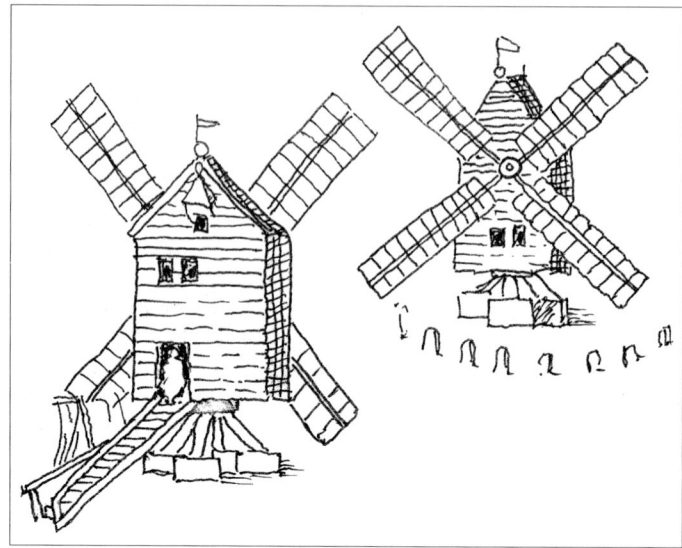

94a Front and rear of two traditional post-mills which existed on Finsbury Field, City of London in the mid 16th century. There were two windmills probably of similar type at Clapham. One was at the rear of the modern Windmill Hotel complex. An indenture of 1652 describes its contents and fittings. The other mill stood in the vicinity of Nightingale Lane. Both mills had disappeared by the mid 18th century. *H.J.M. Green after the Copperplate map of London c.1553-9*

THE CLAPHAM COMMUNITY

In the seventeenth century, there are two groups of documents which provide the first detailed, demographic picture of the Clapham community since the 1326 Customal and Extent. The 1628 Manorial Extent (State Papers – Domestic, Charles I, 154/93) has a detailed description of the demesne property with a list of all the named manorial tenants, the acreage of their holdings and the value of their rents. There is also an itemised rental from all other sources in Clapham associated with the manor. The 1628 Extent is complemented by a parish assessment of 1638 which lists the money payments due from each person for tithes. In all, this provides a fairly accurate indication of the social makeup of the Clapham community in the third decade of the seventeenth century.

Apart from the Lord of the Manor, Dr Henry Atkins, there was the rector, the Rev. F. Taylor and probably two other persons, Sir John Farewell and J. Worfield Esq, who might be described as gentry and perhaps leased Brick Place and the old manor buildings respectively. Below these were the independent farmers who cultivated the land either as tenants of the manor or as owners. They are designated as mister and number 25. They paid between 3*s.* and 5*s.* in tithes and the value of their land varied between £30 and £60 with holdings up to 265 acres. Below them were 23 husbandmen designated by a Christian name and surname paying 1*s.* or 2*s.* in tithes with small holdings of between 1 and 12 acres. Dropping down the social scale, next are 14 labourers, paying between 4*d.* and 8*d.* in tithes with roughly a one-quarter acre of garden. At the bottom of the social ladder were the 12 poor people of the community on outdoor relief (i.e. social security) of between 2*s.* and 3*s.* a week. They rented a small cottage and garden from the manor, as the medieval cottar had before them. These people, mostly elderly and unfit for work, were designated by their surnames and a prefix Goodman or Goodwife (Goody for short).

94b 'Rural scene near Clapham.' The layout of the buildings suggests that this is a mid eighteenth-century view of the Clapham Place farmyard (*colour plate 20b*). The projecting bays indicate that these structures were threshing barns. Note the 'swing-plough' in the foreground. *Courtesy ©Bernard Battley*

Using the Rogers demographic projection of 4.5 individuals per family and counting the poor on parish relief as single individuals, we have approximately 300 persons living in Clapham during the third decade of the seventeenth century, notwithstanding serious attacks of the bubonic plague in 1603 and 1625 which killed 23 and 37 persons respectively according to the burial registers (see the account of parson Coochman's death and that of his family in 1603, Chapter 8). Plague and various agrarian crises in the 300 year interval from the fourteenth century had kept the population levels relatively stable, but there had still been a rise from 184 persons in 1326 to 300 by, say, 1628, an increase of some 40 per cent.

There was consequently considerable pressure on land. In 1628 some 605 acres was farmland (arable, meadow, pasture and market gardens), common land amounted to 275 acres and there were still 200 acres of woods. Buildings and gardens amounted to some 40 acres with 50 acres taken up by public roads. This gave a total parish area of 1170 acres. These figures should be compared with the totals 200 years later in 1838 (Clapham Tithe Award) when there was still a considerable amount of countryside left in Clapham: farmland 53 acres; common land 202 acres; wood, nil; buildings and gardens 360 acres and public roads 74 acres. The Milne Land Use Map of 1801 still shows the essential features of the late agrarian landscape of Clapham (*colour plate 18*).

In the mid seventeenth century Clapham was still essentially a small Surrey village, but by the end of the century not only were suburban mansions beginning to be built around the Common but, in the village, housing was beginning to take on the character of metropolitan development of the day, the characteristic terrace planning. Church

This page and opposite: 95 Drawings by Joseph Powell *c.*1815 of views of Clapham Common. Published 1825 and lithographed by C. Hullmandel. *Reproduced from E.E.F. Smith and J.L. Howgego (1977) Joseph Powell and his drawings of Clapham*

95a Part of the Rookery slum, formerly north-east of the Long Pond. Circa 1740 stable yard complex built by Robert Thornton to serve his establishment on South Side, demolished between 1849 and 1857. Former coach-house with central entrance which was blocked up in the late eighteenth century and converted into two semi-detached cottages, the one on this side with a lean-to kitchen and wash-house extension. Village family in foreground with chicken. Courtesy © Bernard Battley

95b View of Northside, Clapham Common of post-medieval houses all now demolished. Right to left: Late seventeenth-century former farmhouse, gable-end onto the road; was a property of Clapham Place (*colour plate 20a*) – now under the garden of No. 5 Northside. The adjoining house also timber-framed with a jettied first floor is of early eighteenth-century date. The other houses to the west, one weather-boarded, are later eighteenth-century and early nineteenth-century. Courtesy © Bernard Battley

buildings along Northside of *c.*1714-20, are a fine example of such early development (*colour plate 19a*).

The topographical layout of Clapham village and its Common by the seventeenth century was substantially that of today. In terms of the ordinary villager's housing there had been dramatic improvements since the fourteenth century. The squalid longhouses had long been replaced by more substantial, often jettied, timber framed buildings, which, from the sixteenth century onwards, were increasingly clad in brick. Animals

now occupied separate byres, but the family still lived in one or two room cottages with garrets over for sleeping accommodation. The Powell drawing (*95a*) of a late seventeenth-century cottage with scullery outshut at the Rookery, Clapham Common (demolished in 1904) shows a typical, post medieval housing unit.

In 1650, widower Blacklock died and his household inventory survives. Amongst the furniture are tables, forms (benches) storage chests and barrels, two old bedsteads and flock mattresses with bolsters, a cupboard and the spinning wheel of his late wife. The kitchen equipment included a spit, andirons, pothook and bellows. No crockery is mentioned but there were wooden trenchers and ladles, an old frying pan, salt box, four pewter spoons and seven stoneware bottles. Relics of his old agricultural activities are represented by two old sickles, a flail and a pair of old shoes (Rudolf 1904, 44, 45).

Obviously, the manor and parsonage would be much better equipped, not to mention the manorial tenants and other incomers who were beginning to arrive by the later seventeenth century. Something of the lavish furnishings and fittings of Sir Dennis Gauden's house will be mentioned later. However, in this story of social and economic change, Clapham Place, the subject of this chapter, has a special place. Its erection marks the very beginning of the great flood of suburban mansions which were to become such a feature of eighteenth- and nineteenth-century Clapham, and the end of the rural idyll which so captivated John Evelyn and led him to term the village and its landscape 'Paradisian Clapham'.

THE ESTATE

The name of the Gauden establishment first appears on a London topographical map of 1730 by T. Bowles '*A Map containing towns etc 20 miles round London*'. Clapham the village is conventionally indicated by a church with a tower and spire. Beside it, slightly further west, and south of the Wandsworth Road, is a gabled house symbol marked *Clapham Place*. Strangely, this is the only evidence that we have of the contemporary name of the house, perhaps so designated to distinguish it from Clapham Court, the name of the Clapham Manor House.

The early history of this site has been touched on before in this study. It is situated more or less centrally in what had earlier been the West Field of Clapham, and was still referred to in a generic way as late as the eighteenth century as Clapham Field. It is interesting that John Aubrey picked this up on his visit in *c*.1700, but wrongly refers to its being in Battersea Field. As we have seen following the climatic downturn in the early fourteenth century with ensuing agrarian crisis, these lands were put down to woodland *c*.1320 and became part of the 70-acre demesne woods of Stockwood (also known as Lord Montague's Wood after a former manorial tenant). By the late sixteenth century, part of this woodland had been turned over for use as a 15-acre hunting park.

It would appear that the forerunner of Clapham Place started life as a hunting lodge in the woods served by a trackway (The Chase) from Wandsworth Road. The building first appears as *Brick Place* in a conveyance of 1503 from William Ireland to Thomas Marrowe who was, evidently, a tenant (Redstone 1967, 40). Under the same house name, it passed through various hands during the sixteenth century, including the Cokeyn family.

A considerable amount of former demesne land was vested in the property, which, in an inquisition of 1605, included 190 acres of arable, 54 acres of pasture, 32 acres of meadow and 45 acres of woodland: a total of 421 acres. Much of this land is shown on the early eighteenth-century Brayley map (*colour plate 20a*) and apparently formed the core of the Gauden, subsequently Hewer, Estate. In the Extent of 1628, the property appears to have reverted back to the manor of Dr Henry Atkins and was subsequently sold outright to Dennis Gauden (as he was then) who had had a small house in the village since 1648. In 1655 the parochial records indicate that Gauden had lodged money and legal papers in the parish strongbox, which suggests that this was the date when he acquired what was to be termed Clapham Place.

A survey of 1666 by John Coffin indicates that Gauden had also procured with the site of what was to become his new house, 432 acres, 3 rods and 22 perches of land, evidently all the property of the former Brick Place with a few extra acres (Batten 1827, 67).

The Atkins family, who were probably Royalists, were evidently in difficult financial straits during the Commonwealth period (it has already been noted how they leased out most of the former manorial buildings) and hence the outright sale of the former Brick Place. This was clearly an advantageous arrangement for Gauden, not so much for the house premises, but for the large agricultural estate which went with it. Gauden, who was at that stage a leading victualler to the Commonwealth Navy, was able to provide foodstuffs directly to the Fleet (at a considerable profit to himself) instead of having to go through middlemen. The estate, moreover, was usefully situated on the south side of the Thames within easy carriage distance to the victualling yards of the Navy at Deptford. In 1668, Pepys described Clapham Place as the 'victualling office' of the then Sir Dennis Gauden's business enterprise. The extensive farm premises evident in the Brayley and Rocque maps must date to this period, and will have included a substantial dairy providing cheese, to accompany the 'hardtack' of naval tradition. The story which Gauden put around that he had acquired the premises as a 'town house' for his late brother on the expectation that he would be elevated to the See of Winchester was evidently a polite fiction to cover a major business transaction!

With the folding of the Gauden business after his bankruptcy in 1677, later owners, notably William Hewer (d. 1715) and particularly the Hewer Edgeley Hewer family, did not feel the need to run such a large estate. Hewer divested himself of all except 60 acres, keeping only some arable land and meadow:

the produce being applied for housekeeping; the wheat for bread, the barley being exchanged or sold for malt for brewing, the beans and oats for feeding horses and hogs,

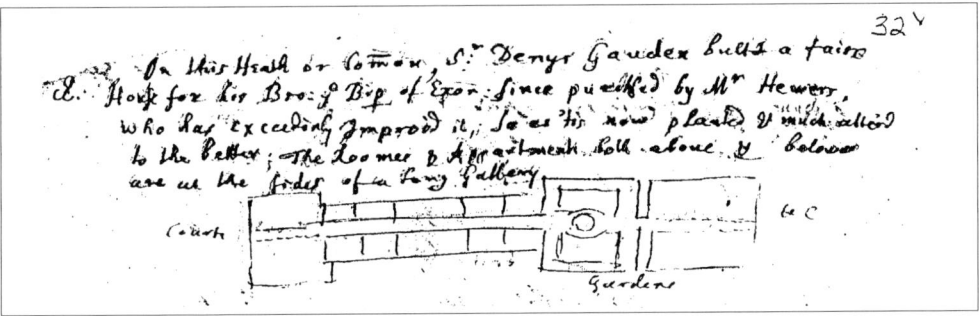

96a The only surviving plan of Clapham Place which appears in MS form with a scribbled note (see text) by John Aubrey (Bodleian 32v). The note appears in *The Natural History of Surrey (1719)*. Aubrey's visit to Clapham Place probably took place in the late seventeenth century. He evidently entered the house at the east end, passed down the ground floor gallery and out of the west door into the garden. It is from Aubrey that we know that it was a five bay house. *Courtesy of the Bodleian Library, University of Oxford*

96b The only definite view (north façade) of Clapham Place by John Ogilby's Road Map of 1675 'Road from London to Portsmouth'. It shows a two-storey symmetrical building with dormers in the roof and a central dome. The building is flanked by two towers with domed roofs. For significance see text. *Courtesy of the Society of Antiquaries of London*

and the meadow ground was partly grazed with some cows, horses and asses, and the rest mowed and spent in fodder for his cattle. The arable land was worth 20*s* per acre, and the meadow land 25*s* per acre.

Dale 1927, 236

What appears to be part of the Hewer farm buildings is shown on an eighteenth-century print of a Clapham farm yard (*94b*).

In addition to the agricultural land, there were a number of properties in the village which were retained by Clapham Place (which are shown on the Brayley map). One of these late seventeenth-century buildings survives, and is probably the oldest house in Clapham. No. 45 Old Town was formerly the end house of a terrace demolished *c.*1880 (*colour plate 19b*). It is of two storeys, rendered with a gabled tiled roof with a gabled dormer. The eaves have a dentil cornice. The ground floor front is modern but the interior retains an original dog-leg staircase with a closed string, turned balusters and square newels.

A house formerly on Northside (also shown on the Brayley map as belonging to the estate) is depicted on an early nineteenth-century drawing by J. Powell. It is very similar in character to the Old Town house, but has retained its jettied first floor. It would appear that the estate buildings of Clapham Place were constructed to a common design, possibly by the same craftsmen who built the main house (*95b*).

THE LITERARY EVIDENCE

There are first-hand descriptions of the Hewer house by three notable literary figures of the later seventeenth century: John Evelyn, John Aubrey and, of course, Pepys himself. In the cases of Evelyn and Pepys, it was a matter of diary entries (23 September 1700. *The Diary of John Evelyn*, E.S. de Beer (ed.); 25 July 1663, 27 July 1665, Pepys *Diary*, Latham & Matthews (eds) 1970-83). The rather later Aubrey notes were prepared for his *Natural History and Antiquities of Surrey* (*96a*). The M.S. folio of this work, now in the Bodleian Library at Oxford, is accompanied by a sketch plan of the house which does not appear in the printed edition. In 1702 the newly appointed Bishop of Carlisle, William Nicolson, also visited the house and described the Pepys library and collection which had been installed, with a description of the gardens (Tomalin 2002, 373).

As already mentioned, Pepys first visited the house when it was owned by Dennis Gauden (knighted 1667), victualler to the Navy. As a client of the Navy Board, he had a close and friendly association with its principal clerk, Samuel Pepys. Pepys called on Gauden at Clapham on 25 July 1663 for the first time:

> ... our first thing was to show me his house which is almost built ... I find the house very regular and finely contrived, and the gardens and offices about it as convenient and as full of good variety as ever I saw in my life. It is true he hath been censured for laying out so much money; but he tells me that he built it for his brother, who is since dead [the Bishop]; who, when he should come to be Bishop of Winchester, which he was promised,

to which Bishopricke at present there is no house, he did intend to dwell there. Besides with the good husbandry in making his bricks and other things, I do not think it costs him so much money, as people think and discourse …

Wheatley 1897, II 220-1

On another visit two years later, on 29 January 1666, when Pepys stayed overnight, he speaks of his pleasure walking in the gardens and reading a book in the later afternoon. On both occasions, he notes the large size of the household, the pleasant wife and 'many pretty children' including a son, a daughter, two nieces and other relatives. On this occasion, he slept in the 'best chamber like a prince' (Wheatley 1897, V 211-12). A third visit is mentioned on 23 January 1668:

At noon with my Lord Brouncker to Sir D. Gauden's at the Victualling-office, to dinner, where I have not dined since he was Sheriffe. He expected us: and a good dinner, and much good company; and a fine house, and especially two rooms very fine he hath built there. His lady a good lady.

Wheatley 1897, VII 290

It is of significance that Clapham Place was designated as the 'Victualling-office' indicating that Gauden was using part of the premises as a centre for his business operations.

John Evelyn, gentleman-scholar of many talents and (in particular) a gardening expert, became a close friend and correspondent of Pepys towards the end of his life. Evelyn's account of a visit in 1700 includes a description of the Clapham Estate, by then owned by William Hewer. He remarks that the house is 'very noble, and wonderfully well furnished … the Offices and Gardens [being] exceedingly well accommodated for pleasure and retirement' (De Beer 1955, V 427-8). This was no mean compliment bearing in mind Evelyn's first-hand acquaintance with most of the great houses of southern England at that period.

Nicolson's description of the Clapham House in 1702 is mainly devoted to a detailed appreciation of Pepys' library and collections which though of interest, do not concern us here (for an account see Tomalin 2002, 373.) Nicolson also admired the 'Gardens, Walks and Bowling-Green, Ponds etc answerable to the House', and the hedges of different heights and woods, bay, yew, holly and hornbeam; and he noted that Evelyn 'own'd himself the causer of a deal of Luxury in these matters' (Tomalin *ibid*). Evidently, these horticultural amenities, introduced by Hewer when he acquired the premises in 1677, were thus after a quarter of a century, of relatively mature growth.

Turning to the Aubrey references, these may belong to any date between 1673 and 1719 when *The Natural History of Surrey* was published. The earlier references in Vol. 1 rather suggest that Hewer was still alive at the time of writing (Hewer acquired the property in 1678) whereas Aubrey's notes in Vol. 5 make explicit reference to Hewer's recent death which occurred in 1715. The Bodleian M.S. copy (32V) has the following note scribbled over the schematic sketch plan of the property:

On this Heath or Common, Sr Denys Gauden built a faire House for his Bro: ye Bsp of Exor: since purchased by Mr Hewer, who has exceedingly Improv'd it, so as 'tis now planted & much alter'd fo the better; The Roomes & Appartments both above & below are at the sides of a Long Gallery.

The printed version (Aubrey 1719, Vol 1; 13, 14) follows the same wording with somewhat improved spelling and punctuation. In Vol. 5 (331, 332) there are some additional notes:

Mr Hewers is since dead, and has left the best part of his large estate to Hewers Edgley Hewers … In this House are still carefully preserved by Mr. Jackson an excellent Collection of Curiosities, much augmented by Mr. Jackson himself … which consist of various subjects relating to English History, Maritime Affairs etc. …

Following Samuel Pepys' instructions, John Jackson (Pepys' younger nephew and principal heir) subsequently catalogued and arranged the library and collection. In 1724, after Jackson's death, the complete collection was transferred to Magdalene College, Cambridge (Tomalin 2002, 380, 381).

County and local histories of the Clapham area from the late eighteenth century onwards tended to repeat the basic information about the House derived from Aubrey, and subsequently that of Pepys and Evelyn as their diaries became available. Daniel Lysons (1796, 162) states:

The Mansion-house of this estate which was pulled down about 30 years since, was a very magnificent edifice. Some of the rooms were wainscoted with japan, and a spacious gallery occupied the whole length of the house, both above and below stairs.

Another historian, but in this case a local man also writing within living memory of the final years of Clapham Place, added some important details, undoubtedly derived from first-hand knowledge. H.N. Batten pinpoints the date of demolition to 1762, and goes on to say:

The situation of the house was on the left side of the Chase, leading to the Wandsworth Road, with very extensive gardens laid out in the Dutch style, reaching to the property now Benjamin Brown's Esq. with one front to an avenue leading into what is now Wix's Lane. The house formed three sides of a square, the principal front looking to the Common.

Batten 1827, 66

Benjamin Brown's property in 1827 was the house known as the 'Cedars' built by John Jackson (aforesaid nephew and heir of Pepys) in the south-west corner of the estate after the diarist's death in 1703. The late E.E.F. Smith gives a date of 1718 (Smith 1976, 38) for the erection of this house, although from where he derived this information is not known. The date is critical since on it hangs the dating of the Brayley map (*colour plate 20a*).

The Grover History of Clapham (Grover 1887, 34) repeats almost word for word the text from Batten's and Lyson's histories. The study of early material (before 1700) by R. de M. Rudolf in 1904, is of value since he includes primary material from the parish records and other sources not covered by the earlier researches of Batten. In respect of the Gauden/Hewer Estate, all subsequent histories and studies of Clapham including the publications of E.E.F. Smith (Smith 1968, 1976, republished 1995), the Clapham Society (Jefferson Smith 1984, 1995) and Gillian Clegg (1998) have tended to repeat the material from these earlier works.

THE TOPOGRAPHICAL EVIDENCE

There are two important early maps which show the Gauden/Hewer Estate and the location of the house. The earliest is an estate plan of the property which I have termed the 'Brayley' map since it occurs as a coloured extra-illustration in a copy of Brayley's *History of Surrey* Vol. III part 2 (1841) in the London Metropolitan Archives (*colour plate 20a*). The drawing covers the north-east corner of the Common (here described as Clapham Heath) and the village of Clapham, and appears to show most of the holdings of the Gauden/Hewer Estate. It is colour-coded to show three distinct properties. Yellow indicates 'Sir R. Atkins Land' i.e. the manorial estate. Pink shows the buildings and immediate curtilage of 'The House', as it is described. Also included are certain agricultural lands to the east of the village and tenements within Clapham itself. Blue covers the outer gardens and fields to the north-west of the estate together with some additional properties within the village. The detailed significance of the colour-coding will be further discussed when the estate is considered in this study. Briefly, however, pink and blue appear to show the estate as acquired by Sir Dennis Gauden *c.*1655; blue shows the land sold off by Hewer and the Hewer-Edgeley-Hewer family subsequently.

The critical issue at this point is the date of the map. The two landowners' names mentioned on the plan, Sir R(ichard) Atkins (1689-96) and Sir W(alter) St John (1657-1708) might suggest a late seventeenth-century origin. However, the plan shows that a land transaction whereby the estate was given a parcel of land from the Common or Heath frontage in exchange for ground used to enlarge the churchyard in 1714 had already taken place (Batten 1827, 129). More significantly, the Cedars House, purportedly built in 1718, is also shown. This might suggest that the latest version of the map should be dated to the period following Hewer's death in late 1715 when the property had passed to Hewer-Edgeley-Hewer.

The second map was that prepared by John Rocque (commenced 1741 and published 1746). The Clapham survey was part of the second London Series which took in some 10 miles of the surrounding countryside. Not only were the Rocque maps reasonably accurate, but they also indicated the appropriate land use showing gardens, arable, pasture and rough 'waste' delineated separately. Unfortunately, the main house is at the junction of two sheets, of which only the western sheet actually shows part of the building (97).

In passing it should be noted that the Brayley and Rocque maps, together probably with the Aubrey plan, may all date to a period after 1715, some 50 years after the House

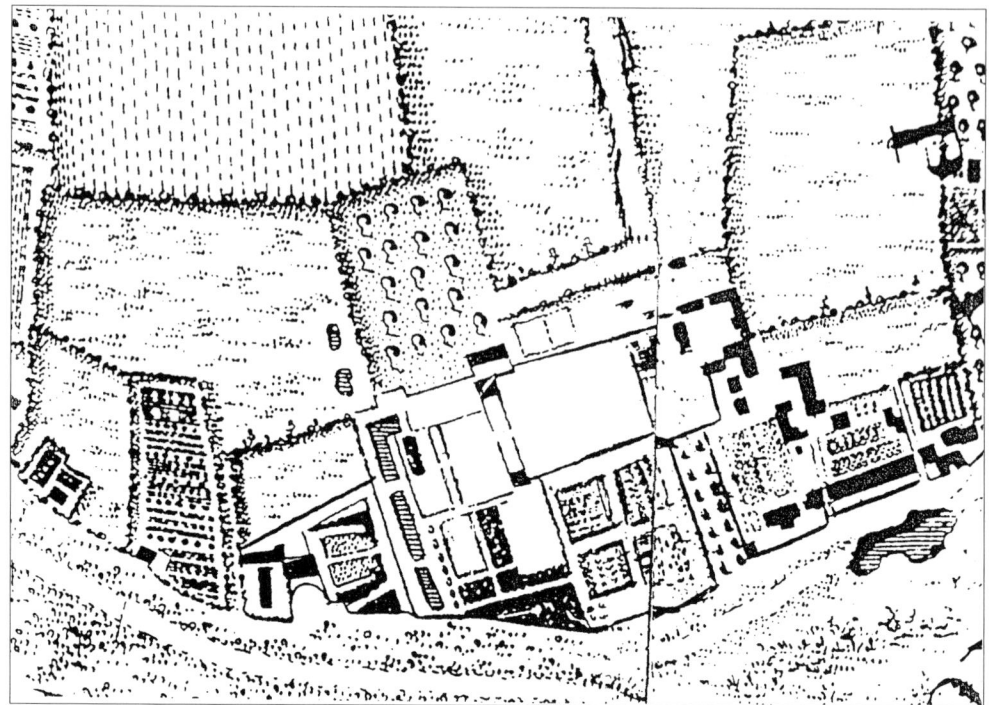

97 Plan of Clapham Place and its environs from John Rocque's map of London 'and the country near 10 Miles Round' published in 1746 and surveyed 1741-45. The vertical line represents a junction between two sheets, of which only the left-hand (western) side shows the house with its rear wings and forecourt (cf. *colour plate 20b*). The gardens are reasonably accurate (not so the fields at the rear) and shows their run-down state towards the end of the building's life (demolished 1762). *Courtesy of the City of London, London Metropolitan Archive*

was built. Indeed, it is possible that the Brayley map may be a copy of the survey recorded to have been made by Mr George Wass in 1725 for the Lord of the Manor, Sir Henry Atkins (Batten 1827, 133). By this date the grounds and estate were at their fullest development just before the property began to be broken up by the Hewer Edgeley-Hewer family and their successors. Indeed, if it were not for the coloured overlays on the Brayley map, it would not be possible to guess at the earlier development of the estate under Gauden.

These are the only maps which actually show the house and grounds in any detail. Large-scale maps of the vicinity do not appear again until some 40 years after the house had been demolished, although traces of the garden features and curtilage walls are still visible on the first accurate, detailed survey, the parish tithe map of 1838. Using this map as the basic template, it is possible in conjunction with the early Ordnance Surveys and other nineteenth century estate and parish maps, to work out the exact position of the house and features of the gardens and estate in relation to the present day topography of Clapham (*colour plate 20b*).

THE ARCHAEOLOGICAL EVIDENCE

This is not the type of evidence which in this instance might be expected to provide much information. The area of the Gauden/Hewer Estate is now intensively built over, with practically every surface paved or covered with well-developed gardens. The topographical survey indicates that the main block of Clapham Place lay under the road surface of the Chase and the adjoining properties on the west side of the road, Nos 5-11. These houses had been built *c.*1887 by the architect John Miller (Wilson 2000, 50) in the grounds of the Elms, now part of Trinity Hospice. The cellars of Nos 7 and 9 were inspected but were clearly contemporary with the development of 1887. The gardens were not suitable for archaeological investigation.

However, No. 13 to the north lies on the site of the west wing of Clapham Place. By a remarkable stroke of luck, the new owners, Mr and Mrs J. Rawlins, were constructing a new rear extension at the time of the investigation. The east-west foundation trench for the extension had been taken down 1m (3ft 3in) from the surface to remove the topsoil. At this depth, the deposits on the floor of the trench consisted of the seventeenth-century levels associated with the House. Cutting across them on a slightly different alignment to the 1887 house was the 0.58m (1ft 11in) wide foundations of the west front of the west wing of Clapham Place.

This was an extraordinarily fortuitous discovery confirming the postulated siting of the house and establishing the position and alignment of the west wing to within a couple of feet of its calculated position (*98*). The trench-built foundations had been set directly on the clay subsoil and survived to a height of seven courses constructed in English bond. The red hand-made bricks (2½in x 4½in x 9in) came, according to Pepys (Diary 23.7.1663) from the immediate area, almost certainly the brickfield described as Brick Mead and Brick Clamp in the Batten survey of 1827 and originally owned by Hewer. The joints were of white chalky mortar. On the west (garden) side of the wall, there was 0.38m (1ft 3in) of garden loam (layer 2). On the east (house) side of the wall, there was 0.56m (1ft 10in) of floor foundation, made up of gravelly loam and rubble with a layer of burning (layer 3). The original floors had been removed, probably for building materials in 1762.

The really important discovery which fixed once and for all the location of Clapham Place occurred in 2008 in service trenches by Thames Water in The Chase.

Fortuitously the narrow service trench on the east side of the street revealed the entire line of the east wall of the house, thereby establishing its exact position and orientation. The overall dimensions of the main block of the house as now calculated appear to be 110ft (32m) in length and 65ft 6in (20.25m) in depth. This should be compared with the same length, and width of 64ft (19.5m) of the dimensions of the house shown in the mysterious plan of a mansion designed by Sir Roger Pratt discussed in Chapter 11. So close are these dimensions that the postulated identification of the Pratt plan with the design of Clapham Place is enormously strengthened (*98* and *105a/b*).

Starting at the northern end of Clapham Place complex, the service trench revealed the substantial foundations of the curtilage wall of the estate (A) which ran east-west

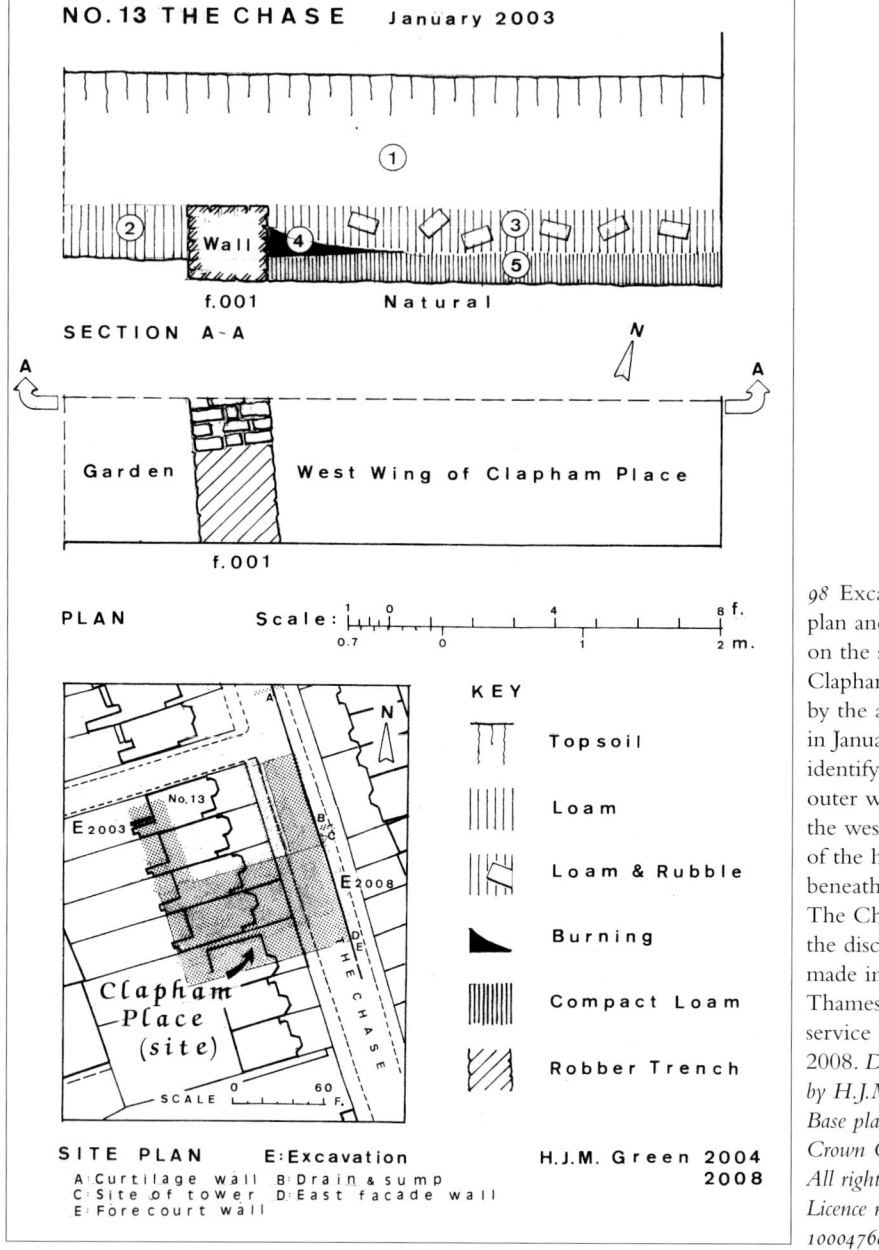

NO. 13 THE CHASE January 2003

①

② ③ ④ Wall ③ ⑤

f.001 Natural

SECTION A-A

Garden West Wing of Clapham Place

f.001

PLAN Scale:

KEY

┌┬┐ Topsoil

║║║ Loam

║║║ Loam & Rubble

◣ Burning

║║║ Compact Loam

▨ Robber Trench

SITE PLAN E:Excavation H.J.M. Green 2004
2008
A:Curtilage wall B:Drain & sump
C:Site of tower D:East facade wall
E:Forecourt wall

98 Excavation plan and section on the site of Clapham Place by the author in January 2003, identifying the outer wall of the west wing of the house beneath No. 13 The Chase. Also the discoveries made in the Thames Water service trench in 2008. *Drawing by H.J.M. Green. Base plan © Crown Copyright. All rights reserved. Licence number 100047602*

beside the north lodge (*Colour plate 20b* 5). Serving as a contractor's boundary wall at the onset of building works, it later would have functioned as an inner estate wall round the house, farm and garden nucleus.

The next major discovery, moving southwards down the service trench, was a drain and well feature (B). The bottom of the service trench broke through the brick roof into the void of a well 3ft 4in in diameter and at least 12ft deep from the surface of the road. This was evidently a major well in the east service wing of the back court and immediately adjacent to the kitchen and dairy premises. At a later stage it was evidently connected to a surface water drain running across the north side of the house serving the court and perhaps the farmyard. At this stage the well may have functioned as a sump (*101*).

Immediately south of the wall was the site of the northeast tower of Clapham Place, 17ft wide, and whose foundations had been robbed out perhaps before the end of the house's life (C). In the debris of the backfill of the robber trench was a chunk of the ground floor string course (*plat* band). This substantial feature with its vertical-coursed, plain-tile work and good quality cement finish clearly functioned effectively as a reinforced strap band holding the structural framework of the building (built of soft local brick) together at its base. A stucco cornice band would have done the same for the upper part of the building.

The main east wall of the house (D) was surprisingly thin, only 13½ inches wide, and hence the need for a strap band – no doubt another Gauden 'economy' noted by Pepys in 1663. It was built (like the curtilage wall) off a thick pad of mortar and rubble. One of the problems highlighted by the new discoveries is the depth of the semi-basement postulated on the basis of the Streater painting (*99*). If the 1660 ground level was approximately the same as today, the basement floor could have been no more than 3ft below ground level. The last feature of Clapham Place revealed by the service trench was the 9in wide foundations of the forecourt wall (E).

THE ARCHITECTURE OF CLAPHAM PLACE

When all the threads of evidence concerning the location, appearance and character are drawn together regarding Clapham Place, there is still a black hole. What precisely did the building look like? A house of this importance would almost certainly have been painted or drawn, but where is this missing evidence? Architectural historians have been assiduous over the last half century in ferreting out every possible representation of historic houses of this period and carefully attributing them. Discussion with authorities in this field indicated that there really was no archive in existence of unattributed major houses dating to the mid seventeenth century. All we had to go on was the sketchiest of plans by John Aubrey suggesting that the building was rectangular of five bays with a central corridor running the length of the building.

There the matter might have rested had it not been for the providential help of Adrian James, Assistant Librarian of the Society of Antiquaries of London. He suggested that the Ogilby Road Map of 1675 should be consulted. Sure enough, on the itinerary of the 'Road from London to Portsmouth' (page 15) there is a note '... pass by Clapham, and Sr. Denis Gauden's House 2F [furlongs] on the left ...'. The description is supported by a map (p. 60, pl. 30) which graphically illustrates the house in question. Now the buildings illustrated on John Ogilby's itineraries are not conventional symbols but actual vignettes, however schematic. As Ogilby puts it 'the mansion houses [are described]..scenographically or in prospect'. Clapham Place as illustrated (*96b*) was as it would have appeared across the fields from the Wandsworth Road (i.e. the north frontage). It shows a two-storey building with dormers in the roof and surmounted by a central dome. The critical features, however, are the two towers with domed roofs

Above and below: 99 Unidentified house, possibly Clapham Place showing the south front and garden layout. Painting by Robert Streater (attrd) *c.*1662-4

Above 99a General view of house and garden

Left 99b Close-up of house. *Courtesy of Sotheby Publications*

which flank the façade. These are most unusual elements in a building of the mid seventeenth century, and at last give us a diagnostic feature on which a search might be based.

The next stroke of luck occurred when Alyson Wilson, architectural historian of the Clapham Society, remembered seeing such a building illustrated in John Harris's *The Artist and the Country House* (1979, p.50, fig. 35). Harris's catalogue description is worth quoting in full:

> 35. Unidentified House with a great fountain
> Robert Streater (attrd.) circa 1662-4
> Oil on canvas

Called Eltham Place, Kent, this does not remotely resemble Eltham, a Dutch-styled house designed by Hugh May, but the front to the garden is obviously an immediate post-Restoration type. The two cupolaed towers behind suggest a new front to an earlier Tudor or Jacobean house.

Although the right foreground parts are obviously staged, the garden is probably a real one, with persons admiring the great fountain, and its pumping tower. The date of this painting is early rather than late 1660s, and this is the type of decorative overdoor that Streater might have painted.

Collection not known

Harris, the doyen of living architectural historians, is not to be faulted in either his attribution or diagnosis. When interviewed, he remembered that the illustration came from the catalogue of an unidentified London dealer, the painting having been sold to an unknown collector. Hopefully, one day it may be located, since the photographic quality might be better and lacks the colour which might be more revealing (*99a* and *99b close-up of house,* see also the reconstruction on the front cover and *100*).

Although there is no absolute, clinching proof at this stage that this painting shows the south façade of Clapham Place, the circumstantial evidence is very strong – the dating, style of building and, above all, the two Jacobean towers flanking the building on the north front, suggests that this is the lost house of Sir Dennis Gauden.

The building is 2½ storeys with dormers. The hipped, tiled roof has a flat viewing platform with either workmen or visitors in a central, balustraded area where the (later) cupola might be expected. There are brick chimney stacks on the corners of the flat roof. The brick façade with dressed, rusticated quoins and a platt band at ground floor level is of five bays. The central bay is wider than the others with a pedimented cornice and carved tympanum. The architraved entrance doorway is approached by a flight of five steps. The first floor window over the entrance is flanked by pilasters and carries a balcony. The flanking window bays have paired casement lights with architraved surrounds. The semi-basement also has paired, architraved windows which appear to have a sunken area in front of them. On the corners of the (north) front are hexagonal, brick turrets or towers rising above the roof, with leaded cupolas surmounted by weather vanes. The turrets appear to have stucco quoins and fenestration at each stage.

The gardens in the foreground are in the French style with an entire scheme of *parterres*, terraces and lesser garden areas subordinated to a central, house-orientated design. There is a central broad walk flanked by cruciform schemes with grass plats and central fountains. As at Clapham, the land falls away from the foreground. The pumping 'tower' to the left of the picture is in the right position to use the water from the stream which at Clapham passed into the garden in this area.

The general impression is that this view shows the domestic garden front at the rear of the building with the main entrance on the north side. If this does represent Clapham Place, it must be at an early stage of its development before the building was completely finished by the addition of a central cupola and a decision had been made to resite the main entrance on the south front with the principal gardens to the west.

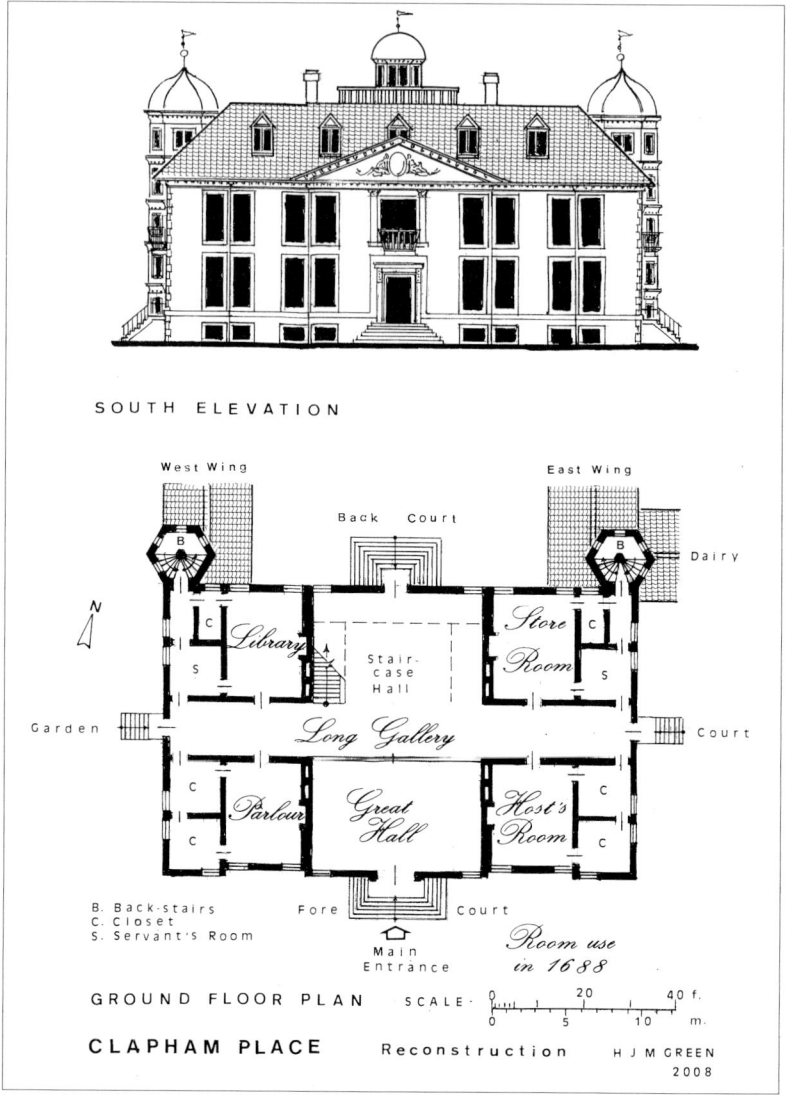

100 Reconstructed ground floor plan and south elevation of Clapham Place showing a conjectural arrangement of rooms, *c.* 1670. *Drawing by H.J.M. Green*

The final piece of evidence is the important discovery of the Probate Inventory of 1688 of Sir Dennis Gauden. The background and summary of this document is described below (see Chapter 10). If the earlier material (descriptions, maps, the Aubrey plan and the Streater painting, not to mention the archaeology) provides the architectural framework of Clapham Place, the Probate Inventory describes in detail each room of the house, its function and furnishings. On the basis of this collected material, it is now possible to provide a conjectural plan of the entire establishment and describe with some confidence the life of its occupants in its formative years during the late seventeenth century.

10

THE PROBATE INVENTORY OF SIR DENIS GAUDEN 7 JULY 1688

Il savio sa Trovar Tutto nel poco.
To the wise man a trifle may reveal all.

Anon.

INTRODUCTION

The discovery of this interesting inventory (listed in full below) was due to the Wandsworth historian, Dr Dorian Gerhold, who told me of its existence in the National Archives (probate 5/3027) in 2004. A search for comparable Probate Inventories for Hewer and the Edgeley-Hewer family, who owned Clapham Place in the first half of the eighteenth century, was unsuccessful.

BACKGROUND

Sir Denis Gauden died in June 1688 and was buried in the vault he had built in Clapham churchyard on 1 July. The probate inventory was evidently put in hand at once and the inspection completed on the 27 July 1688. The version here is the fair copy.

The picture it reveals is of importance, not only in terms of the arrangement and furnishing of the rooms at Clapham Place, but the state of the household and Gauden's financial position at the time of his death.

Gauden built Clapham Place and he and his family were in occupation from the early 1660s (see Chapter 9). Although he was a prominent city businessman and victualler to the navy, Gauden over-reached himself financially and was arrested for debt in 1677. In 1678 he was declared bankrupt, and on the 14 November of that year William Hewer wrote to Pepys that he had acquired the lease of Clapham Place from Gauden at an annual rent and had recovered 'goods and chattels etc' from the Sheriff upon a judgment of one Pilkington and others to whom Gauden was indebted (Tomalin 2002 438 fn. 23 quoting Brit.Lib. Egerton MSS 928, fol 229). By 1683 Hewer had evidently purchased the mortgage outright from Gauden.

For the first 17 years of its life when occupied by the Gaudens, Clapham Place was a happy family establishment, and after Gauden's knighthood in September 1667, a place of some social standing. All this ended in 1677–8 with Gauden's bankruptcy. The Probate Inventory thus reflects the state of affairs at the end of the second phase of the house's history. Hewer generously allowed Gauden to continue living with his family at Clapham Place, but they were clearly in reduced circumstances. In 1684, after Hewer moved from Buckingham St in Westminster, his mother Anne Hewer (who had been his housekeeper) took up residence in Clapham Place, evidently to keep an eye on things on behalf of her son; not a very comfortable situation for the Gauden family! In October 1685 Pepys paid a visit to the 'good Mrs Ewer' at Clapham.

The last mention of Lady Elizabeth (Mary) Gauden is in 1679, when she employed a young servant maid from Clapham parish (Rudolf 1904, 55). At some point between then and 1688 she must have died, since the inventory makes no mention of any apartment occupied by her, or any of her furniture or effects. Furthermore Sir Denis had clearly moved out of the family bedroom. However, Gauden still had a young adult family, some of whom were still at home, including at least two sons and probably more than one daughter. It is possible that at this point in the 1680s Anne Hewer came into her own, giving some measure of support to the stricken family and becoming a close friend – so much so that after her death in 1693 she was buried in the family vault of the Gaudens at Clapham (Dale 1927, 70).

CLAPHAM PLACE

The plan and general layout of the house has been deduced from a number of different sources (*100* and *101*). What the 1688 Inventory identifies for the first time is the actual function of the rooms and their changes of use following the family's altered circumstances, and consequent arrangement of furniture.

The assessors Wallin and Hull started work in the garrets in the roof space. The bedroom furniture for three persons (with the exception of the ironing table) is rather too grand for servants, who would normally have slept in the attics. The likelihood is that it was members of the family, and in particular the sons of the house who were moved up here from the first floor.

Moving downstairs to the Two Pair Stairs (i.e. first floor) there is a description of a main bedroom by the assessors which is not otherwise identified. This is curious since all the other rooms and their functions are described. It is probable that this was the living room of Mrs Anne Hewer who was occupying what was formerly the best room of the house, the Withdrawing Chamber. She was *de facto* (as representing her son's interests) the head of the establishment, but was probably too tactful to press the point. A polite fiction appears to have been maintained until Gauden's death in 1688, that he was 'master of his own house', and that Mrs Hewer was merely a guest! (*102b*)

The other main room on this floor, the 'Great Dining Chamber' was next inspected, together with the other dining room on the ground floor, which was effectively the family living room and known as the living parlour. Next the contents of several closets are described. At this period these small rooms were designed in suites of two: a dressing

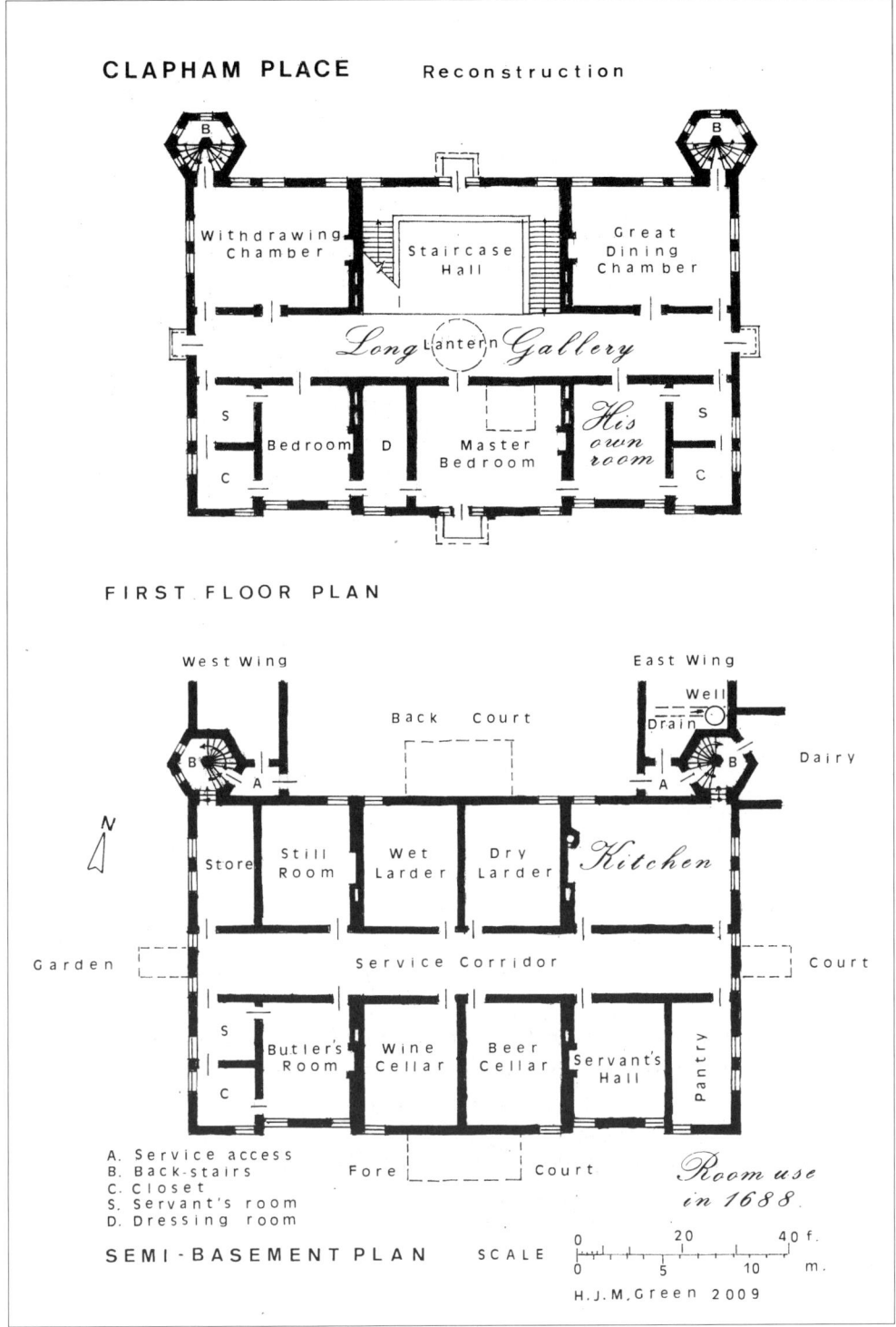

101 Reconstructed semi-basement and first floor plans of Clapham Place showing a conjectural arrangement of the rooms *c.*1670. *Drawing by H.J.M. Green*

102a View of gentlemen's bedroom with barber in attendance. Note French bed, dressing table and farthingale armchairs. *Le Barbier* by Abraham Bosse. Earlier seventeenth-century. *Courtesy of the Trustees of the British Museum*

102b View of Lady's bedroom with occupant at her toilet. Noble Parisian bed, farthingale chairs stand and andiron in the fireplace. One of five plates representing the senses, this one being 'sight', by the English printmaker Edmond Mannion *c.*1653. Pepys owned a set of these prints which he may have had at Clapham Place. *Courtesy of the Pepys Library, Magdalene College, Clapham*

room (sometimes doubling as a personal servant's bedroom) and a 'stool' room or lavatory. There appear to have been six of these suites on the ground and first floors of the house, together with a dressing room for the master adjoining the master bedroom in the centre of the first floor front. By 1688, apart from the stool rooms, which were provided with chair stools, most of these closets were evidently being used for storage of miscellaneous furniture and dining equipment. There are no signs of beds or other furniture for servants, either here or elsewhere in the main part of the house. It would seem that live-in servants had been replaced by local help from the village.

Still on the first floor the 'two rooms over the [Living] Parlour' were next inspected. They contained two beds, and the likelihood is that this was the girl's bedroom. It evidently included the adjacent dressing room no longer used by the master bedroom. Wallin and Hull then moved to the kitchen premises in the basement. There were a number of rooms here, but only the items in the kitchen proper and the contents of the pewter and silver canteens, together with the linen cupboard, are actually described. It raises the question of whether the other rooms had been emptied of their contents, or whether the Hewers had moved in their own furniture. On a wider level it poses the problem of what areas of the house were actually used by the family, whether or not they contained items of the Gauden furniture and fittings. Clearly communal spaces like the Great Hall and the Long Gallery were used by both parties. Perhaps other rooms like the Great Dining Chamber, while still retaining Gauden furniture, were not used by the family at this stage (*103b*).

Next the assessors moved back upstairs to complete the inspection of the first floor. 'In his own Chamber' is clearly Gauden' s own bedroom containing a comfortable bed, perhaps that moved in from the master bedroom next door after his wife's death. The likelihood is that this was the boys' former bedroom, whose beds had been moved upstairs into the garret space. It is significant that no fireplace or furniture is mentioned for Gauden's room, which would fit this location (*102a*). The first floor 'Long Gallery' is next covered. It is the only room where pictures are specifically mentioned, but it is otherwise minimally furnished.

'The Room over the Hall' is, by my estimation, the central first floor room with a balcony used as a former master bedroom by the Gaudens in happier days. Although still retaining its luxurious silk-quilted window curtains, the bed and other furniture had evidently been moved out and the room used as a storage space for chairs (possibly from the gallery). As already suggested, perhaps Gauden had the family bed moved in for himself next door.

The suite of rooms on the ground floor were next inspected in succession. 'The Host's Room', evidently a public reception room, is probably to be identified as the Common Parlour located between the hall entrance and the service entrance from the east court. This utility room would have doubled as a meeting place for members of the household, ordinary visitors, tradesmen, villagers and servants (who would be paid their wages here by the steward) and a cloakroom (hence the looking glass) with toilet availability for grander occasions with access from the Great Hall.

Across the ground floor gallery was a room described in the inventory as a 'Store Room'. This is apparently not a storeroom in the basement, but a large room containing

Above and below: 103 Two seventeenth-century prints of interiors of a kitchen (a) and a dining room with a family meal in progress (b). These views probably provide a good impression of everyday domestic life in the Gauden household. *From Thomas Burke's 'The English Townsman' (1946) figs 20 and 21*

a wide miscellany of household equipment and drapery, but no furniture. The likelihood is that this is the former 'Best Chamber' slept in by Pepys in 1666, now reduced to a lumber room. To such depths had evidently sunk the former famed hospitality of the Gauden establishment! I suspect that the bed and other furniture of this room were now used by Mrs Hewer in her room on the first floor.

Moving further along the gallery westwards towards the family part of the house was the Library. This may have started life as a nursery/schoolroom for Gauden's children, but by now was practically empty except for a book box, a writing desk and a Cypress chest containing rolls of various types of expensive fabric.

The foyer described as the 'Great Hall' was the last to be inspected, and was the central entrance hall entered from the south, with the main staircase on its north side and crossed by the lower ground floor gallery. Its main feature was a display of weaponry and, as was customary, rows of chairs against the side walls.

To round off the inspection of the main house there is mention of a few personal effects of Gauden, including clothing, books, arms and three gold rings.

The inventory of Clapham Place concludes with a visit to the Outhouses and the Stables. The outhouses referred to were almost certainly the east and west wings flanking the back court on the north side of the house. Most of the items are lumber, as is specifically mentioned, but there are suggestions that a live-in servant slept here, perhaps the only one in residence in 1688. The Stable was also probably in one of the wings of the back court. The items listed would only refer to one horse, but there is no mention of the animal itself, let alone a carriage or coach house. Likewise it is also significant that there is no reference to farm buildings, equipment or stock, all of which by this date must have been wholly under the control of the Hewer establishment.

FINANCIAL AFFAIRS

The matter of Gauden's debts and receipts do not form part of this study, and are not included here though they comprise a substantial section of the Probate Inventory. Most concern leases and mortgages at his former victualling yards at his premises in Deptford.

The most poignant clauses come at the end of the schedule and go to the nub of Sir Denis Gauden's financial difficulties. They refer to the debts incurred by him in victualling the navy up to the end of 1671, and the clincher that finally pushed him into bankruptcy, namely victualling the garrison at Tangier until October 1677. The staggering amount of £310,695 16s. 7d. owed to Gauden by the Crown was apparently never paid. Charles II's attitude to naval (indeed all business) affairs was 'arbitrary and capricious' (Tomalin 2002, 358) and in any case he died in February 1685, ending any possible hope of repayment. Quite apart from the claims of friendship, both Hewer and Pepys must have felt some degree of responsibility, due to their official positions at the Admiralty, for this situation. It goes a long way to explain their subsequent generous treatment of Gauden at a personal and private level.

CONCLUSION

After Gauden's death and his own resignation from the Admiralty Board in early 1689, Hewer moved to Clapham to take up residence at Clapham Place. His mother, Anne, who earlier had been his housekeeper in Buckingham Street, left Clapham Place and was provided with a 'little house' in the village of Clapham by 1690, dying three years later (Latham & Matthews, Vol 10, 1970-83, 182). The little house may have been that near the church which the Gaudens had owned 50 years earlier, and was still part of the Clapham Place Estate.

Reading between the lines of the terse legal terminology of the Probate Inventory, it is evident that we are looking at the wreck of a once prosperous establishment and the impoverishment of its owners. However, with these reservations, the 1688 inventory fleshes out and vitalises the lifestyle of a typical, wealthy upwardly-mobile household of the period in a remarkable way. What might otherwise have been a very schematic, indeed hypothetical, plan form for the Clapham Place house is given architectural definition and social immediacy of special importance. It is possible to reconstruct the life and cultural setting of each room and circulation space of the house, and their changing fortunes at a critical period of its history. Under the next occupier, Hewer and the Edgeley-Hewer family, Clapham Place would once again become an important centre of cultural and social life in London, but never again would the intimate domestic life of the household be seen with the clarity supplied by the Probate Inventory entries of 1688.

THE INVENTORY

A true and perfect inventory of all and everyone of those goods, chattels and credits of Sir Denis Gauden, Knight late of Clapham in the county of Surrey, deceased: examined, valued and assessed this 27th day of July 1688 in the fourth year of the reign of our sovereign Lord James II of England, Scotland, France and Ireland, King, Defender of the Faith: and by us Samuel Wallin and John Hull as follows, viz:

In several garrets
Firstly: velvet hangings for 3 beds;
Bed linen;
3 feather beds;
Bolsters;
Linen pillows;
Blankets;
2 rugs;
4 quilts;
Chests;
Close-stools;
Press table.   Total: £14-16-4

Notes

Velvet – The velvet frequently mentioned in the inventory appears to refer to a plain woollen velvet (Thornton 1978, 112).

Feather Bed – A mattress in a bag of canvas ticking filled with feathers, as would have been the bolsters and pillows.

Quilts – Probably Dutch cotton coverlets (Thornton 1978, 179).

Close-stools – chair stools. A *commode* taking the form of a box or chair with a padded ring-like seat beneath which a moveable pewter pan or chamber pot was fitted.

Press table Ironing board or table for pressing linen tablecloths and napkins (Thornton 1978, 286).

Two Pair Stairs (first floor)

Item: velvet quilted bed-hangings;

Bedstead;

Feather bed;

Pillows;

2 quilts;

5 cane-seated chairs;

Cushions;

Table (stained);

Looking glass;

2 hanging shelves;

Bellows;

Chimney irons;

2 tables;

2 chairs. Total: £8–8–0

Notes

Room curtains – In the absence of punctuation it is difficult to differentiate at times between wall-hangings, bed-hangings and window curtains.

Cane-seated chairs – these became popular after *c.*1664, and required cushions (Thornton 1978, 202).

Hanging shelves – these were fixed to the wall and appear to have been used as a substitute for dining room sideboards

Looking-glass – this was often suspended between two windows and accompanied by a table, chair and candlestands formed a dressing suite (Thornton 1978, 231).

In two dining rooms

Item: wall hangings;

12 chairs;

3 tables;

2 hanging shelves;

2 carpets;

Earthenware;

Glasses;

Window curtains of velvet lined with silk quilt.   Total £13–12–0

Notes

Hanging shelves – See above. This item seems to appear only in rooms where food was being served.

Window curtains – curtains using silk material occur from the mid seventeenth century in England as effective blinds against the sun and matching the rest of the upholstery. The only other room at Clapham Place with this expensive feature was the former master bedroom (Thornton 1978, 140).

Several closets

Item: wall hangings;

Tables;

Desks;

Chair stools;

Pewter pan;

3 brass candlesticks;

8 Pictures;

Alabaster images;

3 trunks;

2 pestles and mortars;

Scales and scale weights;

Knives;

Glasses;

2 (window) curtains;

Iron;

Wooden ware.   Total: £5–18–6

Notes

Closets – See Clapham Place. Apart from the chair stools and pewter pan indicating the use of stool rooms, there are a number of references to specialised equipment and utensils suggesting the consumption of food and drink requiring cutlery and glasses. Of greater interest and clearly referring to the dressing rooms for Gauden and his wife which doubled as *cabinets privés* (or secluded private apartments) are the mention of pictures (probably family portraits) and, surprisingly, alabaster images. If these latter were religious rather than 'classical' marble busts, it is a reminder that Elizabeth Gauden, 'a good lady' (Pepys' diary entry for 23 January 1668) was a pious woman who kept up an 'intense seraphic correspondence' with Simon Patrick, a Protestant Divine, who was Rector of St Paul's Covent Garden (Harris 2002, 155).

In two rooms over the parlour
Item: 2 bedsteads;

3 feather-beds;

Bolsters;

Bed-hangings;

Carved bed (head);

4 blankets;

2 rugs;

Quilt;

Table box;

5 cushions.   Total: £8–7–0

Notes

Bedsteads – The presence of two beds suggests a children's room, almost certainly that of
the Gauden girls. The beds had bed-hangings and were probably of French type, i.e. a
plain rectangular box framework with curtains fixed to the top rail (Thornton 1978,
160). One of the beds had a carved headboard, if this does not refer to an entirely
separate bed.

Table box – Probably a games board for backgammon, taking the form of a box with
two tray-like halves hinged so as to open out. When closed the box held the 'pieces'
or 'men' (Thornton 1978, 231).

In the kitchen (103a)
Item: range fender;

Other irons;

Chimney Jack weight;

2 spits;

6 candlesticks;

Pestle (and) mortar;

2 stoves;

Brass pot;

Table;

Chairs;

Wooden ware.   Total: £8–14–6

Pewter
Item: 391 lbs of pewter (at 8*d* per *lb*).   Total: £13–18–0

Linen
Item: 44 pairs of sheets;

31 tablecloths;

270 napkins;

26 pillowcases;

55 towels;

Sideboard (table) cloths.   Total: £17–4–6

Silverware

Item 20lbs 4oz weight of plate.   Total: £25–3–0

Notes

Kitchen – pewter, linen and silverware. All the items tabulated under these headings appear to have been kept either in the kitchen or in locked storage rooms adjacent in the basement.

Fire place equipment – includes chimney jack weight, fire irons and spits, indicating the operation of a mechanised jack in front of an open fire. The mention of a range fender indicates that the fire itself burnt coal and was probably of a single manger or iron basket type. The risk of cinders falling from the fire into the kitchen necessitated the use of a fender often provided with flat bars along the top to carry pots (Wright 1964, 69).

Stoves – Possibly freestanding, tiled 'Dutch' stoves.

Wooden ware – 'treen', turned wooden bowls, spoons etc.

In (his) own chamber

Item: Printed wall hangings;

Cloth bed-hangings;

Bed with double vallour (satin) bedspread;

7 'Court' chairs;

Linens;

9 cushions;

Screen;

2 close-stools;

Quilted blankets;

Table.   Total: £13–18–0

Notes

'Court chairs' – Perhaps wooden sgabello stools popular in Caroline court circles, with carved legs and back. They were evidently used with cushions.

Printed hangings – suggests the use of Indian painted cottons (callico or chinters) for wall hangings. Pepys brought 'chintes' to hang in his wife's study in 1663 (Pepys' Diary 5 September 1663).

Bedclothes – double vallour (ie velvet satin) bedspread and quilted blankets were probably necessary for Gauden in this unheated bedroom.

In the Long Gallery

Item: 6 pictures;

2 stands;

2 dishes.   Total £4–6–0

Notes

Pictures – Large portraits of high-ranking friends and relations were commonly hung in the Long Gallery, and Pepys had a collection of such hung in his library in Buckingham Street, which would later have been transferred to some such context at Clapham Place (Tomalin 2002, 43, 44).

Stands and *dishes* – The stands may have started life as simple candlestands used for dressing room toilet activities, but were evidently used here to support decorative plates of slipware or Majolica (Thornton 1978, 278).

In the Room over the Hall
Item: velvet window curtains;
lined with silk quilt;
6 chairs;
'Holland' plaited matting;
Bellows;
Trunk.   Total: £6–1–6

Notes

Window curtains – The survival of the Gauden's expensive bedroom curtains has already been noted. The hanging arrangements are not mentioned.

Holland matting – Plaited in strips and secured by cross-stitching giving a quilted appearance for carpeting (Thornton 1978, 116).

In the Host's room
Item: Holland wall-hangings;
Looking glass;
Velvet curtains;
(Fabric) covered chairs;
Carpet;
'Press' screen.   Total: £2–3–6

Notes

Holland hangings – for use of plaited 'Holland' matting see previous entry.

Covered chairs – these were probably the ubiquitous 'farthingale' chairs with covered seat and back (Thornton 1978, 186).

'Press' screen – 'Press' as perhaps in 'pressed together' referring to a folding screen.

In the Store Room
Item: 3 warming pans;
Kettle;
Skillet;
Skimmer ladle;
4 brass candlesticks;

3 pairs of snuffers;

Grater;

2 andirons;

2 pairs of (fire) dogs and other irons;

4 Holland quilts;

Feather-bed bolster;

9 pillows;

2 rugs;

Bedshirt;

2 green carpets;

Dimity and calico curtains;

Some wooden and ironware horse furniture;

Fittings (furniture) for velvet curtains;

3 carpets;

Mantles.   Total: £7–8–0

Notes

Warming pan – flat, lidded dish of brass with long handle. When filled with coals or embers would be used to air beds.

Skillet – Three-legged brass or iron saucepan with long handle used for cooking food over an open fire.

Skimmer ladle – flat perforated dish with handle used for separating the risen cream from the milk.

Snuffers – scissor-like implements used for snuffing out candles or rushlights.

Andirons and dogs – Although there is a distinction in the inventory between these two items, it is not clear where the differentiation lay. Both consisted of a front pillar standing on two feet with an iron bearing-bar (*billet*) stretching backwards and ending in a third support. Positioned either side of a fireplace the andirons/dogs supported the burning logs (*102b*). In the kitchen the uprights were notched to carry spits for cooking between them. The ornamental pillars of the fire-dogs were mostly made of brass, and it was perhaps these designed for the best rooms of the house that were distinguished as andirons (from the French *l'andier*). (Thornton 1978, 260).

Holland quilts – Fine quilts of cotton were imported by the Dutch at this period (Thornton 1978, 179).

Feather-bed bolster – A bolster stretched across the full width of the bed and the pillow rested against it.

Bedshirt – The only reference to (male) nightwear in the inventory.

Green carpets – Not necessarily floor carpets, but might refer to any cover that lay flat. The likelihood is that the items here were of a plain woollen stuff from north-eastern France (Thornton 1978, 114).

Dimity and calico curtains – Dimity was a stout cotton cloth, woven with raised stripes and fancy figures, but used undyed for hangings. For discussion of calico see under 'In (his) own chamber'.

Mantles – A shelf or 'mantel-tree' became a feature of chimney-pieces in the last decades of the century; hence our mantelpiece (Thornton 1978, 265).

In the library
Item: 2 chairs;
Trunk;
Secretaire.   Total: £0–10–0

Notes

Trunk – There is no mention of bookcases. Gauden obviously preferred the older system, going out at this period, of storing valuable books in a chest (Thornton 1978, 306).

Secretaire – Writing desks consisting of a box-like nest of drawers were enclosed in the front by a flap that dropped down to form a writing surface. Since no table is mentioned, a stand would have been provided. (Thornton 1978, 312).

In the cypress chest
Item; a pair of tapestries;
5 carpets;
Calico curtains.   Total: £7–17–6

Notes

Cypress chest – The chest (with a flat lid) may have been made of cypress wood. However, since chests were normally covered with fabric, it is more likely that it refers to the material itself. The textile fabrics originally from Cyprus known as the 'satin Cypres' (1603) resembled 'cobweb lawn' or 'crape' (1722) (Shorter OED 1973).

Tapestry – This is the only mention of this expensive woven fabric in the inventory, as is perhaps reflected in the high value of this group of items. The source and type of the two tapestry pieces is unspecified, but given their storage location they are hardly likely to be wall-hangings of any size. Perhaps made up of small panels they may have been intended as firescreens, as became popular in the late seventeenth century (Thornton 1978, 107).

Calico curtains – see note under 'In (his) own chamber' above.

In the great hall
Item: 13 chair-stools;
3 halberds.   Total: £1–3–0

Notes

Chairs/stools. – These may be separate items, but perhaps represent a composite description of a form of upholstered chair with a low back known as a 'back stool' (*102a*), here called a 'chair-stool' (Thornton 1978, 185).

Halberd – A Civil War weapon, a combination of pike and axe which was the sergeant's badge of rank.

Personal Effects
Item: wearing apparel,
both linen and woollen;
Books;
Arms;
3 gold rings.   Total: £16-9-0

Notes

This group of personal effects of the late Sir Denis Gauden may have been stored anywhere in the house, but most probably came from the trunk in the 'room over the hall', i.e. the former master bedroom of the Gaudens.

Books – These may have come from the trunk in the library.

Arms – These may have comprised a dress sword, pistols and perhaps ceremonial armour such as a 'gorget'.

Gold rings – These may have included a wedding ring, a signet ring and perhaps a mourning ring.

In the outhouses
Item: table;
Hangings;
Bedstead;
Blanket;
11 chairs;
Screen;
Lumber.   Total: £1–18–4

In the stables
Item: horse saddle;
Bridle;
2 saddle cloths;
2 halters.   Total £5–0–0

Notes

Horse furniture – Other items were kept in the 'store room'. The items listed here would refer to only one animal. In his heyday Gauden maintained a coach (Pepys' *Diary* 25 July 1663) but by 1688 this had gone together with all the animals: another casualty of the 1678 bankruptcy no doubt.

Total value £211-16- 4

10th November 1688
Benjamin Gauden, juror,
truthfully makes this inventory

in the presence of Richard Raines
By means of
Abraham Nixon & Co, publisher.

Notes

Inspection and publication of inventory – The initial inspection and assessment, carried out on the premises by Samuel Wallin and John Hull on July 1688, collected the basic data in note form, which was then produced in a finished copy on 10 November 1688 by Abraham Nixon & Co, who appear to have been acting as auditors.

Witnesses – The inspection appears to have been monitored and signed by Benjamin Gauden and witnessed by Richard Raines. Benjamin Gauden, eldest son of Denis Gauden, was aged 46 in 1688 (born late March 1642 and baptised 31 March 1642 at St Mary at Hill, City of London). He was still living at Clapham at this stage and did not leave until *c.*1690 (Dale 1927, 223-4).

11

CLAPHAM PLACE &
ROGER PRATT

'Spoiling a custard to save an egg'

Trad. (Anon.)

A MYSTERIOUS DRAWING

In the Pratt archive preserved at Ryston Hall, Norfolk (the family estate since the seventeenth century) is a notebook described by R.T. Gunther in 1928 as 'a Tanner's Fly Almanack for 1672'. It is not clear whether the date refers to the date of publication of the almanac, or more probably, the date of the main entries which contain material from early 1671 to the end of 1672. The contents comprise 'numerous notes on building, farming, finance and a rough sketch plan of Ryston Hall, on 85 leaves' (Gunther 1928, 301). R.T. Gunther, one of the few scholars permitted to examine the 13 M.S. notebooks of Pratt, gave this particular volume the letter J. The sketch plan is of particular interest since it is the only drawing of its type in the notebooks, and for the last 70 years has been firmly identified, on the attribution of Gunther, as an early sketch plan of Ryston Hall 1671 (Gunther 1928, 189).

The interest of this purportedly 'Ryston Hall' plan for our purposes in this study is that it bears a marked resemblance to the reconstructed Clapham Place design discussed earlier. Any possible connection is likely to be indirect and the evidence circumstantial, but in view of the possible importance of such an identification, it requires further examination.

THE RENAISSANCE MAN

Sir Roger Pratt (knighted 1668) was an important gentleman architect in the later seventeenth century (*104*). Consequently he has received considerable attention from architectural historians, not least T. Mowl and B. Earnshaw, who have attempted to reconstruct the likely social and professional background of Pratt, and in particular his relationship with the architectural genius of that age, Inigo Jones (Mowl and Earnshaw 1995, 55). Pratt was away travelling on the continent during the Civil War, only returning

104 Sir Roger Pratt, architect,
by Sir Peter Lely (1668 or
later). *Taken from R. T. Gunther,*
The Architecture of Sir
Roger Pratt *(1928), frontispiece*

in 1649 at the age of 29. With a head buzzing with classical architectural concepts, particularly Palladian, he evidently sought out Inigo Jones, and became involved with the great man on his last important architectural project, Coleshill House in Berkshire. Jones died in 1652, but Pratt continued working on this project for his kinsman, Sir George Pratt, completing the ceilings and generally fitting up the house interior *c.*1657 to 1660. It appears that the revolutionary Renaissance design of Coleshill, formerly attributed to Pratt, is actually that of Jones. The young impressionable Pratt evidently considered the house a touchstone of good design, as is evident in an observation in November 1664 (Mowl and Earnshaw 1995, 50). Coleshill is also of importance in this study because it bears the closest resemblance in plan of any of this period to that of Clapham Place. Pratt went on to design on his own account four great houses ending with Ryston in 1668-1673, each representing a development of his architectural ideas from the Coleshill model.

IDENTIFYING THE PLAN

Notebook J in the Ryston Hall archive contains notes and accounts relating to this house in 1671-2 when it was nearing completion. The 'early sketch plan' is on page 85 on the last sheet of the notebook and follows notes on farming matters dated 16 September

1672 and the tiling of fireplace surrounds in the Great Parlour, Withdrawing Rooms and Bedchambers at Ryston (notebook J page 84v). It is hardly credible therefore that in this position in the book, if any sequential process is followed, this can be an 'early sketch plan' when the Ryston project was already effectively finished, with only some small fitting out jobs to complete. Furthermore the plan bears no resemblance whatever to the recorded plan of Ryston (Gunther 1928, 166). Nor does the sketch appear to relate to the other known layouts of Kingston Lacey (1663-5) Horseheath (1663-6) and Clarendon House (1664-7) designed by Pratt.

The sketch plan in notebook J fills an entire sheet with two annotations, and is untitled, contrary to the implications of Gunther's description in his publication. He has redrawn the plan, tidying it up and removing corrections in the original. In the process some key measurements have been omitted or misinterpreted. A photocopy of the original kindly provided by the Norfolk Record Office (*105a*) is accompanied here by a redrawn plan to scale with the original measurements (*105b*).

RECONSTRUCTING THE SKETCH PLAN

The drawing is a freehand ink sketch roughly in scale lineally, but not in depth, where it is compressed rather like the Aubrey sketch plan. Indeed Pratt must have been aware of this since he has scratched out the rear wall and moved it out, in part to accommodate

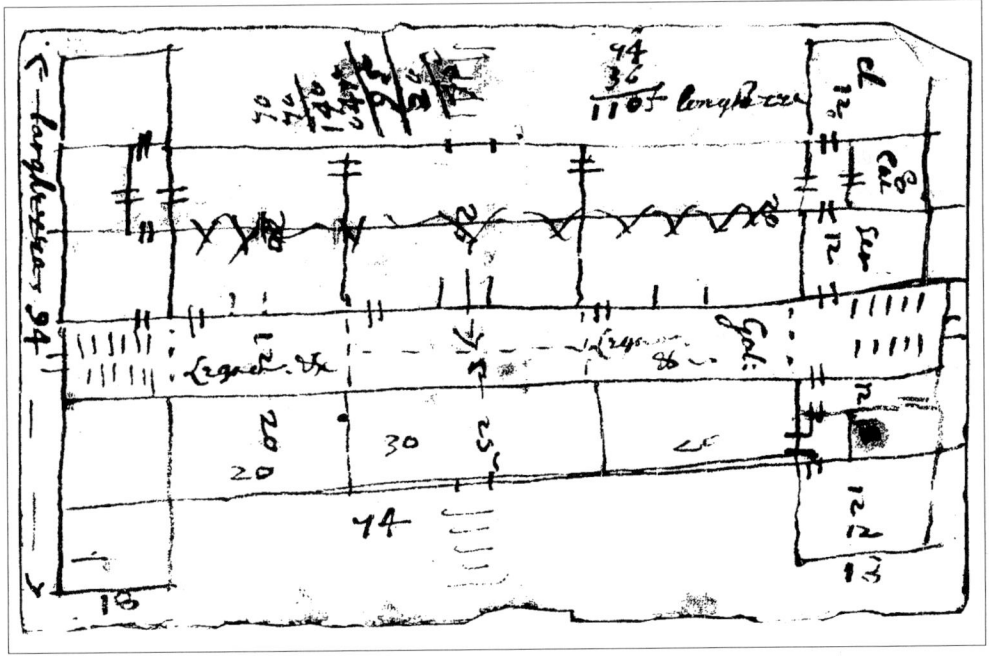

105a Sketch plan by (Sir) Roger Pratt of a house, arguably Clapham Place (see text) in the 'Tanner's Fly Almanac for 1672'. *(Gunther, vol I, 85). H.J.M. Green, 2005*

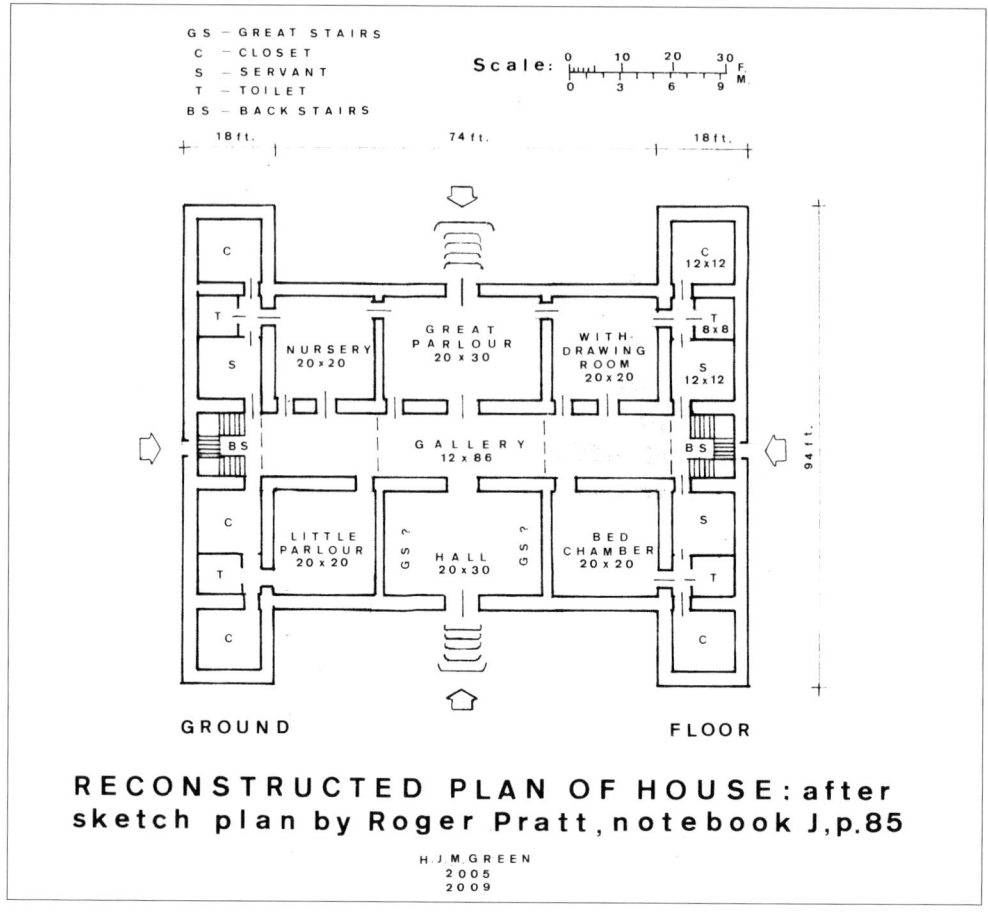

GS – GREAT STAIRS
C – CLOSET
S – SERVANT
T – TOILET
BS – BACK STAIRS

Scale:

**RECONSTRUCTED PLAN OF HOUSE: after
sketch plan by Roger Pratt, notebook J, p. 85**

H. J. M. GREEN
2005
2009

105b Reconstructed plan of house by H. J. M. Green, based on the sketch plan by Roger Pratt in the 'Tanner's Fly Almanac for 1672' (*Gunther, vol I, 85*). *H.J.M. Green 2009*

the service room arrangements in the wings. That it is a ground floor plan, or 'Parlor Flor' as Pratt would have termed it, is shown by the provision of entrance doorways and steps to the principal entries. Pratt appreciated the difficulty of transposing simple room dimensions to overall block sizes and accommodating wall thicknesses, and this was shown in the particular type of numeral shorthand he used. The length of the central section of the main front, based on room sizes is 70ft (20 x 30 x 20) but Pratt has firmly marked it as 74ft externally. The extra 4ft is taken up by the thicknesses (each of 2ft) of the two internal cross walls. Likewise one of the front wing extensions is shown as having a room width of 12ft, whereas the overall length of the projection is 18ft indicating external wall thicknesses of 3ft. To emphasise the overall length (*longhezza*) Pratt has provided on the sketch a short computation 94 + 36 = 110ft. Likewise the width of the building is shown as *longhezza* 94ft. The total room dimensions add up to 76ft (12 + 8 + 12 + 12 + 12 + 8 + 12) so there is an additional 18ft to be accounted for. There are two outside walls plus four loadbearing partition walls. If the outside walls are 3ft wide, as previously estimated, then each of the four main partition walls must also have been

3ft wide (however, no provision appears to have been made for the extra thickness required for internal walls carrying fireplaces and flues). A further scribbled computation in the margin of the drawing (70 + 70 = 140 95 - 20 = 75) may also refer to the house dimensions, but it is not clear in what context.

THE ARCHITECT'S DESIGN SKETCH

When the overall dimensions, room sizes and implied wall thicknesses are all taken into account, a measured, design drawing emerges (*105b*). It is evident that what we are looking at in the 'sketch' drawing is a rough *aide-memoire* from which a finished, scale drawing could be prepared. It is exactly the sort of sketch that an architect at an initial sitting with a client might rough out for basic decision-making. Indeed Pratt himself precisely described such a procedure in his draft treatise on architecture, folio L dated 4 July 1660 (Gunther 1928, 60).

> ... and after you [the client] have pitched upon the number of the rooms and the dimensions of each ... then if you be not able to handsomely contrive it yourself, get some ingenious gentleman who has seen much of that kind abroad and somewhat versed in the best authors of architecture: viz Palladio, Scamozzi, Serlio etc. to do it for you, and to give you a design of it in paper, *though but roughly drawn* [my italics].

Pratt clearly had himself in mind as the 'ingenious gentleman' and had indeed purchased the standard architectural treatises for his library – Vitruvius, Serlio, Alberti, De Muette, the Architecture of Antwerp and Du Cerceau on the 10 January 1658 (Mowl and Earnshaw 1995, 57).

THE ELEMENTS OF THE BUILDING

The building has a simple, five-bay symmetrical plan of double-pile form with the principal rooms grouped in the centre and the service rooms organised in the end bays which are carried forward as wings. The service quarters are identified on the drawing as providing room for a closet (Cl.) and a servant (Ser.) – each 12ft square – and a small, 8ft square room marked Cm, presumably meaning Commode or close-stool, i.e. toilet. In his architectural treatise Pratt goes into some detail over the function and relationships of these rooms:

> Let the whole be so contrived that each room lieth to other with the best convenience, and let it be so furnished with back stairs and passages to them, that the ordinary servants may never publicly appear in passing to and fro for their occasions there; let the little parlour have 2 closets there, the one for the man the other for his wife, and each of the bed-chambers a closet to it, and a chamber for a servant, which has a door as out of his master's chamber, so another landing him upon some other passage near the back stairs,

so that he need not foul the great ones [i.e. The Great Staircase] and whatsoever is of use may be brought up or carried down the back way.

taken from Gunther 1928, 64

The cruciform circulation plan with entrances on four sides is emphasised by providing a central, linear 'gallery' 12ft wide, as opposed to a mere circulation 'corridor'. The 'throughway' from 'Hall' to 'Great Parlour' provides the other axis. No rooms are identified in terms of use apart from the 'gallery' and service room functions. Back stairs are clearly indicated at either end of the gallery. The two central rooms with their entrances approached by steps are the Hall (which may have contained the main staircase) and the Great Parlour, if the precedents set by the Coleshill plan are followed. The room with lateral communication doors (*enfilade*) would be the Great Parlour.

DESIGN PROBLEMS

However attractive the cross-axis plan might appear to an 'ingenious gentleman' with Palladian precedents in mind, it was not a convenient plan form for an English country house. Jones' brilliant architectural solution of placing a palatial winged staircase at Coleshill in the entrance hall by the doorway short-circuited the social conventions beginning to be adopted in polite circles by the mid seventeenth century. As Evelyn put it 'the Vestibule or Porch should precede the Hall; the Hall the Parlor' following a progression of rooms representing increasing degrees of social intimacy (1723, 12-13). In theory the staircase should lie at the inner end of such an arrangement providing access to the Great Dining Room and family apartments, not just inside the front door as at Coleshill (Cooper 1999, 287). Ideally the through-axes of lobby/hall/parlour and (going the other way) outer court/great gallery/garden, if following the Palladian model should be unimpeded by staircases, minor circulation spaces and doorways. However, this was found to be impractical in smaller English country houses and was rapidly abandoned. Contemporary designers of double-pile houses such as Peter Mills at Thorpe Hall, Cambridgeshire (1663-4) had incipient long galleries which were blocked off by staircases and smaller rooms (Summerson 1993, 152 & 157). Even Inigo Jones at Coleshill fills the ends of the Great Gallery with service stairs. The same arrangement is to be found in the notebook J plan, which effectively dates the drawing to a phase of Pratt's developing architectural thinking between the excitement of the Jones' Coleshill model and his later houses where the Long Gallery and central staircase concepts had been completely abandoned. A date of *c.*1660 would thus be appropriate, which was additionally marked by the formulation of Pratt's ideas in his draft treatise on architectural and building practice.

IS THE DRAWING OF CLAPHAM PLACE?

Could then the notebook J sketch plan be a preliminary study, not of Ryston Hall, but of Clapham Place? It is possible; indeed the circumstantial evidence is strong, but it should be emphasised that there appears to be no evidence for the mention of Clapham Place in the voluminous Pratt archive, or any indication elsewhere that it was one of his projects. The date of *c.*1660 would also be about right in terms of the building works starting at Clapham Place, since, according to Pepys, it was almost complete by July 1663 (Diary 25 July 1663). There was also a mutual acquaintance in the shape of John Evelyn who might have introduced the aspiring architect to this wealthy client. Pratt and Evelyn had become acquainted in Rome while on the Grand Tour, and renewed their friendship on their return to England (Evelyn Diary 14 June 1655). Likewise Evelyn was on business and social terms with Gauden from the 1650s onwards (Diary entry for 19 March 1668).

However, if the Streater picture evidence is followed for the appearance of the house, together with the other supporting evidence mentioned earlier, there must have been some significant changes of design between the postulated Pratt sketch and the final building. The eventual house design omitted the wings, but had slight projecting bays for them and the centre bay on the south front. In other respects, however, it is extremely close to the Pratt design with a five-bay front and, in particular, the Great Gallery running the central length of the house, and the overall dimensions of the building.

So what went wrong? Why is Clapham Place not a recognised early work by Pratt? Indeed, how was it that the preparatory sketch found its way into a notebook filled with details of a much later house in 1672?

IDEALIST V. PRAGMATIST

What I think happened was this. In 1659 or 1660 a meeting was set up by Evelyn between Pratt and Gauden to discuss the design of Gauden's new house. Pratt took along a new unused notebook and sketched on a first page his proposals for the layout of the new building and a code of dimensions for working it up as a finished drawing. Either at this meeting or shortly afterwards there was a falling-out between the two men. Curiously, reading between the lines, the reasons for this are all set out in detail in Pratt's draft treatise on architecture drawn up in mid 1660 under 'Certain heads to be largely treated of concerning the undertaking of any building' . Indeed one gets a marked impression from the strength of feeling evident behind Pratt's 'good practice' precepts that they had been formulated as a result of some recent bad experience with a client, who is all too likely to have been Gauden himself!

Following his advice on getting a roughly drawn design from an architect, Pratt sets out two major caveats in connection with the design and siting of a new house.

> But be sure not to be wrought upon either to patch up an old house, at any great expense,
> or to make an addition to it ... the old one ... will look patched and irregular without,
> and within very little convenience, with low ceilings, and unequal floors, and many things
> else of the like ungracefulness.
>
> Taken from Gunther 1928, 61

Evidently the problem at Clapham Place was that Gauden wished to retain the Tudor turrets of the earlier house to function as back stairs for the new building, partly to provide unimpeded entrances at both ends of the Long Gallery, but also to save money. Pratt would have strongly objected to this proposal which in his terms would have ruined the appearance of the north entrance frontage. On this elevation Pratt was prepared to have two small flanking wings, but even these were not designated for use as back stairs.

The second reservation that emerges from Pratt's directions concern the setting of the building.

> ... neither ever be persuaded to set your house in a hole or the like induced thereunto by the neighbourhood of good outhousing there as they call it, for this according to the proverb is 'to spoil a custard to save an egg', and yet a thing much practised amongst us.

Because Gauden wished to build on the site of the old house, Brick Place, in order to retain the use of the two turrets, it meant keeping the new building adjacent to the extensive farmyard complex to the east – the 'good outhousing' sarcastically referred to by Pratt. Pratt, whose professional career showed that he had no compunction in pulling down old, unfashionable buildings and erecting a new house well clear of any farm or service area, would have thoroughly disapproved of Gauden's proposals made primarily on the grounds of economy – hence 'spoiling a custard to save an egg'!

No doubt initially Pratt may have hoped that upon seeking third party advice (Evelyn for example) Gauden might have been prevailed upon to see good sense. Indeed in the same section of his folio Pratt advises just such a procedure.

> ... shew this [the sketch plan] afterwards to men of ingenuity, but withal well capable of judging ... And after you have had the advice and heard the discourses of many such, according to what you shall then be convinced of [then proceed etc.]

It was not to be, and architect and client parted company. Clapham Place was built according to Gauden's wishes, but owing something of its essential character to Pratt's planning ideas. It was never to be accorded an honoured place in the eminent architect's canon of designer houses. Twelve years later while fishing around for an unused notebook for the Ryston project, Pratt found the almanac in which was his old Clapham sketch. Instead of removing the drawing, it was interleaved with the Ryston notes of 1671-2 and thus wrongly attributed by Gunther and all subsequent architectural historians.

However, there is a final connection which should be mentioned in closing. A plan-drawing of the Villa Thiene near Vicenza, built in 1545 by Andrea Palladio, is very similar in its proportions and layout to Clapham Place. Inigo Jones, Pratt's *mentor*, acquired this drawing on a trip to Italy, possibly in 1613–14, and no doubt showed it to his junior partner, who, in turn, proposed a similar plan for Clapham Place. Clapham Place thus has a claim to be regarded as one of the earliest Palladian villas in England.

GLOSSARY

acolyte	trainee priest
andirons	fire-dogs on which burning logs rested to raise them above the hearth
architrave	lowest member of the classical entablature; moulded frame of a door or window
baluster	bellied pillar used for supporting a handrail or coping
benefice	incumbency of a church, or the income derived from it
berewick	hamlet or village within a manor
byre	cow house
carinated	keel-shaped
cartulary	register of lands and privileges granted by charter, usually in roll or book form
chattel	personal property
cowl	hooded cloak worn by priests and monks
cruck truss	pairs of inclined timbers, usually curved, set at bay-length intervals in a building and supporting the timbers of the roof
cupola	small dome on a circular or polygonal base crowning a larger dome, roof or turret
curtilage	land (including yard and outbuildings) in the immediate environs of a house
demesne	land retained by the lord of the manor for his own use
dentil	small square block used serially in classical cornices
denarius	Roman silver coin
flue	smoke-duct in a chimney
Gibbs surround	eighteenth-century treatment of a door or window surround, seen particularly in the work of James Gibbs (1682-1754)
glebe	land held by a priest
hod	receptacle for carrying mortar, bricks etc.
inquisition	judicial or official investigation or inquiry; also the document recording such inquiry
interregnum	cessation or suspension of the usual ruling power; breach of continuity
japan (interior design)	Japanese workmanship, especially with painted or varnished design
leat	artificial waterway
lunette	semi-circular headed window
murrain	infectious disease in cattle, possibly foot and mouth

newel	central post in a circular staircase; the principal post where a staircase meets a landing
ogee	double curve, bending first one way and then another
osier	species of willow used in basket work
palimpsest	surface (or landscape) reused or altered but still bearing visible traces of its earlier form
parterre	formalised garden layout using geometrical patterns
pediment	normally a triangular gable derived from that of a classical temple. Also used over doorways and windows
pilaster	representation of a classical column in flat relief against a wall
Plantagenet	royal dynasty in England from Henry II to Richard III (1154–1485)
platt band	flat intermediate stone or brick course projecting from the surface of a wall
prelate	church dignitary
presentation (ecclesiastical)	the action or right of presenting a priest to a benefice (i.e. parish church)
promontory	point of high land jutting out into the ancient marshes of the Thames floodplain (in this context)
quoin	dressed stones at the angles of a building
reredos	decorated screen behind and above an altar
respond (architecture)	half-pier bonded into a wall and carrying one end of an arch
rood	cross or crucifix, usually over the entry into the chancel
scramasax	Anglo-Saxon sword-knife with tapered point
see (ecclesiastical)	seat or office of a bishop in his cathedral or diocese
seigneurial	pertaining to a feudal lord
stook	bundle of straw
stucco	plaster rendering sometimes with relief decoration
sump	pit for collection of water or other fluids
synod	assembly of clergy convened to decide ecclesiastical affairs
tanged	of an arrowhead, backward shaped points to secure penetration
tilth	land under cultivation
tympanum	surface within a pediment
victualler	merchant who is engaged in providing victuals (i.e. food) to the armed services
worsted	woollen fabric made from well-twisted yarn spun of long-staple wool to lay the fibres parallel

BIBLIOGRAPHY

Aubrey, J. (1719) *Natural History and Antiquities of Surrey* Vol I and V, London

Ault, W.O. (1972) *Open Field Farming in Medieval England*, London

Baker, A.R.M. (1973) 'Field systems of Southeast England', in A.R.M. Baker and R.A. Butlin (eds) *Studies of Field Systems in the British Isles*, Cambridge

Bartlett, R. (2000) *England under the Norman & Angevin Kings 1075-1225*, Oxford

Barton, N. (1997) *Stone Age Britain*, London

Barton, N.J. (1962) *The Lost Rivers of London*

Batten, H.N. (1827) *Plan of Clapham*, Clapham

Batten, H.N. (1827) *Key and Companion to the Plan of Clapham*, London

Battley, J.R. (1938) *Clapham Guide*, London

Beresford, M.W. (1963) *Lay Subsidies and Poll Taxes*, London

Birch, W. de G. (1893) *Cartularum Saxonicum*

Blair, J. (1991) *Early Medieval Surrey: Landholdings, Church and Settlement before 1300*, Stroud

Bowen, H.C. (1958) *Ancient Fields*, British Association for the Advancement of Science

Brayley, E.W. (1844) *A Topographical History of Surrey* Vol. 3 Part 2, London

Brooke, C.N.L. (1975) *London 800-1212: the shaping of a city*, London

Clegg, G. (1998) *Clapham Past*, London

Coghill, N. (1992) *The Canterbury Tales by Geoffrey Chaucer*, London

Cole, F.A.J. (1971) 'Titus Licinius Ascanius', *Clapham Antiquarian Society Occasional Sheet* No. 282, August

Collingwood, R.G. & Wright, R.P. (1965) *The Roman Inscriptions of Britain* Vol. I, Oxford

Cooper, N. (1999) *Houses of the Gentry 1480-1680*, New Haven and London

Coulton, C.G. (1925) *The Medieval Village*, Cambridge

Cowie, R. (2004) 'The evidence for Royal sites in Middle Anglo-Saxon London' *Med. Arch.* XLVIII

Cowie, R. & Blackmore, L. (2002) *Early & Middle Saxon Rural Settlement in the London Region*, London

Cox, J.C. (1905) in *Victoria County History of Surrey* Vol. II, Malden H.E. (ed.), London

Dale, T.C. (1927) *Clapham and the Clapham Sect*, London

De Beer, E.S. (1955) *The Diary of John Evelyn* 6 vols, Oxford

De Windt, A.R. & E.B. (2006) *Ramsey*, Washington

Densem, R. & Seeley, D. (1982) 'Excavations at Rectory Grove, Clapham, 1980-81', *The London Archaeologist*, Vol. 4 No. 7, 177-184

Dudley Stamp, L. (1955) *Man and the Land*, London

Edwards, J. (1801) *A Companion from London to Brighthelmustan in Sussex*, London

Ellison, R.A. (2004) *Geology of London*, BGS Nottingham

Ekwall, R. (1947) *The Concise Oxford Dictionary of English Place Names* (3rd ed.)

Erskine, R.W.H. and Williams A. (eds) (2003) *The Story of Domesday Book*, Phillimore

Estyn Evans, E. (1957) *Irish Folk Ways*, London

Evelyn, J. (1723, first published 1697) *Some Account of Architects and Architecture*, London

Ewart Evans, G. (1956) *Ask the Fellows who cut the Hay*, London

Fagan, B. (2002) *The Little Ice Age*, New York

Farrant, N. (1972) 'The Romano-British Settlement at Putney', *The London Archaeologist* Vol. 1, No. 16

Farrant, N. (1974) 'Roman Roads at Putney', *The London Archaeologist* Vol. 2, No. 9

Farries, K.G. and Mason, M.T. (1966) *The Windmills of Surrey and Inner London*, London

Finucane, R.C. (1977) *Miracles and Pilgrims: Popular Beliefs in Medieval England*, London

Gooder, E.A. (1961) *Latin for Local History*, London

Gower, G. (1995) *Brixges Stane*, London

Gower, G. (1996) *Balham: a brief history*, Wandsworth

Gower, G. & Tyler, K. (2003) *Lambeth Unearthed*, Lambeth

Gray, H.L. (1915) *English Field Systems,* Cambridge, Mass.

Green, H.J.M. (1969) 'A Roman site at Clapham', *LAMAS* 22 pt. 2, 28

Grover, J.W. (1887) *Old Clapham*, Clapham

Gunther, R.T. (1928) *The Architecture of Sir Roger Pratt*, Oxford

Hall, D. (1982) *Medieval Fields*, Aylesbury

Hall, D. (1995) *The Open Fields of Northamptonshire*, Northamptonshire Record Society 38, Northampton

Harris, F. (2002) *Transformations of Love*, Oxford

Hawtrey, V. (1967) in *Victoria County History of Surrey* Vol. IV, Malden H.E. (ed.), London

Heales, A. (1898) *Records of Merton Priory*, Oxford

Horsman, V. (1988) in Aspects of Saxo-Norman London I, *LAMAS spec. paper 11f*

Hunt, R. (2002) *Hidden Depths: An Archaeological Exploration of Surrey's Past*, Surrey Archaeological Society

Hurst, J.G. 1967 'The Kitchen Area of Northolt Manor, Middlesex', *Med. Arch.* Vol.V, 211-299

Hutton, R. (1991) *The Pagan Religions of the Ancient British Isles*, Oxford

Imber, D. (1968) 'Stane Street in Clapham', *The London Archaeologist* Vol. 1 No. 1

Imber, D. (1974) 'Excavations for Stane Street in the Clapham area 1966-71', *LAMAS* 25

Jenkins, J.G. (1976) *Life and Traditions in Rural Wales*, London

Jefferson Smith, P. (1984, 1995) *Clapham: Then and Now*, The Clapham Society

Jefferson Smith, P. & Wilson, A. (2007) *Discovering Clapham*, London

Johnson, H.C. (ed.) (1932) 'Surrey Taxation Returns' *Surrey Record Society* pt. XXXIII Vol. 26d

Jones, T. (2003) *Who Murdered Chaucer?*, London

Jones, T. and Ereira, A. (2004) *Medieval Lives*, London

Jones, G. and Jones, T. (trans.) (1949) *The Mabinogion*, London

Jordan, W.C. (1996) *The Great Famine*, Princeton

Kent, W. (1948) 'John Burns as an Antiquary', *Clapham Antiquarian Society Occasional Sheet* No. 11 (March 1948)

Knowles, D. (1949) *The Monastic Order in England*, Cambridge

Latham, R. (sel. & ed.) (1986) *The Shorter Pepys*, London

Latham, R. & Matthews, W. (1970-83) *The Diary of Samuel Pepys, a new and complete transcription*, London

Loobey, P. (2003) *Battersea Park*, London

Lysons, D. (1796) *The Environs of London* I, London

Madden, T.F. (2004) *Crusades*, London

Malone, C. (2001) *Neolithic Britain & Ireland*, Stroud

Merrifield, R. (1969) *Roman London*, London

Mowl, T. & Earnshaw, B. (1995) *Architecture without Kings*, Manchester

Opie, I. & P. (1951) *The Oxford Dictionary of Nursery Rhymes*, Oxford

Oxford English Place name Society (EDNS) (1934) Vol XI *Place Names of Surrey*

Oxford University Press (1973) *The Shorter Oxford English Dictionary*, Oxford

Parker Pearson, M. (ed.) (2005) *Bronze Age Britain*, Batsford

Peate, I.C. (1946) *The Welsh House*, Liverpool

Platt, C. (1978) *Medieval England*, London

PRO (Public Record Office) (1898) *Calendar of the Close Rolls for Edward II AD 1323-1327*, London

MacCana, P. (1970) *Celtic Mythology*, London

Rackham, O. (1976) *Trees and Woodland in the British Landscape*, London

Rackham, O. (1986) *The History of the Countryside*, London

Redstone, L.P. (1967) 'Battersea with Penge' in *Victoria County History of Surrey* Vol. IV, Malden H.E. (ed.), London

Richardson, G. (2003) *The Local Historian's Encyclopedia* (3rd ed.) Historical Publications

Rogers, A. (1972) *Approaches to Local History*, London

Royal Commission on Historical Monuments, Bowen, M.C. & Butler, R.M. (eds) (1960) *A Matter of Time*, London

Redstone, L.J. (1967) 'Battersea & Penge' in *Victoria County History of Surrey*, Malden H.E. (ed.), London

Renier, H. (2006) *Lambeth Past*, London

Round, J.H. (1895-6), *The Genealogist* (New Series), Vol. XII, H.W. Forsyth Harwood (ed.), London

Rudolf, R. de M. (1904) *Clapham before 1700*, London

Savage, A. (1983) *The Anglo-Saxon Chronicle* (translated and collated), London

Saxby, D. (2005) *Merton Priory*, London

Siddell, J., Cotton, J., Rayner, L., Wheeler, L. (2002) *The Prehistory and Topography of Southwark and Lambeth*, MoLAS mono. 14

Sheldon, H. (1973) 'Further excavations at No. 31 Clapham Common, South Side', *LAMAS* 24

Smith, E.E.F. (1968, revised editions 1969, 1970, 1973 and 1975) *Clapham: an historical tour*, London

Smith, E.E.F. (1976) *Clapham*, Lambeth

Stenton, F.M. (1950) *Anglo-Saxon England* (2nd ed.), Oxford

Stenton, F.M. (1960) 'Norman London' in Barraclough, G. (ed.) *Social Life in Early England*, London

Stringer, C. (2006) *Homo Britannicus*, London

Stuart, A.J. (1988) *Life in the Ice Age*, Aylesbury

Sullivan, D. (1994) *The Westminster Corridor: The Anglo-Saxon story of Westminster Abbey and its lands in Middlesex*, Historical publications

Sullivan, D. (2006) *The Westminster Circle*, London

Sumbler, M.G. (comp.) (1996) *British Regional Geology: London and the Thames Valley*, London

Summerson, J. (ed.) (1993) *Architecture in Britain 1530-1830*, New Haven and London

Taylor, C. (1973) *The Cambridge Landscape*, London

Taylor, C. (1974) *Fieldwork in Medieval Archaeology*, London

Taylor, J.C. (1925) *Our Lady of Batersey*, London

Thornton, P. (1978) *Seventeenth-Century Interior Decoration in England, France and Holland*, New Haven & London

Thurley, S. (1993) *The Royal Palaces of Tudor England*, London

Tomalin, C. (2002) *Samuel Pepys: The Unequalled Self*, London

Wheatley, H. B. (1897) *The Diary of Samuel Pepys*, MA Proceedings of the Royal Society of London

Williams, A. and Martin, G.H. (1992) *Domesday Book*, Penguin Books

Wilkinson, P. (2006) *England's Abbeys*, Swindon

Williamson, T. (2003), *Shaping Medieval Landscapes*, Macclesfield

Wilson, A. (ed.) (2000) *The Buildings of Clapham*, London

Wilson, A. (2007) *Discovering Clapham*

Wetherby, C.T. (1946/7) 'Stane Street in Clapham', *Surrey Archaeol. Collect.*

Whitelock, D. (1879) *English Historical Documents* Vol. I (2nd ed.)

Wood, M. (ed.) (2005) *The Domesday Quest*, London

Wright, L. (1964) *Home Fires Burning: The History of Domestic Heating and Cooking*, London

Ziegler, P. (2003) *The Black Death*, Stroud

INDEX